Homeland Security & militia-204
Very interesting, if idealistic & ignorant
of some crucial facts faced.

Restoration of the Republic

RESTORATION
of the REPUBLIC

The Jeffersonian

Ideal in

21st-Century

America

Gary Hart

OXFORD
UNIVERSITY PRESS

2002

OXFORD
UNIVERSITY PRESS

Oxford   New York
Auckland   Bangkok   Buenos Aires   Cape Town   Chennai
Dar es Salaam   Delhi   Hong Kong   Istanbul   Karachi   Kolkata
Kuala Lumpur   Madrid   Melbourne   Mexico City   Mumbai   Nairobi
São Paulo   Shanghai   Singapore   Taipei   Tokyo   Toronto

and an associated company in Berlin

Published by Oxford University Press, Inc.
198 Madison Avenue, New York, New York 10016

www.oup.com

Oxford is a registered trademark of Oxford University Press.

Library of Congress Cataloging-in-Publication Data
Hart, Gary, 1936–
Restoration of the republic : the Jeffersonian ideal in 21st-century America / by Gary Hart.
    p. cm.
Includes bibliographical references and index.
ISBN 0-19-515586-6
1. United States—Politics and government—2001–   2. Jefferson, Thomas,
1743–1826—Political and social views. 3. Democracy—United States. 4. Political
participation—United States. 5. Republicanism—United States. 6. United States—Social
conditions—1980–   I. Title.
E902 .H37 2002
973.4'6'092—dc21   2002017095

9 8 7 6 5 4 3 2 1

Printed in the United States of America
on acid-free paper

THIS I HOPE WILL BE THE AGE OF EXPERIMENTS IN GOVERNMENT. . . .

—Thomas Jefferson,

Letter to John Adams,

Monticello,

February 28, 1796

FOR A NUMBER of years I have been preoccupied with the question of how ordinary citizens can participate in a mass democracy. Reading in both classical political literature and the writings of America's founders led me to reexamine the basic principles of the republic and the qualities of republicanism. This reflection in turn led to the production of two previous books, *The Patriot* and *The Minuteman*, and then to the writing of this work as a thesis, for which I was granted a doctor of philosophy degree from Oxford University in Trinity term 2001.

These years of study brought me to the doorstep of Thomas Jefferson, in many ways the most radical of the founders and, on the issue of republicanism, the most literal. Rather late in life, around age seventy-three, Jefferson initiated a series of letters proposing the notion of "ward" republics, local forums patterned loosely after the Greek city-state, in which citizens could directly and immediately participate in the public life of their communities. It is a matter for conjecture whether Jefferson, had he been actively participating in the Constitutional negotiations instead of representing his Confederacy in Paris, might have insisted on this notion as a means of guaranteeing popular sovereignty while the federal Union of States was being formed.

The central question of this book is whether now, at the beginning of a new century and a new era, the notion of the local republic might be revived as a means for renewing democracy and restoring the republic. It is fully intended to be a radical inquiry, for I am among those who believe that globalization, the information revolution, the evolving nation-state, and the transformation of war all are combining to place unique stresses on both democracy and republicanism. My central thesis is that the republican ideal, and the American republic, must now become more democratic.

While writing this book, I also served as cochair of the U.S. Commission on National Security/Twenty-first Century whose mandate was to conduct the most comprehensive review of national security threats, opportunities, and potential responses since 1947. In its first public report, dated September 15, 1999, our commission's finding was that the United States would be attacked by terrorists using weapons of mass destruction and that Americans would lose their lives, possibly in large numbers, on American soil. The watershed tragedy of September 11, 2001, in which this prophecy in fact came about, announced the new world of the twenty-first century and demanded new political thinking for this precarious new age.

The examiners of my thesis made the following comment in their report to the politics faculty at Oxford: "The thesis is an unusual combination of textual analysis, contextual study, contemporary political theory, and policy prescription. Hart clearly believes that the Jeffersonian picture is one of increasing relevance to the United States, and the thesis is at times a powerful piece of advocacy for that picture. However, the thesis is firmly grounded in a scholarly literature, and it makes its argument within a context of contemporary debate on the character of the American polity in the twenty-first century." The whole idea of this project was to test the practical implications of a historical ideal against high scholarly scrutiny.

In this effort, the guidance and counsel of a number of significant contributors must be acknowledged. Two advisors, Gerald Cohen, Chicele Professor of Social and Political Thought at All Souls College, and Alan Ryan, warden of New College, helped shape and guide this work according to the highest traditions and standards of their great university. Professor Cohen asked perceptive and penetrating questions at the outset; then Professor Ryan assumed the responsibility for requiring a mature student to replace the mantle of advocate with that of critical scholar. He provided a shaping influence through his precise questions, hours of review, editorial suggestions, and guiding intellect, and he deserves credit for whatever merit this book may possess and no blame for its errors, frolics, and detours. Mark Philp, chair of the politics faculty, offered important early direction and lectures that helped shape and mold. John Gaddis, Eastman Professor at Balliol, provided the critical historical eye otherwise not available, and the warden and fellows of St. Antony's College warrant great thanks for their more than kind hospitality. Not least, Jane Boulden, research fellow at St. Antony's, proved an invaluable editor and computer demystifier. To all of them and to the Oxford University community, I express thanks and appreciation.

Most of all, for her continued patience, understanding, and support, I state my love for and thanks to Lee Hart.

Contents

Restoration of the Republic

Introduction:
"The Republic
for Which
It Stands"

"I PLEDGE ALLEGIANCE to the flag of the United States of America," U.S. schoolchildren are taught to recite, "and to the Republic for which it stands." Almost all can describe the flag, but few can describe the republic for which it stands. Nor, for that matter, can the students' parents. In the aftermath of terrorist attacks against the American homeland, the renewal of patriotism invites an inquiry into "patriotism toward what."

My argument for the restoration of the American republic is based upon several propositions. First, America in the twenty-first century is a procedural republic deficient in the qualities of civic virtue, duty, citizen participation, popular sovereignty, and resistance to corruption. Second, the centralized state, based upon a large-scale federation among national and State governments, mass democracy, and representative government, provides no recognized public space for the exercise of these republican virtues. Third, Thomas Jefferson offered a proposal—the ward or elementary republic—for incorporating republican qualities into the federal structure. Fourth, new economic, political, and social realities warrant reconsideration of a proposal such as Jefferson's for the creation of authentic democratic republicanism.

In an authentic democratic republic, the rights of citizens are protected by the duties of citizenship. As the Cambridge scholar Quentin Skinner has written: "The reason for wishing to bring the republican vision of politics back into view is not that it tells us how to construct a genuine democracy, one in which the government is for the people as a result of being by the people. That is for us to work out. It is simply because it conveys a warning . . . we can hardly afford to ignore: that unless we place our duties before our rights, we must expect to find our rights themselves undermined."[1] It is the voice of duty, the sense of citizen responsibility and, therefore, of empowerment that is silent in recent democratic, rights-dominated discourse. American schoolchildren do not know what a republic is because no one wants to tell them that they must earn their rights by performance of their duties. This has particularly been true in the past quarter century during which the values of the marketplace have replaced the values of the republican forum. It is difficult to hold that the "government is the problem" and a kind of enemy of its citizens and, at the same time, challenge young citizens particularly to give something back to their national community through public service. When all is being privatized, including the notion of virtue, it seems contradictory and heretical even to breathe the notion of civic virtue.

America's founders knew the republic to be the ancient alternative to monarchy and adopted its forms of mixed government and its language of popular sovereignty with a fervor that only a revolution against monarchy could inspire. Montesquieu reminded them that all republics throughout the ages had been small in scale, but he also provided the suggestion of a federation of republics. That idea of federation, when combined with the then-novel notion of elected representation, laid the structural foundation for an expansive new republic possessing a consolidated government whose branches were checked and balanced by a written Constitution, which also guaranteed a republican form of government to the various States of which it was composed. It was, all in all, a political feat that remains, even today, amazing.

But its success in both ratification and duration has rested in part on what are often admired as its compromises but which are, in truth, its embedded paradoxes. Few have noted the contradictions with greater fluency than the scholar Michael Kammen, who found among these institutionalized paradoxes a mistrust of "the people" by certain founders that was at least as strong as that of kings, aristocrats, and priests. This contradiction produced both "democratic elitism" and "aristocratic liberalism," or what Kammen calls "biformities"—the paradoxical coupling of opposites.[2]

These institutionalized paradoxes may also account for the persistence of America's preferred self-description of being a democracy rather than a republic. Whereas Woodrow Wilson considered America as democracy's defender around the world, late twentieth-century presidents have sought to make democracy America's leading export and America itself the Vatican of a secular religion whose cardinals, bishops, and emissaries are meant to spread the democratic gospel to "heathen" nations far and wide.

Even as America became democracy's missionary, its own definition of democracy was narrowing in two ways. Democracy was increasingly defined as a synonym for capitalism; and democracy was increasingly seen as a guarantor of rights. The second half of the twentieth century will surely be described by historians as "rights based." That is, patterns of discrimination by whites against minorities, men against women, and straights against gays were attacked and substantially diminished through judicial decision and statute. More subtle forms of discrimination, including neglect, such as those by an advantaged majority against various disadvantaged minorities, have also been addressed. In myriad ways, the complexion of American political discourse throughout this half century has been heavily conditioned by a laudable focus on individual and group rights. Thus, as America was emerging as the world's great promoter of democracy, democracy was in the process of being increasingly defined by a set of ever more precisely calibrated rights.

But there is a deeper ideological reason for America's preference for *democracy* over *republic* as a term of self-reference, and it relates at least in part to both an ambivalence toward citizen duty and a paradoxical attitude toward the military. America's military power was better at defeating fascism and thwarting the spread of communism than it is at imposing a democratic value system of rights on nations and cultures that do not necessarily share those values. Indeed, the twenty-first century's clash of cultures presents the American military with a challenge and a threat that exposes this limitation, as it illuminates the paradox inherent in the military's dual Constitutional nature. Perhaps most important, it underscores the principal distinction between democracy and republicanism. One of the most divisive, but least remarked, Constitutional debates was inspired by the Federalists' (especially Alexander Hamilton's) demand for a standing army and navy and the Antifederalists' (especially Patrick Henry's) insistence that a standing military in peacetime was a threat to republican government. The Antifederalists had history on their side; the Federalists had commercial interest on theirs. It is no particular surprise who won. Also not surprisingly, a compromise that created yet another paradox was reached. America would have two armies, a standing regular military to protect its commercial interests abroad and a militia, an army of the people under the control of the States, to defend the homeland and thus preclude the necessity of regular military forces ever being used on the homeland, the greatest fear of republicans throughout history.

Thomas Jefferson, founder of the Democratic Republican party but not a leader (as many still suppose) of the Antifederalists ("we are all republicans, we are all federalists"), has been criticized throughout history for wanting to keep the standing regular forces small and the militia strong. In his first annual message to Congress, Jefferson advocated that the militia be the natural first line of defense against hostile attack on the homeland and that it "maintain the defence until the regulars may be engaged to relieve them." A fiscal conservative, he resisted the costly maintenance of a large standing force principally designed to protect the commercial interests of financial speculators. Regardless, as America's role in the world expanded, so did its standing army and navy until, in the struggles against fascism and communism, they became the centerpiece of a "military-industrial complex." In the process, in the late nineteenth century, the militia became the National Guard, and in the following century it became an auxiliary expeditionary force in its own right.

America's two armies are significant in the democracy-versus-republic debate for at least two reasons. First, a new set of realities in the twenty-first century—dramatically demonstrated on September 11, 2001—may, in effect, reverse their roles; and second, the two armies illustrate the distinction between a rights-based democracy and a duty-based republic. As democracy has come to be defined in recent times principally by individual and group rights, the republic has been characterized since the

Greek city-state twenty-five hundred years ago by citizen duties. Classic republicanism is characterized by norms of civic virtue, duty, citizen participation, popular sovereignty, and concern for corruption. Civic virtue is the essence of citizenship ("ask what you can do for your country"). Duty, the performance of public service, is the obligation of citizenship. Participation is narrowly defined as tax paying, jury service, and military service and broadly defined as voting, involvement in the public dialogue, and active engagement in the life of the community. Popular sovereignty holds that the government works for the people, not vice versa. Concern for corruption holds that a national government dominated by special interest lobbyists paying huge sums in campaign cash for access to the corridors of power is unacceptable.

It is at this point that the paradox of America's two armies comes into play. The most immediate threat to American national security in the early part of the twenty-first century, according to the U.S. Commission on National Security/Twenty-first Century (of which I was cochair), is not the Red army plunging through the Fulda Gap, or even Saddam Hussein launching rogue missiles, but rather that of terrorists using weapons of mass destruction, whether nuclear, biological, or chemical (or perhaps even cyber), upon America's homeland. Our commission's first conclusion was: "America will become increasingly vulnerable to hostile attack on our homeland, and our military superiority will not entirely protect us. Americans will likely die on American soil, possibly in large numbers."[3] This conclusion was the result of almost three years of intensive study and the most far-reaching analysis of U.S. national security since the end of World War II. It went largely unnoticed by the American press and, therefore, the American public until terrorists attacked the symbol of American capitalism, the World Trade Center towers, and the symbol of American military power, the Pentagon.

The commission concluded that superior clandestine intelligence, especially human intelligence, might help prevent some terrorist attacks. Statutory creation of a new National Homeland Security Agency, embracing the Border Patrol, Customs, the Coast Guard, and the Federal Emergency Management Agency, could help detect and deter others. But if, as the commission warned, terrorists evaded intelligence and avoided detection, the first line of defenders should be the National Guard, the original Constitutional militia believed by Antifederalists and Jeffersonian republicans alike to be the best protectors of the homeland. This conclusion was less the result of Constitutional orthodoxy and more the result of pragmatic utilitarianism. The National Guard is forward deployed on the American homeland in twenty-seven hundred different units located in virtually every city in the nation, and such proved true in New York City.

Dependence on the National Guard also avoids a messy statutory problem. After the last razor-thin national election in 1876, fear of the use of regular military units to control unrest led to the enactment of the Posse Comitatus Act of 1878, which precludes the use of professional soldiers on American soil, yet another facet of America's republican heritage. The Posse Comitatus Act specifically provides: "It shall not be lawful to employ any part of the Army of the United States, as a posse comitatus [the power or force of the county], or otherwise, for the purpose of executing the laws, except in such cases and under such circumstances as such employment of said force may be expressly authorized by the Constitution or by an act of Congress."[4] Unquestionably, the president as commander in chief can and will call out the full resources of the military services in times of national emergency or catastrophe. But Constitutional structure, statutory mandate, practical necessity, and republican philosophy all dictate that the army of the people, the citizen-soldiers, be the frontline of homeland security.

Perhaps the most literal, and radical, of America's founding republicans, Thomas Jefferson thought that the elementary, or ward, republic was the appropriate forum for direct citizen engagement in public schools, human welfare and relief, and constabulary and judicial systems, among other functions. Were Jefferson here to argue his case today, he would begin by pointing out, as he often did, that laws and institutions must keep pace with changing times and the progress of the human mind. He would surely not seek a reversal of the undertakings by the national community to bring economic justice through social service programs created during the New Deal and Great Society eras. He would argue that national standards for education, the environment, care for the elderly, poor, and dependent children, among many other progressive commitments, and the equitable distribution of national revenues to achieve those standards, need not and should not be relaxed in an effort to revitalize the republic. He would argue, instead, that active citizen participation in the local community's (the ward republic's) achievement of those standards is the best means to combine ancient republican virtues with modern social justice.

Jefferson also considered defense of the community against outside interference to be a preeminent obligation of the authentic republic. Although achievement of the common good for the true republic requires citizens' commitment of time and energy to the common concerns of the community, the obligations of homeland defense and the duties of the citizen-soldier involve the ultimate sacrifice. The first specific demand of civic virtue, according to Skinner, is "the need to defend our community against the threat of conquest and enslavement by external enemies. . . . no one else can be expected to care as much for our own life and liberty as we care ourselves. . . . It follows that a willingness to cultivate the martial virtues, and to place them at the service of our community, must be indispensable to the preservation of our own individual liberty as well as the independence of our native land."[5]

The changing nature of conflict from that of war by nation-state against nation-state to that of terrorism or low-intensity urban conflict among tribes, clans, and gangs presents the historical irony (and paradox) that the citizens of the world's sole superpower are now hostage to the threat of terrorism, a threat whose seriousness is compounded by the availability of weapons of mass destruction. A restoration of republicanism will not alleviate this threat. However, this threat and the most plausible Constitutional and practical response to it, in the form of the citizen-soldier, do offer a powerful argument for that restoration. There are other factors as well. Fewer than half of those eligible to vote in the world's leading democracy bother to do so, which means that the leaders of the free world are elected by a quarter of America's citizens. Even that pathetic figure declines markedly among younger voters and in nonpresidential elections. This massive apathy is directly traceable to the sense, indeed the conviction, that special interests through their lobbyists and campaign contributions enjoy easy access to executive and legislative offices and dictate policy on matters of importance to them. Placing narrow interests above the common good is classic corruption in republican terms. The message that the national interest is but a collection of all of the special interests leads in turn to disengagement and detachment by the citizens from their own government and thus to the sacrifice of popular sovereignty.

A republican restoration in America promises, though it does not guarantee, the reengagement and empowerment of ordinary citizens in matters of community and national concern. It offers the hope of the restoration of integrity to government. It teaches future generations of schoolchildren that their democratic rights are best protected by the exercise of their citizen duties. It couples opportunity with obligation and rights with responsibilities. It gives content to the idea of civic virtue and to the ancient notion of the commonwealth.

Though I here place great emphasis on the martial virtues of the citizen-soldier as an illustration of how twenty-first-century realities may make a republican renaissance plausible, that by no means exhausts the content of the commonwealth. Throughout my active life I have advocated some form of national service for young people. Before the stage of family and career, most young people possess a natural idealism untapped by conventional politicians. Despite opposition from some, the success of President Bill Clinton's Americorps program demonstrates this assumption. If called upon and given concrete opportunities, many young people will provide some form of community service to their country. Arguments of coercion, cost, and management probably preclude this service being mandatory. But surprising numbers of young people, and even retired elderly people, are searching for some means to express the natural sentiments of citizenship. For those politicians who continue to preach individual autonomy and the government as enemy, however, it is difficult to encourage young people into public service.

Disillusionment with the ethos of materialism, privatism, and personal aggrandizement coupled with a renewed sense of community, the common good, the national interest, and the notion, most notable in wartime, that we are all in this together may spark the renaissance of the republic. Unlike the ancient republic, however, a twenty-first-century Jeffersonian republic must be democratic in character, open to all and owned by all. Founded on the classic qualities of civic virtue, duty, popular sovereignty, citizen participation, and resistance to corruption, the new American republic can and should be the forum in which the government is *for* the people because it is *by* the people. Most of all, this republic will be worthy of the allegiance of future generations of young people, who will come to know what they are saluting and why they are saluting it.

Thomas Jefferson's theory of the elementary or ward republic is relevant to the politics of twenty-first-century America. Jefferson's republicanism was uniquely democratic, liberal, and congruent with a federal governmental structure supporting a unified nation. It was democratic in that all (land-owning, white males) could participate in the local republic. It was liberal in that individual rights were to be protected by citizens exercising civic virtue. And it was explicitly intended to be the foundation of a pyramid of republics extending from the ward up through the individual States to the federal republic.

Jefferson's republicanism was radical but not reactionary. He was among the most revolutionary of the founders and saw in the local republic the political space in which the American revolutionary spirit could be preserved. For him, local republicanism, combined with each generation's responsibility for recreating its laws and constitutions, was a guarantee that political structures would keep pace with the expansion of human knowledge.

America's founders preserved the form of republican government by two measures: adoption of the principle of representation and creation of a federated structure. In so doing, however, they neglected the only public arena in which citizens could exercise civic virtue through direct participation. Jefferson sought to preserve authentic republicanism through elementary or ward republics in which all citizens could participate in matters of common concern.

The current age is not characterized by continuity with past arrangements and institutions but is instead one of political, economic, and social transformations sufficiently profound to make reconsideration of Jefferson's ideal of the republic timely. As the nation-state's traditional sovereignty over economic and political matters migrates upward to the international arena, we must consider whether democracy might now be preserved by Jeffersonian means—restoration of the republican ideal and, with it, civic duty, virtue, and citizen participation in government.

Thomas Jefferson had a Constitutional strategy. He understood and endorsed the imperative to create a unified nation based upon a federation of State republics. Yet his knowledge of history provided no instance of a republic on such a national scale. Other than sharing James Madison's concern for Alexander Hamilton's Caesarean ambitions, he was not caught up in the foundational Federalist-Antifederalist struggle. He was concerned instead to create a public space where classical republican qualities of civic virtue, duty, citizen participation, popular sovereignty, and resistance to corruption could be protected. His solution, devised only after reflecting on the shortcomings of representative government as provided for in the Constitution, was the ward republic, a truly democratic republic at the most local level.

Thomas Jefferson proposed that a layer of American government composed of elementary, pure, or ward republics should provide the foundation upon which individual State republics and the federated republic would be based.[6] His proposal was heavily influenced both by classic republican theories of civic virtue and citizen participation and by the belief that local public affairs were best managed locally. His views, explicated most thoroughly following his retirement from public office, were not considered during the Constitutional debates and were thus neither explicitly accepted nor rejected during America's founding era.

Federalist proponents of the new Constitution, principally Jefferson's ally James Madison, argued for a Constitutional structure based upon a federal republic whose allocation of power among branches of government would check and balance each other, a republic strong enough to unite the various States and sufficiently consolidated as a national government to resist local factions and interests. Whereas Madison saw citizens as fractious, potentially oppressive, and neither enlightened nor virtuous enough to restrain their natural self-interest, Jefferson saw them as both virtuous enough and sufficiently enlightened for self-government. Madison saw democracy as a door through which chaos might enter; Jefferson saw it as the only means by which to prevent ownership of government by "interests" and the resulting citizen alienation from government.

More than any of the other founders, Jefferson sought to reconcile a citizen's rights with his duty to secure those rights by participation in governance. Indeed, civic duty was, for him, the guarantor of rights. The most effective protection of individual rights, civil, legal, and political, was widespread democratic participation in the affairs of governance. The greatest danger to rights was in citizen detachment and in the political resolution of public concerns by interested forces dominating a remote central government. But meaningful citizen participation can only be achieved in a "pure republic," that is, one accessible to all at the local level. For Jefferson, the more remote government became and the more dependent the citizen became on elected representatives, the less republican the government and the greater the danger of corruption, narrow self-interest, and the erosion of democratic rights. In the context of the American founding, Jefferson's ideal of the republic was radical and *sui generis*. He took the core issues of virtue, participation, and duty seriously and sought a Constitutional locus for them as a barrier to corruption.

Jefferson was not, as some scholars have argued, a simplistic exponent of yeomanry seeking to recapture or preserve an idyllic agrarian age. He was, rather, an active advocate of national expansion, international trade, commerce, and diplomatic engagement, a sophisticated politician and statesman, and a complex political theorist. His republicanism was radical but also highly sophisticated within the context of a complex federal structure.

Classic republican values of civic virtue and citizen participation were subordinated during the adoption of the Constitution to the imperatives of national unification, and a public space for direct citizen participation was not, therefore, expressly protected in the Constitutional formulation. The tempestuous political and economic circumstances of the founding era made popular sovereignty and local citizen control frightening; the ambitions of commercial interests made dispersed political power unacceptable. For these reasons, a specific arena for the practice of democratic republicanism was never seriously contemplated in America's founding era.

The founders' attentions were focused on the challenge of creating an extended republic, on unifying thirteen confederated former colonies with disparate regional interests, and on suppressing local secessionist sentiments. The resolution of this experiment, for which little if any historic precedent offered itself, was sufficiently complex as to cause the Federalist founders to neglect consideration of a Constitutional space for local self-governance or for a public forum for democratic participation. Subsequent history reinforced federal consolidation, concentrated national power, and representative government—at the expense of citizen empowerment and civic participation—as the pillars of American government.

This book proceeds as follows: (1) consideration of the revolutionary economic, social, and political changes in the early twenty-first century; (2) an examination of whether America in the twenty-first century is an authentic republic; (3) consideration of the objections to small-scale republicanism during the founding-era debate and discussion of the impact of these new realities on early objections to small-scale republicanism; (4) rebuttal of the objections to the Jeffersonian vision in light of early twenty-first century political, social, and economic realities; (5) explication of Jefferson's theory of the republic, with special emphasis on the issue of scale; (6) application of the Jeffersonian model to selected public issues as a test of the model's current plausibility; and (7) a concluding discussion of the relevance of radical democratic republican ideals to America in the current age.

This volume will not consider a wide range of related issues and arguments, including the general nature of American republicanism in the founding era; the details of classical influences on American republican thinking; a detailed analysis of the Constitutional debate; a detailed treatment of the Federalist-Antifederalist struggle; a survey of influences on Jefferson's comprehensive and complex political philosophy; a comprehensive review of the debate between liberalism and republicanism; or the history of confederacies or federal structures. Each of these topics has received extensive scholarly attention over the years. They are, however, only tangentially relevant here. Previous scholarly work is addressed throughout this study where it illuminates the specific subject addressed, but elaborate discussion of these topics would represent a diversion from the principal concern.

Jefferson's republican structure does not threaten rights and liberties, is neither a formula for chaos nor a challenge to national authority, is compatible with justice, is a means of securing rights through duties, and strengthens national purpose by empowering citizens. No attempt is made, because there is no need for it, to reconcile republicanism and liberalism. A common view is that republicanism of the sort that Jefferson proposed is at odds with the liberal concern for individual rights, but it is argued here that Jefferson understood no such incompatibility and rather believed in a republic of rights founded on duties. Certain fundamental questions and the arguments responding to them will be dealt with individually in more specific detail below.

First, does the restoration of Jeffersonian republicanism require a reconciliation of classical Aristotelian republicanism with modern Lockean liberalism? The answer is no. Jefferson did not envisage the sacrifice of individual rights in order to promote civic duty. Indeed, in his formulation, the most effective means of guaranteeing the rights he himself espoused in the *Declaration of Independence* and the *Bill of Rights* was through active participation in the public life of the community. His early demand for Constitutional inclusion of the rights of free speech, a free press, and freedom of assembly was principally a demand for recognition of the public character of these rights. Jefferson considered access to property as central to man's pursuit of both liberty and happiness and called radically for distribution of land to the landless. But his rights theory went well beyond the property-centered rights theory propounded by Locke. Jefferson's concern was principally for the right of political participation and the right to resist unjust authority. The Jeffersonian rights "embodied in the first ten amendments to the American Constitution are addressed to the public activity of a naturally social being whose concerns extend beyond his own private interests."[7] Civil, legal, and political rights are most in jeopardy, for Jefferson, when government becomes detached and remote from the citizenry, when elected representatives fall under the sway of interests, when the concerns of the powerful, usually commercial, elites outweigh the common good in the halls of power, and when individual citizens lose their sense of participation in the public life of the community and nation.

Jefferson saw no tension between the rights espoused in the *Declaration* and the *Bill of Rights* and the duties attendant upon the local republic. Insistence upon a venue for participation and a forum for the voice of the citizen could scarcely, for him, be considered a means of political coercion. Remote government, not the government closest to hand, most jeopardizes rights. Today, recognition of a more vital public space for direct citizen participation would in no way challenge the central role of the Supreme Court in interpreting the laws, including interpretations affecting individual and group rights, nor the role of the federal legislative and executive branches in enacting laws guaranteeing and expanding civil and political liberties.

Second, how can political notions from the very different era of the eighteenth century be relevant to the twenty-first century? Are not the interests of national unity even greater today than then? The answer is that the realities of the present age are even more conducive to the idea of local republicanism than those of the early federal era. Then, the concern for unity and union, the establishment of a federal structure to replace the confederation of former colonies, the creation of a national government to conduct the new nation's foreign commercial and political relations, and the suppression of rebellion and factionalism all overrode any concern to establish a public space for citizen participation. Today, America has matured well beyond these concerns and faces the dark side of the Hamiltonian vision in the form of a corrupt national state.

Sufficient federal power exists today to regulate concentrated industry, to tax concentrated wealth, to establish national standards of social performance, to enforce national laws, to unify the nation against external threat, to represent the nation's interests abroad, and to participate in the councils of the world. Indeed, America in the early twenty-first-century, vastly unlike the early, fragile republic from which it evolved, is widely accepted as the world's only superpower. The question now arises as to the political and social price being paid for these national goals. This price includes citizen apathy, a lack of interest in and disengagement from public affairs, a minimal sense of public duty, and the corruption of national politics by special interests, in short, a retreat from a sense of the commonwealth—all variations on the issues of concern to republicans throughout history. Addressing these concerns by the creation of an accessible republican forum does not jeopardize democratic rights. Instead, it would substantially help secure them.

Further, no inevitable contradiction exists between a revival of democratic republicanism and America's role as early twenty-first-century superpower. Consolidated authority and power in the national government is required for America to play its current stabilizing role in the world, as well as to ensure uniformity of the rights and opportunities of all of its citizens. But that consolidated power need not frustrate republican values of civic virtue, duty, and citizen participation. Concern must rather now be expressed for the health of American democracy. Citizen alienation is a disease that attacks the roots of even the greatest superpower.

Third, is it necessary to use Hamiltonian means to achieve Jeffersonian ends? This formula, identified with the work of Herbert Croly in *The Promise of American Life* (1909), essentially holds that centralized national government is necessary to achieve national purposes and to guarantee the democratic rights of citizens. This question requires the following complex responses. Yes, this might have been so in the founding era, and central authority continues to be imperative when a mass democracy confronts a crisis from within, as in the American Civil War, periods of economic concentration, and the Great Depression, or from without, as in world wars. But no, Croly understood neither Jefferson's ends, a democratic republic, nor his means—full citizen access and involvement at the local level in the governing process. Indeed, the current age might require the formula to be reversed: Jeffersonian means might be required to achieve Hamiltonian ends.

Croly and those who preceded him (back to Hamilton) and who followed him (up to Arthur Schlesinger, Jr.) saw Jefferson as the embodiment of antifederalism, decentralization, and fragmentation. As a leading advocate of progressivism, Croly sought not only the centralization of federal governmental power but also "the nationalizing of American political, economic, and social life" and an "increasing nationalization of the American people in ideas, in institutions, and in spirit."[8] All of this nationalization of the American spirit was to be undertaken in the interest of "the national purpose."

Undeniably, Jefferson would have been suspicious, to say the least, of such an undertaking. It would not be too many years before the rhetoric of "national purpose" would be found on the lips of European dictators. But the basic flaw of Croly's argument is its misrepresentation of Jefferson. Croly could more authoritatively have attacked Thomas Paine, but Jefferson offered a larger target. Jefferson, in reality, was both a Republican and a Federalist. Confronted with the proposed Constitution in 1787, he wrote Madison, "I like much the general idea of framing a government which should go on of itself peaceably, without needing continual recurrence to the state legislatures," "I like the organization of the government into Legislative, Judiciary & Executive," "I like the power given the Legislature to levy taxes," "I am captivated by the compromise of the opposite claims of the great & little states," and "I am much pleased too with the substitution of the method of voting by persons, instead of that of voting by states."[9] These are scarcely the sentiments of a man opposed to the new federal structure.

Supporters of the Hamiltonian vision, including Croly, are not to be faulted for their insistence upon a strong central government. But to set Jefferson up as the antithesis of this notion is to erect a false and misleading dichotomy. To resurrect Jefferson's proposal for ward republics is not to challenge either the federal structure or the role of the central government. It is to contend that the Hamiltonian means have not achieved the Jeffersonian ends.

Fourth, can an antique notion such as the ward republic be practical in modern urban society? The answer is yes, and this notion may help address problems of fragmentation in urban government. Most American metropolises are constituted by neighborhoods. Many of these neighborhoods retain their original names. They are the venues for local school districts, fire and police districts, local hospitals and health services, water and sewer districts, and other functional government units. Even as political power has gravitated toward Washington, D.C., a plethora of sub-municipal governments, councils, and districts have sprung up. Local government has thus become fragmented, and both authority and responsibility have become confused and confusing. Consolidation of these public functions under local republics, as argued here, can harmonize and rationalize fragmented municipal governments. More challenging is the post–World War II rise of suburban America. Even for those neighborhoods, however, proposals will be provided for introducing republican government to suburban communities.

The issue of city and town is a real one for neorepublicanism. From Aristotle forward, republican theory has struggled with the issue of scale, an issue at the core of this book. Twenty-first-century America is neither ancient Athens nor republican Rome. Nor is it Venice, Holland, or Switzerland. The argument contained herein is neither nostalgic nor utopian. Small towns with clearly defined borders, low mobility, stable and secure populations, and community memories are more easily adapted to the Jeffersonian ideal, and, in many cases they are already close to it. But to restore republicanism at the community level, communities must be identified or created in urban and suburban America.

Fifth, is Jeffersonian republicanism not simply another name for today's communitarianism? The answer is no, although the sharpness of the differences between them depends on which definition of communitarianism one employs. Unlike communitarianism, republicanism is a political even more than a social doctrine. Republicanism is a form of government founded upon popular sovereignty, resistance to corruption, and a commitment to liberty as nondomination. By most understandings, communitarianism is based upon collective action, possibly by nongovernmental associations, on matters of common concern, whether matters of public policy or not, that may or may not require official governmental forms, structures, and procedures. Both have the goal of uniting neighboring and like-minded citizens to address issues of common concern, to achieve the common good, and to share responsibility for resolving local problems. Republicanism, however, stresses duty over voluntarism, government over association, and popular sovereignty over informal collaboration. Given often-similar objectives, too much can be made of the differences. But the republican ideal has, for twenty-five hundred years, offered a formal political alternative to monarchy and related forms of centralized power. Communitarianism recognizes the void in the political and social structure created by the perverse combination of concentrated political power and the individual's social isolation from a detached polity. Republicanism offers a political remedy for that void in the form of space for citizen participation in government. The Jeffersonian republican formulation was specifically proposed as a foundational layer of government in an already sophisticated federal structure.

Sixth, is not recourse to Jeffersonian republicanism simply an argument for subsidiarity by another name? Once again, much depends upon one's definition of subsidiarity. Suffice it here to acknowledge the question and to answer it as follows: Jefferson's ward republic is not an instance of subsidiarity, because subsidiarity is meant to achieve efficiencies of function by the delegation of responsibility to associations—not necessarily democratically elected or accountable—for the purpose of undertaking functions that, in a republic, would be matters of common, public concern to all citizens. Subsidiarity might become an excuse for the avoidance of governmental responsibility, a subtle form of privatization, or an argument for reliance on private mechanisms to achieve public goods (for example, "a thousand points of light" or governmental use of "faith-based organizations"). These may be plausible social and even political objectives, but that does not eliminate the differences between them and Jefferson's distinctly classical republicanism as the foundation of the commonwealth.

Even as it addresses these and other challenges and questions, this volume explores the applicability of radical democratic republicanism to the present age, which is characterized by antirepublican trends and yet is a time when the resolution of those political dilemmas might profit from a reconsideration of republican political values. The Jeffersonian republican ideal is not held up as a perfect political model. Rather, it represents a road not taken at a critical early juncture, indeed a road not even fully explored or understood.

A series of historic events in the political evolution of the United States over two centuries inhibited reconsideration of this model. Those events included consolidation of the union in the face of continued foreign pressure, particularly from Great Britain, which culminated in the War of 1812; expansion of the national frontier; expansion of international trade and the search for foreign markets; the mounting crisis of States' rights and slavery, which culminated in the Civil War in the mid-nineteenth century; the era of Reconstruction followed by extreme economic turbulence; industrialization, mass immigration, and labor strife; emergence from isolation into the turbulent European strife of World War I; economic depression and the New Deal recovery; and World War II and the cold war that followed. All contributed to national consolidation and resistance to the distribution or devolution of political power. Especially after the Civil War, resistance to the dominance of the federal government was sporadic at best.[10] Throughout America's complex history, there has been little motivation for reconsideration of the nature of republicanism or revisitation of the Jefferson elementary republic model.

However, early in the twenty-first century, new realities confront advanced democracies generally and the United States specifically. The authority and sovereignty of the nation-state is waning. Two centuries of the neglect of civic virtue and republican values have caused America to become a procedural republic more attentive to individual rights than to the common good and to citizen duties. The price of this neglect has been the corruption of government by interests, loss of popular sovereignty, and erosion of civic virtue. Now, citizen alienation from remote and uncontrollable international and national institutions has created renewed interest in local autonomy and authority. New threats to security require much more attention to homeland defense at the local level than to international expeditionary capabilities. Information technologies may now enhance community solidarity, provide a surplus of information required for local decisionmaking, and strengthen the claims for local self-governance. These and other new realities invite reconsideration of the

Jeffersonian model of the republic in the United States of the twenty-first century.

Though an effort is made here to suggest how certain issues, including public education, social welfare, and local security, might be administered in a modern ward republic, this book is an exercise in political theory not political science. The many practical questions relating to the workings of the small-scale republic within the large-scale federal democracy are not addressed here. Those public functions—education, social welfare, and local security—are addressed for the purposes of demonstrating how the local republic might operate, not how it must operate, and of demonstrating that the theory of authentic republican government is not implausible in the current age.

Two approaches set this work apart: first, its focus on Thomas Jefferson's theory of radical democratic republicanism in the form of the ward republic, and second, its exploration of this theory as it might apply to distinctively new political, social, and economic realities in twenty-first-century America. Except on the part of a very few scholars, there has been little focus on Jefferson's idiosyncratic republicanism. As one of these scholars says: "No one has adequately linked Jefferson's theory of local ward democracy with his conception of American federalism." A search of the literature reveals no scholarly consideration of the viability of Jefferson's theory of local republicanism in the modern age.[11]

The immense body of scholarly literature on Jefferson has focused upon much else: on the sources of and influences on his political philosophy, his enlightened and revolutionary liberalism, his expansion of America's territory through the Louisiana Purchase and sponsorship of the Lewis and Clark expedition, his complex views and behavior regarding slavery, his educational theories, and, to a somewhat lesser degree, his ideas on land distribution and generational responsibility. Thomas Jefferson's political philosophy consisted of a foundational liberalism, a radical distributionist economic theory, generational accountability, and elementary democratic republicanism. His liberalism is most notably articulated in the *Declaration of Independence* and his advocacy of many of the core principles of the *Bill of Rights*. His economics are based on his proposal for the distribution of land to landless households. His generational idea, that "the earth belongs in usufruct to the living," argued that each generation is responsible for adopting its own laws and constitution in keeping with the changing realities of the times. And his republicanism is founded upon the elementary republics of the wards.

This book contains both a detailed analysis of the nature of Jefferson's republicanism, particularly its elementary (local) and democratic (inclusive) character, and an application of that republican theory to current American political conditions. This speculative venture of transposing a political theory two centuries forward considers the original objections to Jeffersonian republicanism, proposes responses to those objections, especially in the light of transforming new realities, argues that American republicanism is being hollowed out, and considers specific ways in which foundational republicanism might operate in practice in the complex federal structure of a twenty-first-century superpower.

Even though care is taken herein to distinguish analysis from advocacy, this is not always a sharp distinction when the central effort is to rescue from two centuries of neglect an ideal that might be seen to possess political relevance to our nation in an age whose challenges invite fresh approaches. This effort requires both presenting Jefferson's ideal with clarity and precision and propounding it as politically relevant and institutionally plausible. Although the distinction between analysis and advocacy may not always be as sharply drawn as perfection might require, this volume is principally intended to contribute to an understanding of Jefferson's theory of the republic, a theory unique to America's founders, and only secondarily to explore its current political plausibility.

Among America's founders and original political thinkers, Jefferson alone championed a radical republican ideal within the context of the complex federation. In part because his ideal was never seriously considered in the founding debates, no public space for civic virtue, duty, and citizen participation is recognized in the U.S. Constitution. Such republican qualities are largely missing from current public life. However, as noted, new political, economic, and social realities, including, *inter alia*, globalization, eroding nation-state authority, and a renewed desire for community empowerment, may now make local republicanism viable. Among those new realities are a technological revolution that might be used to empower citizen governance, financial globalization that increases public desire for greater control of community functions, and diminishment of the nation-state, which might release the dynamic of local republican government.

Adoption of a democratic republican model in twenty-first-century America might establish a forum for direct democracy, restore popular sovereignty, create a public space for citizen participation, establish a capacity for citizen-initiated reformation,[12] restore civic virtue, create a remedy for corruption, and guarantee rights through performance of civic duties.

In the current age, Jefferson's democratic republican ideal might yield a new political culture or a polity founded upon humanity's essentially social nature; a new destiny founded on participation in community life; the restoration of a public ethic that supersedes the private, commercial self; and the elevation of the common good and of commonwealth institutions, such as public schools as instruments of civic education, community welfare as a political and moral function of the ward, and local security provided by the citizen-soldier. This book seeks to explore the plausibility of this eighteenth-century idea in the twenty-first century.

AMONG A NUMBER of unresolved issues in structuring an American federal system based upon representative government was the question of the locus of sovereignty. The new federal government would clearly be sovereign in certain matters, such as foreign policy, national defense, and even the general welfare. But to the degree powers were not delegated by the Constitution to the national government, sovereignty would remain in the States constituting the new union. But then, there were the people. Are not the people themselves sovereign in an authentic republic? And if they are, how should that core sovereignty be acknowledged and guaranteed? Thomas Jefferson, as we will see, came, *ex post facto*, to comprehend this conundrum and to seek to resolve it. The central question of this volume is whether the revolutionary tides of the early twenty-first century may not now make his revolutionary solution viable.

Much of the political tension within the U.S. system during the more than two centuries since its founding has surrounded the federal-State relationship. With rare and sometimes colorful exceptions, States have left foreign policy and national defense to the na-

New Realities in Twenty-first-Century America: Economics, Politics, and Society

I

tional government, thus the political struggle has occurred over issues of domestic authority. Though this struggle occasionally surfaces in current times, it does so with much less frequency since the series of Supreme Court decisions during and following Franklin Roosevelt's New Deal, which broadened the federal role in domestic affairs much more widely. The twentieth-century Supreme Court, relying to varying degrees on the original intent of the founders, has evolved a relatively stable federal-State Constitutional relationship. However, below this federal-State struggle, a less audible friction has persisted between State governments and the municipal and township governments operating by charter under the various State constitutions.

The broader question is whether social, economic, and political trends in the late twentieth and early twenty-first centuries may now open the way for at least partial consideration of the recreation of authentic republics at the local level, according to the Jefferson ideal. Or, in other words, can and should U.S. citizens participate more immediately and directly in matters "within their reach and competence"? What are the factors that reawaken this possibility? What are the continuing factors that militate against it?

Economic Globalization, the Evolving Nation-State,
and the Decline of Ideology

The dual forces of integration and fragmentation are powerfully at work in the world of the twenty-first century, but they are not new. Ian Clark, citing John Gaddis, finds their roots as far back as, at least, the eighteenth century:

> He [Gaddis] traces a "fault line" between "the forces of integration" and the "forces of fragmentation" back to the eighteenth century. This results from an essential duality in human existence between the integration required "for the satisfaction of material wants" and the "particularization . . . that is required to satisfy intangible . . . needs." . . . Reformulated, this remains close to the standard dichotomy between the unifying dynamic

of the economic universe as against the divisive dynamic of the political realm.[1]

Thus, even as economic globalization integrates and compresses the trading world, political particularization fragments previously unitary national states. Clark further cites Francis Fukuyama to the same effect: "He [Fukuyama] suggests that nationalism once fulfilled an integrative role that met the needs of early capitalism, but that 'those same economic forces are now encouraging the breakdown of national barriers through the creation of a single, integrated world market.' "[2] The casualty in this continuing tension between globalizing economics and fragmenting politics are national borders, the nation-state itself. The state finds itself struggling to accommodate economic pressures from without and political pressures from within. Many scholars conclude that only political innovation—new structures and new systems of politics—will achieve this accommodation: "The so-called contemporary crisis of the state is a product of its shouldering the political costs of globalization. This is but a reflection of the tensions between international disciplines and domestic needs and the higher political price that states are now having to pay for the levels of globalization that have already occurred."[3] As a backdrop for the exploration of a republican restoration, it is necessary to consider the full impact of these increasingly competitive forces.

Globalization

The turn of the century witnessed the massive internationalization of finance and capital flows. Private banking systems and multinational financial institutions, all operating within an ad hoc framework of cooperating central banks, now finance public and private undertakings around the clock. Most large corporations in developed countries are now multinational enterprises conducting manufacturing, distribution, and marketing through global networks.

In just the past few years corporate giants have emerged across all industries. Citibank and Travelers, Bank of America and Nationsbank, and Deutsche Bank and Bankers Trust are among the major mergers that have reshaped banking. In other industries, Daimler-Benz has linked up with Chrysler; AT&T with MediaOne; British Petroleum with Amoco; Aetna with Prudential Health. Still awaiting regulatory approval are some of the biggest combinations of all, including those between Exxon and Mobil, MCI Worldcom and Sprint, and Viacom and CBS.[4]

Citing these massive mergers, since followed by others, the author, Jeffrey Garten, continues: "But by itself, sheer size—whether in finance or in other industries—should not be a concern. The real problem could be the unchecked political influence of the global goliaths. . . . The see-saw of private and public power is seriously unbalanced." Not only have these megacompanies begun to expand "beyond the law," they have also "become too big to fail. Were they to falter, they could take the entire global financial system down with them."

Multinational conglomerates have accumulated financial and political power beyond the reach of even national regulatory structures and, therefore, have emerged into a new, uncertain, and nonaccountable international regime. Trade between nations and private entities is now conducted directly through bilateral negotiations or, more likely, through regional quasi governments such as the North American Free Trade Agreement (NAFTA) or the European Union (EU). New international governmental organizations (IGOs), created to respond to this financial internationalism, are only nominally democratic and are organized and operated by multinational bureaucracies not directly accountable to any electorate:

> The European Union offers telling evidence. There, such nominally democratic structures as popular elections and a parliament are formally in place. Yet virtually all observers agree that a gigantic "democratic deficit" remains. Crucial decisions mainly come about through bargaining among political and bureaucratic elites. Limits are set not by democratic processes but mainly by what negotiators can get others to agree to and by considering the likely consequences for national and international markets. Bargaining, hierarchy, and markets determine the outcomes. Except to ratify the results, democratic processes hardly play a role.[5]

Under the aegis of the World Trade Organization, NAFTA, the EU and the European Community, and a de facto trade bloc in Asia, nations are attempting to organize international commerce. Hundreds of billions of dollars, yen, deutsche marks, and francs move from bank to bank instantaneously. Capital, once the province of national treasuries, mints, and central banks, now is virtually unregulated, and national currencies are themselves the objects of speculative exchange.

Underscoring these trends, the U.S. Central Intelligence Agency, in a report published in December 2000, reached this conclusion: "The elements of globalization—greater and freer flow of information, capital, goods, services, people, and the diffusion of power to nonstate actors of all kinds—will challenge the authority of virtually all governments. At the same time, globalization will create demands for increased international cooperation on transnational issues." This report also deals in depth with the impact this new transnational cooperation will have on traditional nation-state governmental structures.[6]

Massive infrastructure projects are conceived, financed, constructed, and operated by corporations—themselves evolved from late thirteenth-century guilds—chartered in the Isle of Man; supported by banks in Singapore; employing construction workers from the Philippines, engineers from India, architects from Italy, and technicians from Russia; with shareholders throughout the Western world. These corporations pay often nominal taxes in the United States, the United Kingdom, or Japan but owe no particular fealty to any national flag. Software is conceived in Sunnyvale, California, written in Bangalore, e-mailed back to another anonymous building in the suburbs of Seattle, produced and installed in Taiwan. Screenplays are written in Beverly Hills, financed in Tokyo, filmed in Montreal, edited in a studio outside London, and distributed in twelve national capitals simultaneously. "Corporations like Exxon-Mobil will negotiate with oil-producing countries almost as equals, conducting the most powerful private diplomacy since the nineteenth century, when the British East India Company wielded sovereign influence in Asia."[7] In confirmation, the CIA report concludes: "States continually will be dealing with private-sector organizations—both for-profit and nonprofit. These nonstate actors increasingly will gain resources and power over the next fifteen years [the timeline of the report] as a result of the ongoing liberalization of global finance and trade, as well as the opportunities afforded by information technology."[8]

Multinational enterprise has led to multinational finance and banking in the form of the European Bank for Reconstruction and Development, the Asian Development Bank, the World Bank, and the International Monetary Fund, as well as to quasi-official gatherings, such as the World Economic Forum where private financiers meet with national leaders to discuss international priorities and agendas.

But as multinational enterprise must be financed, increasingly there will be demands that it be regulated. International regulatory organizations trace their origins to the creation of the International Telegraph Union (ITU) in 1865, followed by the International Postal Union in 1874, and the International Bureau of Weights and Standards in 1875. Now a specialized agency of the United Nations, the ITU allocates radio spectra worldwide. Since their first creation in the mid-nineteenth century, the number of IGOs has risen to almost four hundred, and they span every kind of activity from air traffic control to management of the sea beds.

The greatest enemy of state borders has been trade. The largest and most successful multinational organization for the abolition of economic and, to a degree, political borders has been the European Union. The EU has, however, been preceded and accompanied by the European Free Trade Association (EFTA), the Latin American Free Trade Association (LAFTA), the Central American Common Market (CACM), the Union Douaniere et Economique de l'Afrique Centrale (UDEAC), the Association of South East Asian Nations (ASEAN), the Andean Common Market (ACM), MERCOSUR in Latin America, the Economic Community of West African States (ECOWACS), and, in 1994, the North American Free Trade Agreement (NAFTA). "The larger the fraction of GNP [gross national product] that a state exported and imported—in other words, the better it used modern technology in order to maximize its comparative advantage—the greater by and large its economic success."[9] The escalation of international trade has led to the increased empowerment of the World Trade Organization, the only body capable of imposing any rules in the trade arena although it is not democratically accountable to any popular constituency. According to the forecast of the U.S. national intelligence community:

International or multilateral arrangements increasingly will be called upon in 2015 to deal with growing transnational problems from economics and financial volatility; to legal and illegal migration; to competition for scarce natural resources such as water; to humanitarian, refugee, and environmental crises; to terrorism, narcotrafficking, and weapons proliferation; and to both regional and cyber threats. And when international cooperation—or international governance—comes up short, the United States and other developed countries will have to broker solutions among a wide array of international players—including governments at all levels, multinational corporations, and nonprofit organizations.[10]

If economics has escaped the bonds of national regulation and is now occupying an international venue defined, if at all, by IGOs without the responsibility of democratic accountability, what does this mean for the future of politics defined by national boundaries? "Sooner or later—perhaps starting with the next serious economic downturn—the United States will have to confront one of the great challenges of our times: How does a sovereign nation govern itself effectively when politics are national and business is global?"[11] As profound as this question is today, it is made doubly complex by a further question: What if politics is no longer national?

The Evolving Nation-State

As economic power spirals upward, political authority is devolving downward and the nation-state—the post-Westphalian political building block for three and a half centuries—is undergoing a long, gradual but perceptible process of evolution. The fate of Yugoslavia—an artificial post–World War I construct—is but one instance of the fate of created nations. In a literal sense, however, all states are artificial. Even as it cedes power and authority to an emerging network of barely accountable international government organizations, the nation-state is in the process of redefinition.[12] Most Western democracies have been engaged for at least two decades in massive privatizations of state-owned and -operated enterprises and state services. The so-called neoliberal revolution of the 1980s among Western democracies was in large part a response to the pressures of economic competition and the sacrifice of systems of wealth distribution to market demands for deregulation and open markets. "In this intensely competitive environment, the state could no longer so readily afford the economic costs of national welfare programmes, and so the 1980s and 1990s were associated with the attack on the welfare state; deregulation and privatization extended the operation of the market into the provision of essential social services," or those social services were contracted or even abandoned.[13] Communications, transportation, and financial systems are increasingly privatized and internationalized. Previous state monopolies on services and functions as disparate as prisons, security forces, air and sea traffic-control systems, welfare programs, worker-training programs, and publicly administered health and retirement accounts—the centerpieces of twentieth-century social safety nets—are being privatized. Increasingly, administration of health, safety, and environmental regulations are passing from state to regional and interstate bureaucracies. International governmental organizations are also being rapidly supplemented by national and international nongovernmental organizations.

Underscoring these trends, the U.S. Central Intelligence Agency, in the report cited earlier, predicts a different and somewhat diminished role for the state in the twenty-first century: "States will continue to be the dominant players on the world stage, but governments will have less and less control over flows of information, technology, diseases, migrants, arms, and financial transactions, whether licit or illicit, across their borders. Non-state actors ranging from business firms to nonprofit organizations will play increasingly larger roles in both national and international affairs. The quality of governance, both nationally and internationally, will substantially determine how well states and societies cope with these global forces."

Nation-states are also losing their historic monopoly on violence and war, and the distinction between war and crime is being obliterated. Traditional wars between nations are being replaced by low-intensity urban conflicts between tribes, clans, and gangs. To a degree, this process is exacerbated by regionalism. The European project to create a single market, in which its citizens

can move themselves, their money, goods and services freely around the Union, has dramatically altered the pattern of cross-border crime in Europe. By lifting internal barriers . . . the EU's members have pushed their border controls to the outer rim of the Union. By, in turn, tightening up the periphery, they have driven certain cross-border activities underground, sometimes sending even genuine refugees into the hands of criminals, who now traffic them for profit alongside illegal migrants. And, by creating a single internal market, Europe has also created for itself a new single market in crime.[14]

Even as previously national concerns such as criminal justice become regionalized, state-owned enterprises are being privatized and often internationalized in large numbers. Throughout Europe, currencies are being unified. The traditional services and obligations of the state—education, health care, communication and transportation systems, prisons, and even police and safety functions—are increasingly carried out by private contractors. The state's welfare function is in retreat, as was made clear by the U.S. welfare "reforms" of the mid-1990s. Technology, especially communications technology, does not recognize political borders. The state's shell of sovereignty is increasingly hollowed out.

As further evidence, the state's loss of its monopoly on war and the privatization of state functions has resulted, especially in Western democracies, in a dramatic increase in reliance on private security forces. Within the last decade, at least 40 percent of the personnel of American airlines operating in Europe were engaged in security operations. In Germany between 1984 and 1996, the number of private security firms more than doubled to a total of fourteen hundred. In Britain, there are measurably more private security guards than the 237,000 uniformed, active-duty military personnel (as of 1995). In the United States, the private security industry's revenues totaled $52 billion in 1995 and reached about twice that amount by the turn of the century. As early as the 1970s the private security industry had twice as many employees and 1.5 times the budget of all local, state, and federal police forces combined. The 1.6 million people employed in this industry exceeds the number of U.S. troops on active duty in the armed forces, and the total amount spent on private security is close to the total national military budget. Even these numbers do not disclose the full political consequences of this trend. Following riots in Los Angeles in the mid-1990s, Korean-American merchants created their own private security force, which amounts to nothing less than a foreign army on U.S. soil.[15] The U.S. intelligence community believes:

> Criminal organizations and networks based in North America, Western Europe, China, Colombia, Israel, Japan, Mexico, Nigeria, and Russia will expand the scale and scope of their activities. They will form loose alliances with one another, with smaller criminal entrepreneurs, and with insurgent movements for specific operations. They will corrupt leaders of unstable, economically fragile or failing states, insinuate themselves into troubled banks and businesses, and cooperate with insurgent political movements to control substantial geographic areas. Their income will come from narcotics trafficking, alien smuggling, trafficking in women and children, smuggling toxic materials, hazardous wastes, illicit arms, military technologies, and other contraband, financial fraud, and racketeering.[16]

Even as domestic security is being privatized, efforts are under way to create an international civil and criminal justice system. The United Nations has enacted human rights and sanctions resolutions, which are treated by the larger international community as having binding force on nations. Member nations are ceding to the EU authority over currencies, banking, communications, customs, tariffs, transportation, and other regional matters, including criminal justice. International courts are now trying national political criminals, and efforts are under way to increase their authority. Nongovernmental organizations are increasingly assuming responsibility for a range of social services, including police protection.

One of the state's most important functions, providing security to its citizens, has also become suspect. This is true of conflict suppression, peacekeeping, and the exertion of national interests abroad:

> Over the last half-century, the change [in national military authority] that has taken place is momentous. From France to the United States, there has scarcely been one "advanced" government in Europe and North America whose armed forces have

not suffered defeat at the hands of underequipped, ill-trained, ill-organized, often even ill-clad, underfed, and illiterate free-dom fighters or guerilla [sic] terrorists; briefly, by men—and, often, women—who were short on everything except high cour-age and the determination to endure and persist in the face of police operations, counterinsurgency operations, peace-keeping operations, and whatever other types of operations . . . were dreamed up by their masters.[17]

The U.S. experience in this regard stretches from Vietnam in the 1960s and 1970s to its failed humanitarian effort in Somalia in 1993 and its subsequent refusal to intervene, either unilaterally or through a con-sortium, in Rwanda shortly thereafter. The former Soviet Union was de-feated in Afghanistan by forces considered "inferior" by conventional stan-dards. And what has been said about the (lack of) potency of the military forces of major powers in foreign operations must now also, in the wake of the World Trade Center and Pentagon attacks, be said about homeland security. Conventional, and even strategic, military force is insufficient to deter attacks on the homeland.

For Jean-Marie Guehenno, a scholar with practical political experi-ence, the year 1989, the beginning of the collapse of both the Soviet and Russian empires, "marks the close of an era that began not in 1945 or 1917, but that was institutionalized thanks to the French revolution, in 1789. It brings an end to the age of the nation-state."[18] Guehenno sees on the global level not "postnational" political structures in Europe but, instead, "aggregates of networks linked together, like the interlinked rings that are the symbol of the Olympic Games."[19] The traditional definition of the state in geographic and spatial terms, by boundaries and perime-ters, is being destroyed by cross-border networks driven in large part by communications technologies: "The nation-state, in its pretensions to combine in a unique framework the political, cultural, economic, and military dimensions of power, is prisoner to a spatial conception of power, even as it tries to redistribute its competences according to a federal prin-ciple. Space has ceased to be the pertinent criterion."[20] Traditional political boundaries are being overwhelmed by instant communications, massive capital flows, and multinational corporations, and they are being supplanted by new transnational networks supporting these functions. The state no longer regulates and supports these functions, for it has lost authority over them.[21]

Within the context of the rise of new regional governments, the European Union especially, issues of federalism and, particularly, new forms of federalism arise. These issues in turn open discussions of the doctrine of subsidiarity. The relation of Jefferson's ward republic to the notion of subsidiarity rests in large part on how it is defined. According to one source, it is "the notion that authority should be given to institutions covering a wider area only if it cannot effectively by exercised by units covering a smaller area."[22] In this definition, much depends on a further understanding of the nature of "authority." According to another definition: "Subsidiarity derives from the Latin subsidium, meaning 'support, help, protection.' The constituent units of society are to be nurtured and protected. They are helped to grow in inner strength, or to recover failing strength—that is, the capacity to perform their distinctive functions. They are protected as objects of moral concern and as social units whose well-being demands self-determination. Thus the underlying model is parental."[23] For Philip Selznick, implementation of the doctrine of subsidiarity does not require citizen consent or agreement; local groups and institutions are considered to have intrinsic worth (according to a canonical doctrine pronounced by Pope Pius XI in 1931); these groups are protected units designated to perform (according to the underlying parental model) distinctive functions; the doctrine is not equated with delegation or decentralization and is not principally concerned with democracy; and there is no expectation that democracy will be nourished in federated communities governed by norms of subsidiarity.[24] Whether one accepts the simpler form of subsidiarity as a presumption in favor of units of government at the lowest level or the more elaborate definition provided by Selznick, neither seems to equate with the classic republican notion of Jefferson.

Jefferson saw the ward republic as a distinctly democratic institution, a foundational layer of government embedded in the federal Constitutional structure, and a forum very much dependent on consent and agreement. Like classical republicans before him, he demonstrated little concern for fostering citizen associations, public or private, and he was not concerned with the republic as an instrument of pluralism or with the perpetuation of quasi-private, quasi-public organizations for their own sake. It is highly doubtful that Jefferson would have seen any relationship of the ward republic to the concerns of the papacy. However, he would have sympathized with the Catholic church's concern for the support, help, and protection of citizen associations of all kinds in addition to, but separate from, the local republican government.

The Decline of Ideology

For our purposes, Daniel Bell's definition of *total ideology* will suffice. It is, he states, "an all-inclusive system of comprehensive reality, it is a set of beliefs, infused with passion, and seeks to transform the whole of a way of life. This commitment to ideology—the yearning for a 'cause,' or the satisfaction of deep moral feelings—is not necessarily the reflection of interests in the shape of ideas. Ideology in this sense . . . is a secular religion."[25] Although social and political conservatism, the impulse to prevent the erosion of traditional values over time, and social and political progressivism, the instinct toward the improvement of society, are deeply embedded in the souls of strong minorities in most democratic societies, the grasp of ideologies as comprehensive belief systems represented by one or another political party, the notion of politics as the arena for deeply felt causes and parties as the vehicles upon which those causes might ride, has weakened noticeably in early twenty-first-century America. Not least among the causes for the emergence of distrust in secular belief systems was the lurid, maniacal appeal of fascism and the failed utopian dreams of socialism. Nor did it help that ideology offered a convenient mask for mass murderers. Even as the two most dangerous ideologies of the mid–twentieth century were destroyed or self-destructed, workers, "whose grievances were once the driving energy for social change," according to Bell, entered the middle class and became "more satisfied with society than the intellectuals."[26] Even as distrust of political systems mounted, a cult of personal self-fulfillment arose to takes its place, a cult that found its cause and its fulfillment in market economics.

As the twentieth century ended, containment of communism as a central organizing principle of American society had lost its cogency and relevance. Politically, the end of the cold war signaled a shift away from nations organized individually and collectively (as in the North American

Treaty Organization) around common ideologies and political belief systems toward sub- and transnational groups identified by culture, history, religion, and tradition. The importance of political ideology in the twenty-first century is thus waning under the pressures of radicalism, tribalism, fundamentalism, and a narrower, more ethnic definition of nationalism. In the decade following the end of a half century of cold war, national dis-integration in venues as diverse as Yugoslavia and Rwanda unleashed tribalism, fundamentalism, factionalism, and the resurrection of ancient hatreds. In the minds of some, this epoch is marked by the triumph of democracy and thus "the end of history."[27] In the minds of others, a century of ideological conflict has been replaced by the "clash of civilizations."[28] But in virtually all cases historians see the Western world stepping across the threshold of history into a totally different and as yet undefined era.

Perhaps most important, even those nations claiming a republican heritage are finding it hollowed out. In the United States, there is declining citizen exercise of the most fundamental democratic right, the franchise. Even in national elections, no more than half of all eligible U.S. voters participate, and the percentage is much lower in off-year (that is, nonpresidential) State and local elections. There is widespread belief, supported by considerable data, that the election and governing systems have been corrupted by powerful, monied interests and that concern for individual citizens is being displaced by interest-group politics. Popular sovereignty is increasingly expressed through opinion polls, and such polls are used by candidates for office and officeholders to define the public agenda. Such civic virtue as exists, exists primarily in the community.

A recent survey of U.S. citizens entitled "Americans Unplugged— Citizens and Their Government" found that "more than twice as many Americans (64 percent) feel 'distant and disconnected' from government than feel 'close and connected' (30 percent)." Among younger citizens, aged eighteen to thirty-four, 68 percent of those surveyed said they felt disconnected from government. A majority of those surveyed spoke in terms of *the* government as opposed to *our* government. The report concluded: "To talk about government as 'ours' is to state—even if unconsciously—a sense of ownership, and perhaps also a sense of belonging or involvement. People who think in terms of *the* government, by contrast, are revealing their feeling that government is not accountable to them."[29] Disempowerment is caused by the loss of any influence on day-to-day economic affairs, the flight of capital to international networks, the rise of political regionalism, the fragmentation of nation-states, the nondemocratic process of resolution of issues of consequence by negotiation among remote political and bureaucratic elites, and the loss of convincing political belief systems. Certain groups of the disempowered have found voice in grassroots resistance to the globalization of economics, finance, politics, and bureaucracies and in the rise of "Seattle man," the prototypical protester against globilization. As a result, there are signs of politics migrating from national capitals downward. In partial response to the loss of control of their economic lives, some protest at meetings of the International Monetary Fund and the World Bank. Others insist on increased control of local, public institutions, such as schools, hospitals, transportation systems, and security forces. Basques, Chechnyans, and Kurds demand autonomy. Scottish and Welsh parliaments have been established in the United Kingdom. Neonationalism at the tribal level has found expression in many ways, including the revival of ancient languages. "This is one of the more intriguing side effects of a uniting Europe: as national boundaries fade within the fifteen-member European Union, more political power flows to Brussels and more countries beg to join the group, local cultures and languages are re-asserting their strength. And, while a blanket of sameness has settled over consumer trends and styles in Europe, historians say that more people are interested in protecting minority languages and asserting local differences than at any other time in this [twentieth] century."[30] According to Hans Magnus Enzensberger, a German writer on European and regional identity, "The more global and uniform our civilization, the more people want to anchor themselves in their own culture. The fact is, Europe has a few thousand years of settled cultures—it can't simply turn into an American-style melting pot." The ancient languages being revived include Breton, Occitan, Basque, Corsican, and Alsatian in France, Gaelic in Scotland and Wales (it was previously reinstated in Ireland), Friulian in northern Italy, Frisian and Limburgs in Holland, Saami in Finland, and Catalan and Basque in Spain. Teaching regional languages is "an enterprise that can destroy the unity of a nation," according to the head of the French Academy. In many cases the language revival has been accompanied by ethnic cultural revivals as well.[31]

In the United States, devolution of political power from national to local levels has been under way since the 1980s. Massive interstate by-passes can no longer smash local neighborhoods with impunity. The siting of nuclear waste dumps can no longer be determined by bilateral negotiations between the national and State governments. There is a clamor for charter schools, vouchers, and home schooling. Hospitals are being taken over by local communities. Supported by increasingly vocal voters, throughout much of the Western democratic world, local units of government are insisting on greater authority and flexibility in the solution of local problems.

The Scope of Twenty-first-Century Change in Historic Perspective

The sixteenth and seventeenth centuries, the era of Dutch, Spanish, Portuguese, and English colonial expansion, were a period of commercial integration parallel to that of the early twenty-first century. The early nineteenth-century industrial revolution was an economic transformation analogous to that brought on by information technologies. The Florentine Renaissance was a period of political revolution not unlike the present age. The era of empire in ancient Rome offers a precedent for one nation possessing unrivaled economic and military power, such as that enjoyed by the United States. However, one searches in vain, certainly through modern history, for a period in which so many similar revolutions occurred simultaneously—as they are at the beginning of the twenty-first century.

The implications of these simultaneous revolutions have yet to be fully understood. The first implication is the potential demand for the regulation of international financial markets when the failure of mega-conglomerate financial institutions threatens to "take the entire global financial system down with them." This might lead to the rise of even more undemocratic, nonaccountable governmental institutions. The second is the potential demand for international security forces to prevent further bloodshed, which could be produced by the decay of the cold war, bipolar world. The third is the need to fill the vacuum created by the erosion of the nation-state and to design a new political architecture for citizen empowerment.

Why even discuss the need for market regulation in an age that has deified free markets? Unregulated markets in the 1920s contributed to market abuses and to collapse and depression. Out of the financial wreckage of the 1930s, Western governments created banking and securities regulations, currency stabilization mechanisms, strong central banks, and social safety nets. As a consequence, the United States has not had an economic depression in seventy years. Postdepression, market-regulating institutions have largely dispelled the myth of genuinely free markets.

Even though finance is increasingly global, save for the World Trade Organization and ad hoc consultation among central bankers, there are few institutions to regulate the international market. A former secretary of the U.S. Treasury is given credit for "saving" Mexico, stabilizing Asian markets, and bailing out Brazil and other countries. These accomplishments are the result of ad hoc coalitions of willing Western central bankers. In a precarious financial world, the adequacy of this approach will be tested.

Instability in the international financial structures may require that consideration be given to building a regulatory superstructure before catastrophe strikes. This superstructure might include an international banking regulatory authority, an international securities and exchange authority, and an international currency stabilization authority. It might require a crisis in the global network, a collapse of the international financial architecture, for public demand for new governing structures to emerge. Perhaps a catastrophe that wipes out the earnings and savings of hundreds of millions of people would produce the political demands that will breach the barrier to global economic stability, the barrier of national sovereignty.

What of security threats? If the world no longer faces the possibility of nuclear exchange between ideological superpowers, is it now at peace? The U.S. Commission on National Security/Twenty-first Century concluded as early as September 1999 that the U.S. homeland would be attacked sometime in the next quarter century, sooner rather than later, and that "Americans will likely die on American soil, possibly in large numbers." Should it occur, the commission warned, this attack would be by a small group of nonstate terrorists using weapons of mass destruction.[32] The fate that visited the United States on September 11, 2001, may await other powers. This commission presented recommendations for the reform of the U.S. national security establishment—including military structures, intelligence capabilities, and deployment policies—which it deemed necessary to implement this new strategy. An effort such as this has not been undertaken in the United States since the end of World War II and the beginning of the cold war in the mid-1940s.

Two major reforms are considered in this volume. For the U.S. homeland defense, consideration must be given to returning once again to the citizen-soldiers, the Jeffersonian local militia with its historic roots in seventeenth- and eighteenth-century England, the reserve army acknowledged in the Constitution and renamed, in the late nineteenth century, the National Guard. Second, a new international security agency, a multinational peacemaking force empowered to prevent the slaughter of civilians, to separate warring factions, and to restore the peace might be considered. These multinational forces, possibly operating under U.N. command, could be rapidly deployable, highly maneuverable, and specially trained in quick-intervention conflict suppression. Forces currently used for peacekeeping operations are generally not equipped or trained for this mission. The United States might well become reluctant to intervene, even with token support from other nations, as it did in Somalia, or unilaterally, as it did in Haiti. The United States will not always be able to form coalitions of the willing as it did in Kosovo or have the time to do so as it did in the Persian Gulf. Alternatives to the creation of a new international peacemaking military police force have yet to be proposed in any detail by the political leadership of Western powers.

Discussions of this alternative have not led to concrete action for much the same reason that few steps have been taken to establish international market regulatory institutions. That reason is national sovereignty. At a time when the authority of the state is already under challenge, national leaders will resist ceding power to as yet unstructured international financial or military institutions. Yet, it is not unprecedented. During only a few years in the mid–twentieth century, the United Nations, the World Bank and International Monetary Fund, NATO, the European Organization for Security and Cooperation, and other organizations were all created. But the cold-war world is being replaced by the world just described, a world of integrated economics and disintegrating nation-states.

Western democracies may find it necessary to attend to the integrated and integrating international financial and security world and leave more of the day-to-day government of the local activities of local people to the citizens themselves. What are the barriers to this kind of devolution? It is certainly not talent or capability. In most Western democracies, local citizens are better educated on a wider range of issues than at any time in history. It is not access to information on complex matters. There has seldom been better or more instantaneous means of communications both at the global and the neighborhood levels. It is not mobility. Through public and private transport, virtually every citizen can participate in the local councils of government. It is not access. In the era of "sunshine" laws, little or no public business is, or should be, conducted behind closed doors.

In the last two centuries, power and authority have gravitated to national governments for several reasons: the need for centralized authority to combat depression and social misery; the need for national unity to fight world wars and defend democracy; the ineffectiveness and occasional corruption of local governments; and the preservation of unions against secession. None of these conditions presently prevails. Furthermore, in recent years, the system of concentrated political power has been seriously corrupted in the United States by the amount of money necessary to sustain it. In a revolutionary political era in which a republican ideal was restored, how would power be distributed and where would authority reside?

What would be the responsibilities of the national government? Primarily, it would defend the borders of the nation and ensure the domestic tranquillity. Second, it would raise and equitably distribute revenues required by local republics to meet local educational, health, safety, transportation, environmental, and other social responsibilities. Third, the national government would establish and enforce standards for these social undertakings sufficient to guarantee that no student, elderly person, worker, or parent would lack the necessities of life, and it would also ensure that all citizens of the republic have equality of access to its protections and benefits. As a twenty-first-century democratic republican ideal should not be based on property ownership, gender, or race, it also must not result in measurable social inequities.

Even presuming a revival of local democratic republicanism, the national government remains the powerful, unifying national force. But the revival would open up the base of the republican pyramid to local citizen involvement in the creative and innovative administration of federal undertakings best carried out by those actively engaged in local community affairs. Thereby, the national community would be strengthened rather than weakened. Neorepublicanism is not proposed as a means to erode national unity or the strength of the federal government.

Establishment of local republicanism, under the federal umbrella, could restore political initiative to the citizens. Traditional excuses for nonparticipation in government—remoteness, lack of access, lack of information—are all taken away. All citizens would be able to participate in the decisions affecting the public's business. An argument might even be made that the scope of compulsory public service, such as jury duty, could be expanded to include, for example, service on public oversight boards. Restoration of the notion of civic virtue could gradually create a culture of participation.

If one premise of this book is correct—namely, that economics is migrating upward and politics is migrating downward—the issue of national sovereignty becomes greater. What happens to the state if it cedes part of its authority to international institutions to regulate an increasingly complex international marketplace, part of its military authority to international peacemaking forces, and part of its authority to local republics so that citizens are empowered to govern their communities? The future structure and role of the state remains uncertain.

The nation-state emerged to give order to a decaying feudal age. The great danger in the erosion of state power is the emergence of a neofeudal era in which loyalties and allegiances are commanded by powerful individuals and private interests. On the other hand, restoration of a classic model could conceivably occur:

> Nations as we know them have existed for only a few hundred years. But cities have been with us since the dawn of civilization. And while the future of the city is not in doubt, modern nations will probably continue to weaken in the 21st century.

By 2100, the organizing principle of the world will be the city-state, along with the urban radials of prosperity that follow major trade routes. Indeed, loyalty toward the polis will gradually overwhelm the traditional state patriotism of the 20th century. Empires will be agglomerations of urban areas. Cities and their hinterlands will make alliances and fight wars with and against each other—less over territory than over bandwidths in cyberspace and trade privileges.[33]

This vision of "the age of high-tech feudalism," more understandable by the map makers of the ancient and medieval worlds than by the politicians of the twentieth century, may seem farfetched. But, given the new realities outlined above and the social, economic, and political tensions and transformations they represent, it is not unreasonable.

Stated somewhat differently, and less provocatively, another observer of long-term trends reaches something of the same conclusion regarding the new century:

The challenge of the next millennium, or rather the next century (we won't have a thousand years), is to preserve the autonomy of our institutions—and in some cases, like transnational business, autonomy over and beyond national sovereignties—while at the same time restoring the unity of the polity that we have all but lost, at least in peacetime. We can only hope this can be done—but so far no one knows how to do it. We do know that it will require something that is even less precedented than today's pluralism: the willingness and ability of each of today's institutions to maintain the focus on the narrow and specific function that gives them the capacity to perform, and yet the willingness and ability to work together and with political authority for the common good.[34]

This requirement to rediscover the common good causes the reconsideration—indeed, the restoration—of something like the classic republican ideal that establishes *res publica*, the "public thing," the common good, the commonwealth, and most of all, the deep and real sense of civic virtue. As Robert Putnam points out, there is precedence for such a restoration in American history: "By the turn of the twentieth century, complacency bred of technological prowess was succeeded by dissatisfaction, civic inventiveness, and organized reform efforts fueled by a blend of discontent and hopefulness. Over the succeeding decade this flourishing, multifaceted movement—sprouting from seeds sown in the Gilded Age and dependent on new tendrils of social connectedness—would produce the most powerful era of reform in American history."[35]

Original Objections to Small Republics

The central forum for debating the future structure of government in the emerging United States was the Constitutional convention in Philadelphia in 1787. Eleven years had passed since the revolutionary war, sufficient time to reveal that the confederacy of thirteen semiautonomous States would either negotiate a federation or be driven toward further autonomy by local, sectional, and regional self-interests. For the Federalists, the leaders of the movement toward a consolidated national government, the enemy of centralization was primitive republicanism, the notion that the republican spirit to which all subscribed—at least rhetorically—could only survive in a venue no larger than an existing State. Therefore, the Federalists' task was to mount arguments against both the existing confederacy and the notion that republican principles could survive only in a small *polis*. For the Federalists, James Madison argued that there was such a political evil as being too "democratical": "The passions [of the public] ought to be controlled and regulated by the government."[36] Direct democracy practiced through local governance was subject to chaos and mob rule. Mass citizen participation in government permitted hysterias of the moment, calculating despots, and petty grievances to overcome sound judgment, detached decisionmaking, and national unity. There was contemporary evidence to support this view. The confederacy at that time was troubled by rebellion, most notably Shays's Rebellion in New England, which featured local resistance to taxation.

> Nationalists like Madison became convinced during the 1780s
> that popular self-government, the essence of political freedom,
> threatened the security of property and must be restrained so
> that freedom might flourish. . . . Madison had in mind the bois-

terous state-level democracy of the 1780s and collective attacks on public order like Shay's [*sic*] Rebellion of 1786–87, when debt-ridden farmers, many of them former soldiers in the War for Independence, closed the courts in western Massachusetts to prevent the loss of their property to creditors.[37]

The overriding issue of which layer of government had the right to make and enforce the laws was very much an open one.

Closely allied to the question of "democratical" excess was the threat of faction. In the minds of Madison and his fellow Federalists, small republics were by their nature more inclined to factionalism and division than large ones: "Among the numerous advantages promised by a well-constructed Union, none deserves to be more accurately developed than its tendency to break and control the violence of faction. The friend of popular government never finds himself so much alarmed for their character and fate as when he contemplates their propensity to this dangerous vice."[38] Their argument was to the effect that the untutored local citizen, participating in "popular government," was subject to being emotionally swayed by narrow causes and movements, which offered purpose and direction, however much in error.[39] Only duly elected representatives, removed by distance from the excesses of local clamor, could weigh the merits and calculate the cost of this or that temporal excitement.

Overriding these concerns regarding the weakness of popular democracy and ephemeral local politics, however, was the greater cause of formation of the union. For the Federalists, construction of a credible national government, a contractual federation of States, was by orders of magnitude a more powerful concern than the preservation of local prerogative. Republican values could be preserved in a large central republic, they believed, just as easily as in the local *polis*—perhaps, given common cause and purpose, even more so. The Federalists also founded the cause of federation on the needs of the new nation to become a commercial power. Hamilton went so far as to describe the proposed union as a "commercial republic," one that will be "governed by mutual interest, and will cultivate a spirit of mutual amity and concord."[40] As it fell to Madison, among the Federalists, to spell out the political arguments for union, so it fell to Hamilton to articulate the more immediate, commercial ones. The "speculative trader," he wrote, "will acknowledge that the aggregate balance of the commerce of the United States would bid fair to be much more favorable than that of the thirteen States without union or with partial union." In sum, Hamilton argued that a central union was required to present a unified commercial face to the trading world, particularly to Great Britain, that a national navy would be required to protect the maritime aspects of those growing commercial interests, that revenue from taxation of those interests would pay for the costs of protecting maritime activities, and that the net result would be a thriving, expansive, and powerful nation. "Let the thirteen States, bound together in a strict and indissoluble Union, concur in erecting one great American system superior to the control of all transatlantic force or influence and able to dictate the terms of the connection between the old and the new world."[41]

Finally, in opposition to the perpetuation of a confederacy of thirteen States, Federalists argued that only a national union could maintain sufficient defensive power to deter external threats to the new nation's security. Thirteen independent republics were both vulnerable to manipulation by foreign powers seeking to capitalize on internal discontent and susceptible to dissension among themselves. "Wisely, do [the people of America] consider union and good national government as necessary to put and keep them in such a situation as, instead of inviting war, will tend to repress and discourage it," argued "Publius" in the Federalist. "That situation consists in the best possible state of defense, and necessarily depends on the government, the arms, and the resources of the country."[42] The Federalists were as concerned with friction among States, regions, and sections as they were by the threat of foreign attack and felt that the best defense against both was union and common defense.

Thus, of the many arguments for an extended federal republic and against a confederacy of smaller republics, the principal ones were (1) popular democracy as exercised in the local *polis* is subject to chaos, mob rule, and instability; (2) small republics are susceptible to factionalism and division; (3) formation of the union was a higher priority than preservation of local prerogatives; (4) a strong federal government is required to advance national commercial interests; and (5) only a central government can maintain sufficient defense forces to maintain internal security and deter foreign aggression.

Responses to Original Objections

The Federalists' arguments for a national federation of State republics all presupposed a single choice—either continuation of a confederation of States with little central cohesion or creation of a federal government of the States. From that viewpoint, any appeal to traditional republican theory or ideals was seen as subversive of the principal objective. Antifederalists relied on republican history, theory, and practice to argue against centralized authority, large-scale and remote government, loss of popular sovereignty, and replacement of the commonweal by narrow interests.

In response to the claim that "democratical" participatory government necessarily meant chaos, Antifederalists argued that the citizens of a republic were either to be trusted or they were not. Given sufficient right to participate in the decisions affecting their lives, they had the good judgment to avoid excesses of passion and emotion and to make sound decisions. There was indeed a natural aristocracy, but it was an aristocracy to which all, not merely a few, belonged. Further, reliance on representation promotes narrow interests at the price of citizen participation in government. With regard to the Federalists' claims that factionalism was rampant in the local republic, Antifederalists responded that the inevitable subversion of a large centralized government by interests was itself a form of factionalism. Interest groups were every bit as much factions as political movements or causes. They simply were more inclined toward commerce than ideology. A nation divided into narrow financial and commercial interests—and which identified citizens as members of those interest groups—was every bit as faction-ridden as a nation divided by political ideologies.

In response to the need for a strong union, it might have been argued (though it largely was not) that the needs of unity and solidarity did not preclude the preservation of a polity in which citizens could participate directly, namely, the polity of the local republic. At this point—the reduction of the formulative Constitutional debate to a choice between a strong federation and a loose confederacy—the debate proved too narrow and exclusive. Since neither Jefferson nor any other founder had formulated the pyramid of republics in which the ward formed the base of the ascending representative republics of the States and the national government, serious consideration was not given to the possibility that the classic republican values of civic duty and participation could be preserved even as a strong union was being formed. Thus, neither Antifederalist arguments against the union nor Federalist responses to them fully addressed the possibility of combining a federal union with an elementary republic. Similarly, the Federalist contention that a federal government was required to protect and promote the emerging nation's commercial interests, like other Federalist arguments, saw the opposition arguments based on classic republicanism as a threat to be crushed rather than as a structure and set of values to be assimilated. The idea that there could be a federal government, one of whose delineated powers would be the promotion of national commercial interests, and a system of ward republics empowered to manage local public affairs seems not to have been thoroughly considered in the Constitutional forum. As a collection of small republics could not adequately support the nation's international commercial activities and interests, so a centralized national government could not appropriately resolve the particular concerns of the local communities.

Finally, in response to the Federalists' concerns for national security and the need for a united defensive front, Antifederalists argued that defense of the homeland was still the responsibility of the local militia, in collaboration with a small standing army, and that the maintenance of a large standing army in peacetime had continuously been viewed as a threat to republican liberties. Stating the traditional republican argument against standing armies during the ratification debate, "Brutus," the Antifederalist counterpart to the Federalists' "Publius," made this case: "The liberties of the people are in danger from a large standing army, not only because the rulers may employ them for the purpose of supporting themselves in any usurpation of power, which they may see proper to exercise, but there is great hazard, that an army will subvert the forms of the government, under whose authority they are raised, and establish one according to the pleasure of their leader."[43] For historic evidence, "Brutus" cited Julius Caesar's use of the lawfully constituted republican army to create "the most absolute despotism" and Cromwell's use of the army, previously employed against a tyrant king, to establish his own autocratic protectorate.

Once again, however, a synthesis, whereby a standing army and navy might protect America's international commerce and an integrated system of local militias might defend the homeland, was considered only in the final Constitutional compromise. The new Constitution authorized a standing national army and navy (Article I, sec. 8) and, after acknowledging State militias in the same article, later the Bill of Rights recognized the right of the various militias to maintain their own armaments (Second Amendment). Of the principal objections to small republics raised, and refuted, in the Constitutional adoption and ratification debates, only this one, having to do with standing armies and militias, resulted in compromise.

In sum, the responses to the objections to small republics in the Constitutional era were (1) primary reliance on representative government reduces civic virtue and citizen participation, which are necessary for republican government and are themselves the greatest guarantors against chaos and mob rule; (2) the danger of factionalism is greater in a distant, remote government, and factions are more likely to be narrow interests than political movements; (3) it is possible to have a central or federal government and still preserve republican ideals in a small *polis*; (4) a federated government can promote national commercial interests without sacrificing popular sovereignty in the local republics; and (5) local militias are greater guarantors of homeland security than standing armies, which are always a danger in a peacetime republic.

Having raised the most important arguments for an extended, federated republic and against small, autonomous, confederated republics, and having then summarized the responses to those objections, it is necessary to restate a principal premise of this volume. The Jeffersonian model, encompassing specific, tiered roles for the national, the State, and the local republics, was only elaborated later in Jefferson's career, following his presidency, and thus was not considered in the Constitutional debates. Those debates generally featured Federalists favoring a national government with recognized Constitutional powers and Antifederalists favoring the preservation of a loose confederation of thirteen States. Though the Constitution as ratified and amended preserved for the States all those powers not entrusted to the national government,[44] following the resolution of the States' rights struggle in the Civil War, the national government emerged preeminent. Unresolved paradoxes embodied in the Constitution and a myriad of Supreme Court decisions seeking to resolve them continue to permeate American public policy debates concerning the locus of sovereignty.

Revisitation of the ideal of local republicanism in the United States has been deferred by more than two centuries of intermittent pressures fostering political consolidation and the evolution of power upward. The Federalists' arguments had merit. The new nation did require union, it did have legitimate concerns about political fragmentation, it was threatened with factionalism, it did need to emerge quickly into international commerce, and it did have real threats to its security. Then came foreign invasion in 1812, frontier expansion in the early and mid–nineteenth century, the emergence of new States, the slavery debate leading to the Civil War, Reconstruction and economic turmoil, followed by industrialization, immigration, and rapid urbanization, emergence into a turbulent world and engagement in world war, then the Great Depression followed by another world war, the perceived threat of communism, and the cold war. Many of the dominant political and economic realities of the nineteenth and twentieth centuries produced greater centralized, consolidated authority and sovereignty and necessarily led to the expansion of the powers of the national government.

These trends were not, of course, without exception. The history of America has been by no means an uninterrupted pattern of consolidated federal power. The first seventy years of the nation's existence represented a continuing struggle between the national and the State governments over the allocation of authority and power, a struggle, as noted, culminating in the ultimate fragmentation, the Civil War. Resistance to the centralization of power during the New Deal era by States' rights interests was considerable, but the resistance was eroded by the exigencies of the depression and then was largely swept away by world war. Even though the argument here is that *overall* the trend has been for greater consolidation, unification, and strengthening of federal authority, a trend that all but a few would consider both inevitable and benevolent, it has been far from an uninterrupted or continuous one.

Throughout two centuries, the old Constitutional struggles continued to be fought, often on badly chosen battlefields. At few periods was the drumbeat for national unity and national purpose heard more loudly than in the Progressive Era of the late nineteenth and early twentieth centuries. Great wealth was being created and held in few hands. National and State governments were dominated by powerful commercial interests. The interests of citizens, consumers, and taxpayers were perceived to be unheard. During this period, progressive scholars and writers parsed America's founding era in search of meanings and patterns possessing some enduring insight into the nation's soul. Among these, Herbert Croly is notable for his effort to achieve an overarching synthesis. Croly saw American life as a persistent struggle between national purpose and rampant individualism. Naming the prototypes of these two polar opposites, he saw Alexander Hamilton as the ultimate representative of national purpose and Thomas Jefferson as the classic instance of what Arthur Schlesinger, Jr. (who wrote the introduction to a modern edition of Croly's work) called "indiscriminant individualism."[45] In Schlesinger's words, Croly sought "to use Hamiltonian means to achieve Jeffersonian ends," a dubious enterprise since both Croly and Schlesinger seem suspicious, at best, of Jeffersonian ends.

Croly saw "nationalism" as a unifying theme for a disparate nation, not as a slogan for consolidation of power. He favored economic concentration and the supremacy of organizations, especially in their emerging business forms, as the touchstones of national life. He perceived in Jefferson's writings a surpassing emphasis on "individualism" to an extent antithetical to national unity and national purpose. For Croly, Jefferson was the ultimate "democrat," neither a friendly nor a benign appellation, and as a committed Hamiltonian, saw Jefferson through Federalist eyes. Jefferson's espousal of democratic principles and ideals represented nothing less than an invitation to chaos, upheaval, rampant individualism, and antipathy to central authority.

Croly characterizes Jefferson as shallow, insincere, lethargic, superficial, and adrift. He was "an amiable enthusiast," favoring "extreme individualism" and possessing "amiable credulity." Jefferson's first inaugural address, held by many scholars of American history to be a sublimely unifying statement following a bitter campaign, is, for Croly, a "bewildering document." Given the stark bipolarity of Croly's world, the idea that Jefferson could be both a Federalist and a republican would indeed be bewildering. Jefferson's egalitarianism is, for Croly, simply a guise for leveling, for reducing Americans, and particularly American leaders, to the lowest common denominator. Above all else, Croly's favorite, Hamilton, had a political philosophy much "more clearly thought out" than that of Jefferson.

Although he claimed to seek a synthesis of Hamiltonian and Jeffersonian beliefs, Croly took little care to conceal his biases. "On the whole," he wrote, "my own preferences are on the side of Hamilton rather than of Jefferson."[46] Hamilton, he thought, "is much the finer man and much the sounder thinker and statesman." On top of that, Jefferson "was incapable either of uniting with his fine phrases a habit of candid and honorable private dealings or of embodying those phrases in a set of efficient institutions." Efficiency is very much on Croly's mind throughout *Promise*. To round out his assessment, he concluded: "Jefferson's policy was at bottom the old fatal policy of drift, whose distorted body was concealed by fair-seeming clothes, and whose ugly face was covered by a mask of good intentions. Hamilton's policy was one of energetic and intelligent assertion of the national good."[47] Croly repeatedly juxtaposes "Jefferson's policy of drift"[48] with Hamilton's "nationalistic organization and principle."[49]

All of this either neglects or distorts both facts and scholarly consensus. Whatever else Jefferson was, "amiable" would not spring to mind as a consistent qualifier (except perhaps to his family and close friends). The same must be said for "insincere," "shallow," "lethargic," "superficial," and "adrift." Croly overlooks Jefferson's repeated references to a "natural aristocracy" of leaders. He further neglects the possibility of the employment of republican ideals and principles—of civic virtue, citizen participation, popular sovereignty, and resistance to corruption by powerful interests—as the means to achieve national purpose and unity. Croly's appeal to an elite of national organizers effectively rules out the contributions to be made by ordinary citizens to national life.

Further, Croly is guilty of a common historical fallacy, the assumption that Jefferson led and spoke for the Antifederalist forces, those most resistant to the formation of a union and suspicious of national leadership. In fact, though he shared their concerns for concentrated wealth and power in a national government (as well as their suspicion of Hamilton's readily evident ambitions), Jefferson was separated by geography and philosophy from the Antifederalists. Jefferson was on the other side of the Atlantic Ocean from the Constitutional debates, and his republicanism was *sui generis* and idiosyncratic. It did not derive from radical Antifederalist rhetoric. Jefferson supported the founding of a new nation.[50] His contribution to the Constitutional debate, made largely through letters to his ally James Madison, emphasized principally the need for term limits for the presidency and a bill of rights, soon thereafter adopted. Unquestionably, Croly is right in one observation—Jefferson's antipathy toward Hamilton, whom he saw as a self-aggrandizer and potential Caesarean menace. But Jefferson was not alone in this assessment.

Croly completely misreads Jefferson's foreign policy as isolationist and regressive. Croly calls it "international democratic propagandism," a characterization even Croly's defender Schlesinger describes as "incorrect." It was neither isolationist, regressive, nor propagandistic. Nor is it true that, as Croly asserts, Jefferson "shirked the necessity and duty of national defense."[51] And to say that Hamilton's political philosophy was more clearly thought out than Jefferson's is equally wide of the mark.[52]

By making Jefferson, wrongly, the enemy of an effective national government, Croly makes him responsible for chaos, disorder, drift, and a lack of national purpose. But Jefferson as president, and thereafter, went far toward achieving the very consensus Croly claims to desire. It was Jefferson not Hamilton who expanded America westward through the Louisiana Purchase and the Lewis and Clark expedition, thus contributing quite markedly to the Crolyan version of manifest destiny. Croly finds Jefferson's first inaugural address calling for unity between Federalists and republicans "bewildering" because it directly counters Croly's warped picture of Jefferson as a divisive, that is, not "national," figure. The idea that Jefferson was a nationalist who sought to replace "national organizers" and financial elites with popular sovereignty is not compatible with Croly's formulation.[53]

This idea, *contra* Croly, is supported by Joseph Ellis's later clarification, which notes the discrepancy between the version of Jefferson's inaugural address printed by newspapers and Jefferson's own handwritten version. The newspapers capitalized the two operative references—Federalists and Republicans (as Croly does)—but the handwritten version has them in lowercase:

> By capitalizing the operative terms, the printed version had Jefferson making a gracious statement about the overlapping goals of the two political parties. But in the handwritten version of the speech that Jefferson delivered, the key words were not capitalized. Jefferson was therefore referring not to the common ground shared by the two political parties but to the common

belief, shared by all American citizens, that a republican form of government and a federal bond among the states were most preferable.[54]

Croly has neither a sense of nor an appreciation for Jefferson's sophisticated republicanism and how that view might have achieved Croly's ends. It is not that America was to use Hamiltonian means to achieve Jeffersonian ends. It is rather that one might better use Jeffersonian means to achieve Hamiltonian ends. The strength of American political purpose in the current age is arguably to be achieved through the re-engagement of ordinary citizens in public life and the common purpose rather than through continued reliance on a remote elite to manage national affairs for a society increasingly detached from national life and national purpose. Croly makes no attempt to understand Jefferson's democratic republicanism and the purposes to which Jefferson sought to apply it. Instead, he badly mischaracterizes Jefferson, indeed reduces him to a caricature and a political straw man to be toppled in the interest of raising up Hamilton, whose successes mark the current age much more than they did the founding era. Croly seems to erect this caricature of Jefferson in order to discredit it.[55]

To the degree that Croly perceives Jefferson's individualism as "selfish," he misperceives Jefferson altogether. The Aristotelian Jefferson saw humans as thoroughly political animals living in, and therefore required to participate in, the life of society. How thoroughly wrong Croly is about Jefferson is further revealed in Croly's assessment that Jefferson was responsible for offering the public the "seductive example of triumphant intellectual dishonesty" that "democracy is a happy device for evading collective responsibilities by passing them on to the individual."[56] Yet he previously had described a Jefferson whose "faith in human nature was exceedingly restricted," a Jefferson who fostered a "cordial distrust of a man of exceptional competence, training, or independence as a public official."[57]

In his effort to reduce Jefferson and raise up Hamilton, Croly blames excessive "money power" in the politics of his day (and, indeed, it might be said, of ours) on Jefferson's "chaotic individualism," not on Hamilton's preference for national financial and political elites.[58] Yet, in a statement calculated seriously to chill any friend of liberty, Croly states his own nationalistic creed: "Like all sacred causes, [the American idea] must be propagated by the Word and by that right arm of the Word, the Sword."[59]

Herbert Croly's insistence on promoting Alexander Hamilton and centralized "nationalism" is worth attention for two reasons. First, it illustrates the unresolved paradoxes inherent in the Constitutional compromises, and second, it illustrates a perceived need to marginalize, if not demonize, Jefferson to further a particular set of national objectives. This may be because, against this continuing backdrop of nationalism, there has been an intermittent and unresolved concern for citizen rights, popular sovereignty, and participatory democracy on the part of varying (some believe, growing) numbers of Americans, who consider the national government to be principally the instrument of interest groups.

A far more cogent challenge to a Jeffersonian ideal of republican virtue than the imperatives of national consolidation is raised by those who question, *ab initio,* the coherence of the ideal of virtue in a modern, liberal, commercial society. Bernard Mandeville offers the platform for this view with his claim that private vices lead to public benefits and that only "cunning Management" by skilled, but self-interested, politicians can socialize inward-directed individuals toward any common good—and that only fleetingly.[60] Using the Mandeville paradigm, one scholar argues for making "a privately oriented conception of civic virtue a plausible and desirable alternative to public, virtue" by making "thrift, honesty, and industry the characteristics of a good citizen." To qualify as a good citizen, on this account, one is expected only to "keep vigilant watch on the behavior of elected officials, inspect public policies for any unjust or tyrannical designs and protest government activity that harms the public good."[61] This view of private virtue expects the good citizen to prepare herself for participation in public debate but principally for the purpose of "defending through political action" her "rights and privileges." This restrictive, self-interested (one need not say selfish, but one might say Hamiltonian) view of citizenship certainly does not comport with Jefferson's more classic understanding of both virtue and citizenship within which the common good is tangible, identifiable, and in need of continuous attention. That common good was defined by, *inter alia,* public education, the health and welfare of the community, and its collective defense. Jefferson's understanding of public virtue was not characterized by making it "the center of their [the citizens'] reflections and affections," as this account suggests traditional civic virtue requires.[62] As the contemporary commercial republic does not require, but does certainly encourage, private virtue as a substitute for civic virtue, so the classic republican view does not require the good citizen to make the commonwealth a substitute for private interest. The public virtue considered here places the concerns of the commonwealth side by side with the citizen's private concerns and understands, in the scale of social values, their inseparable relationship.

Original Objections to Small Republics in the Light of Twenty-first-Century Realities

Given an extensive history of consolidated political power in a strong national government, do the same objections to small republics raised by Federalists in the Constitutional debates obtain today? Have circumstances changed sufficiently to warrant reconsideration of Jefferson's republican pyramid? Are there now deficiencies in the federal-State system of governance to which Jefferson's ward republics might respond?

The Jeffersonian republican pyramid was a sophisticated political construct that overcame the traditional struggle between large and small republics and combined the virtues of both. It assumed Montesquieu's federative structure and gave sufficient authority to the federal government to counter arguments about fragmentation drawn from other, weaker federative models. It recognized well-defined roles for national, State, county, and ward governments, each to perform its own defined functions.

Jefferson consistently acknowledged, including during the Constitutional debates, the need for a strong and cohesive national government. In this respect his views were not articulated by the Antifederalists with whom he is usually associated. The ardent Antifederalists simply opposed consolidated federal power as antirepublican but offered no plausible alternative other than continuation of the confederation.

Thus, the Federalists' arguments were not directed against Jefferson's theory but against the Antifederalists who feared a dominant central government. Antifederalist arguments were a classic restatement of traditional concerns about the scale of republics, that is, once a republic becomes large, it is no longer a republic. Jefferson overcame this argument by preserving a well-defined role for the ward republics within the federal-State structure. The ward republics were, if anything, more of a threat to State sovereignty than to federal sovereignty.

Jefferson uniquely devised a system that preserves republican virtues within a large, complex federative system. The present issue is whether Jefferson's structure might be revived to restore those virtues. Rather than restate at greater length the original Federalist objections to small republics, objections in any case only indirectly relevant at best to the Jefferson scheme, the next step must be to respond to those objections in the light of current realities.

First, in the present age, fear of chaos and mob rule is, absent a disastrous economic downturn for example, remote at best. Even in that eventuality, there is more than sufficient governmental power at both national and State levels to maintain order. Using Jefferson's adage about the therapy of a little revolution now and then, one might even argue that greater resistance to unjust wealth distribution, for example, is warranted. America suffered little and arguably gained much from organized citizen resistance to unjust racial laws, discrimination against women, destruction of the environment, and U.S. participation in the Vietnam War.

Second, restoration of civic virtue in and through local republics might counterbalance the increasing power of interest groups over national political affairs. Those interest groups now represent the factionalism feared by Federalists in the founding era. "Madison's fear which reverberates among today's critics of Washington lobbyists and special interest groups," observes Robert Putnam, "was that elected representatives, swayed by these 'factions,' would sacrifice the good of the whole for the pet projects of the few."[63] Competition among interested elites, all with access to power provided by elaborate campaign contributions, often creates gridlock in government, preventing resolution of complex social and economic issues. The original fear of factionalism at the local level has given way to the modern reality of factionalism at the national level: "In classic civic America, millions of ordinary men and women could interact with one another, participate in groups side by side with the more privileged, and exercise influence in both community and national affairs. . . . In recent times the old civic America has been bypassed and shoved to the side by a gaggle of professionally dominated advocacy groups and nonprofit institutions rarely attached to memberships worthy of the name.

Ideas of shared citizenship and possibilities for democratic leverage have been compromised in the process."[64] By contrast, resolution of as many local issues as practicable at the local republic level would complicate the efforts of interested factions to dictate policy among so many dispersed polities.

Third, a strong union exists, unthreatened by the devolution of responsibility to revitalized local governments. The strengthening of local republican spirit would not weaken the national government. Indeed, properly composed, the elementary republics would strengthen national political and communal life. Citizens alienated from remote government, as feared by Antifederalists, would find a venue for participation in a government readily at hand.

Fourth, support by the U.S. government for American commercial interests is not incompatible with increased citizen participation in local republican government. Jefferson himself granted that role to the national government in his pyramid scheme of republics. This is the very kind of activity a national government should undertake, one that he himself advocated, in expanding America's role in the world. Jefferson did not count himself among the ardent Antifederalists in this regard. He understood and accepted the need for a unifying national government and only feared it as it encroached upon republican liberties and values.

Finally, the contentious world of the new century raises threats to homeland security every bit as immediate and serious as those to U.S. interests abroad. America has no peer politically, economically, or militarily, and it will be a considerable period of time before one might appear. The need for a massive, cold war–style, standing army is suspect in the meantime. The much greater concern—as demonstrated by the savage attacks of September 11, 2001—is about additional assaults on the homeland by terrorist organizations using weapons of mass destruction, whether nuclear, chemical, biological, or cyber. The logical—and Constitutional—force to deter such attacks and to confine their damage should they occur are the National Guard, successor to the original State militias, and the military's reserve forces.

Thus, a consideration of the original objections to small republics and the responses to those objections in the Constitutional era is instructive in assessing the modern viability of a Jeffersonian redistribution of political authority. According to that redistribution and Jefferson's own mature theories, the national government would continue to conduct the country's foreign relations, protect its legitimate interests, establish national policies and priorities, and carry out the functions spelled out in the Constitution, including to "provide . . . for the General Welfare" and to "make all Laws . . . necessary and proper" to execute the powers spelled out in the Constitution.[65] The States would be free to carry out the political functions under their respective jurisdictions. The same would be true of the counties into which they are subdivided. But the innovation would be the revitalization of popular sovereignty and participatory democracy, the commonwealth and the common good, citizen participation and political inclusiveness, and a sense of civic virtue in and through the ward republic.

Current political conditions in the United States make original Constitutional-era objections to small republics now seem less relevant. But what of the future? There is little reason to believe that the twenty-first century will present merely a continuation of twentieth-century realities and every reason to believe it will not.

Restatement of the Elements of
Authentic Republicanism

Popular sovereignty is based upon a genuine degree of democratic deliberation and therefore participation in the definition and attainment of the common good or the public interest. Sensitivity to corruptibility does not assume the inevitability of corruption but rather maintains a keen awareness of the danger that interests represent to the commonwealth and democratic values. The values of civic virtue represent the ideal of the republic, the sense that the citizen has a duty to participate in the common life of the community as the best means of protecting his and his fellow citizens' rights as free citizens. Rather than seeing law as a restraint on freedom, a view of liberty as nondomination requires a resilient and qualitative engagement in the process by which liberty is guaranteed.

It remains then to consider whether restoration of the township republic, within the context of the greater national republic, may provide a forum for the restoration of these qualities of republicanism. Before pursuing that possibility, however, two questions must be raised. First, is America still a republic in substance as well as form? Second, what exactly did Jefferson have in mind when he proposed his elementary or ward republics?

IT WAS NEVER an issue whether America—loosening itself from the colonial tentacles of the English monarchy—would be a republic. Its founders outdid each other in acclamations of their dedication to the wisdom of Cato and Cicero, to the genius of Polybius and Livy, and to the republican ideal. Madison, Hamilton, and Jay collectively wrote the Federalist Papers as "Publius." The country's first president was an American Cincinnatus. Political structures were constructed on the foundations of representative government. The oligarchical "few" of the mixed republics were replaced by a "natural aristocracy." Property ownership was recognized to be critical to the stability of the new republic and became a condition of participatory citizenship in most new States. In almost every way, structures and procedures were designed to emulate those of the traditional republic. "Reading the political pamphlets and private correspondence of the 1790s, one gets the impression that 'republican' was a label to be fought over, a prized appellation to claim for one's own views."[1]

Having established the republic as the political touchstone of the new democracy, however, the founders quickly fell out over the *kind*

Is America Still a Republic? Sovereignty, Corruption, Civic Virtue, and Liberty

2

of republic it should be. The Federalists had in mind an extended republic, a republic large enough to expand geographically, to undertake commercial enterprises abroad, and to make its mark on the world. This extended republic would have a national capital, a national bank, national taxing powers, and a standing army to protect the republic's national interests. Within the complex structure of federalism, this grand republic would exercise hegemony. On the issue of the scale of republics, James Harrington set a standard when he called Oceana "a Commonwealth for increase." James Madison, seeking to bridge a chasm between the classic city-state and the "extended" American republic, relied on an observation by Montesquieu that "the republican form of government, if based upon the federal principle, was appropriate for large and growing territories."[2] Thus, individual States, which might have become their own republics, could voluntarily and constitutionally declare themselves to be part of a greater republic, which itself could continue to grow. It was an innovation or, perhaps more accurately, a political invention never before attempted on such a scale.

But one cannot separate the theory of the extended republic from its promoters' commitment to market liberalism or liberal capitalism. This is especially true of Alexander Hamilton, who saw the need for a central government backed by a central bank and a national army as crucial to the establishment of an extended American commercial empire. "Hamilton advocates a powerful national sovereign based on the expansion of capitalism," writes Richard Matthews. "Once established, this system would spread its largesse to all, becoming the envy of the world."[3]

Hamilton's political economics led inexorably to his philosophy of governance: "Take mankind in general, they are vicious. . . . Our prevailing passions are ambition and interest; and it will ever be the duty of a wise government to avail itself of those passions, in order to make them subservient to the public good."[4] Common human viciousness must be harnessed for the public good, said Hamilton, and the only power capable of doing so is a large sovereign government. Although there is little difference in virtue between the rich and the poor, he claimed, there is a difference in the quality of their vices. Hamilton concluded that the vices of the rich—accumulation of exorbitant wealth, disproportionate political influence, and so forth—"are probably more favorable to the prosperity of the state than those of the indigent and partake less of moral depravity."[5] Then, having heard the voice of the people and deeming it depraved, Hamilton concluded: "The people are turbulent and changing; they seldom judge or determine right. Give therefore to the first class [the wealthy] a distinct, permanent share in the government."[6] Since Hamilton believed in a strong executive, his support for a "distinct share" in government for the wealthy effectively resurrected the ancient mixed republic composed of the one, the few, and the (morally inferior) many as the basis for the extended American republic. In the rhetoric and logic of the Federalists, the extended American republic was commensurate with the vision of an extended American commercial empire. Both required a strong sovereign state supported by national taxation and national armaments. To the Antifederalist opposition, this formula sounded ominously like the Court party of seventeenth-century England.

The issue of the scale, and therefore of the power, of the new republic was the central matter for Constitutional-era republicans. If Hamilton's view prevailed, there would be a powerful central state, a large standing army to support it, high taxes to maintain the state and its army, a central bank to finance its state-sponsored enterprises at home and abroad, and, according to the historical laws of republics, a court class, which would manipulate the levers of state power. For Jefferson and his heirs, this was not the republic they had made a revolution to create.

The Jeffersonian republic guaranteed individual freedom by popular participation in a government accessible to all, a government whose limited powers focused on the common good and the commonwealth, a government that both permitted and strongly encouraged civic virtues and duties to be exercised in the local republic, a government, moreover, that was democratic. Not for Jefferson the republic of the "mixed constitution" favored by John Adams, a republic that, like Hamilton's, would rely on an aristocratic hierarchy for governance to diminish the perils and uncertainties of widespread public participation. Though Jefferson believed in a "natural aristocracy," essentially composed of those with virtue and a talent for governance, political levers of power were to be accessible to all free men.

By and large, Antifederalists thought an "extended republic" to be an oxymoron. Using Montesquieu's "federal principle," however, Madison forged the Constitutional compromise that sought to satisfy Federalists and Antifederalists. Article IV, section 4, of the new Constitution provided: "The United States shall guarantee to every State in this Union a Republican Form of Government." A formulation such as this was necessary to achieve a majority at the Constitutional convention but was not sufficient to satisfy those opposed to consolidation.

This is not to say, as we have seen, that Jefferson was opposed to national expansion and conquest. To the contrary, much of Jefferson's consistent optimism rested not on the reduction of centralized power in the new nation east of the Appalachians but on the opening of the frontier to agrarian pursuits, which, in turn, could produce commodities to be bartered in commercial (including international) markets to provide capital for the westward expansion. But Jefferson could reconcile expansion with limited republican government by insisting always that the first line of government was the ward republic, the local council and authority in which all could and should participate. In one of several summaries of his views, Jefferson wrote:

> The article . . . nearest my heart is the division of counties into wards. These will be pure and elementary republics, the sum of all which, taken together, composes the State, and will make of the whole a true democracy as to the business of the wards, which is that of nearest and daily concern. The affairs of the larger sections, of counties, of States, and of the Union, not admitting personal transactions by the people, will be delegated to agents elected by themselves, and representation will thus be substituted, where personal action becomes impracticable.[7]

The principal determinant in the debate over the scale of the republic was susceptibility to corruption. The Federalists saw little danger to republicanism in a strong, centralized national government. For them, corruption could take root in a political hothouse of any size. The more remote and removed the government, countered the republicans, the more susceptible it would be to corruptibility. Corruption in the classical republic was the opposite of civic virtue, that is, it was the *absence* of citizen duty, responsibility, and participation and the triumph of interest. Corruption represented the failure of civic duty, and civic duty was more difficult to exercise the larger the government became. And the larger it became, the more it was susceptible to subornation by a certain kind of concentrated wealth: "It would be an error to conceive of the Republicans as foes of either capital or wealth. The objects of their condemnation . . . were not merchants or manufacturers, but speculators, bank directors, and holders of the public debt. The target was not business enterprise, nor wealth itself, but a particular variety of paper wealth that seemed too closely tied to government favor."[8] For the republicans, corruption was not simple garden-variety graft or bribery of individual legislators. It was the superseding of the interests of the commonwealth by the narrow but powerful interests of those—such as the modern-day military-industrial complex, powerful financial institutions, or resource industries—that profited from the procurement of weapons systems, manipulation of interest rates, disposition of public resources, or any distribution of government largesse. Thus, historic, Constitutional-era republicanism concerned itself with the scale of the new republic as a determinant of its corruptibility.

For Jefferson, a true republic was "restrained to very narrow limits of space and population," with a government popularly controlled by "citizens in mass" with equal rights of participation, within which such citizens could act "directly and personally," "according to rules established by the majority" through popular elections.[9] He acknowledged both the role and necessity for other gradations of government—counties, States, and the union—to be managed by elected representatives of the people, but they would represent "other shades of republicanism." "The further the departure from the direct and constant control by the citizens," Jefferson continued in the same letter, "the less has the government of the ingredient of republicanism." Thus, scale was directly related to citizen access and control, to personal participation, and to popular sovereignty. As distance and scale grew, access and participation waned, and corruptibility waxed. Scale could not be divorced from the purity of the republican enterprise; indeed, it was central to it. The contrast of Jefferson's view of the people with that of Hamilton's could not be more stark, and it was to mark a deep divide in American politics for more than two centuries.

Jefferson's definition of republicanism is straightforward: "government by its own citizens in mass, acting directly and personally, according to rules established by the majority." This central quality of popular sovereignty was elucidated on other occasions: "Every member composing [the government] has his equal voice in the direction of its concerns," and every member of society "has an equal right of participation, personally in the direction of the affairs of the society." To popular sovereignty as the central element of republicanism, he added, in vivid language, civic virtue: "When every man is a sharer [in government] he will let the heart be torn out of his body sooner than his power be wrested from him." The principle aim of education was to enable the citizen to "understand his duties to his neighbors and country." The aim and focus of republicanism was individual and collective liberty, defined as "unobstructed action according to our will, within the limits drawn around us by the equal rights of others." To popular sovereignty, civic virtue, and liberty, he added the classic quality of concern about corruption: "Either force or corruption has been the principle of every modern government." He warned against "the gamblers in corruption who take advantage of public finance" and insisted that republics "guard against corruption and tyranny."

These standards can be used to measure the nature and quality of republicanism in current-day America. Tracking Jefferson's thinking closely, Bill Bruger finds that the republic's "distinctive feature is a view of political life which affirms popular sovereignty, is sensitive to corruptibility, asserts the value of civic virtue and upholds a view of liberty as non-domination."[10] With regard to the first category, he writes: "At the centre of republican thought is a strong Constitutional state based on the rule of law and opposition to arbitrariness and with a clear notion of the common good or the public interest which is not simply the result of group pressure. . . . Popular sovereignty, moreover, requires some degree of what is nowadays called deliberative democracy."[11] A view of history concerned with systematic corruptibility, he continues, no longer sees history as cyclical but has now accommodated to the concept of progress. Nevertheless, "it preserves a sensitivity to what is now called Contingency." Civic virtue, a third characteristic, is exercised in the "relatively autonomous political sphere," is "practical and situational," and is possessed by citizens at large. Finally, he says, "The republican tradition maintains a qualitative rather than a quantitative view of liberty as non-domination which has to be enjoyed resiliently," a view that "law is constitutive of liberty rather than being simply a restraint upon it."[12]

In assessing the nature of republicanism in early twenty-first-century America, the application of both Jefferson's and Bruger's qualities of republicanism yields two sets of results, one procedural and the other substantive. The procedural American republic certainly affirms popular sovereignty, is sensitive to corruptibility, asserts the value of civic virtue, and sees liberty as the basis of its existence. The American people insist on teaching succeeding generations that their government is of, for, and by the people. There are professional rewards for journalists and prosecutors who sniff out turpitude in public places high and low. Schoolchildren are required to submit to lectures on "civics." And "Don't Tread on Me" is a popular revolutionary slogan capturing the essence of the more abstract notion of liberty. But a more thorough, penetrating examination of the substance of American republicanism—its heart and its core—reveals a different picture.

Popular sovereignty is waning. There is a distinct multidecade trend of declining voter participation in national elections. Since 1960, the average turnout of the voting-age population in all U.S. national elections has been under 48 percent and in presidential elections just 55 percent. In 1960, more than 63 percent of those eligible voted. In 1996, that number was just 49 percent, and in 2000, it rose only slightly above 50 percent of eligible voters. The third political party, nonvoters, now represents a majority of eligible voters. Candidates for national office are themselves selected by the small minorities of voters registered in the two major parties.[13] The day-to-day concerns of citizens are managed (or ignored) by special-interest lobbyists in Washington and in State capitals who gain access to legislators through increasingly large campaign contributions to both candidates and parties. It has become fashionable and routine for lobbyists to draft legislation—always favorable to their own interests—that affects their industries. "Public opinion," as measured by polling (recently the weather vane of policymakers and at best an ephemeral means of testing the public pulse), is increasingly discredited by revelations of rising and massive citizen resistance to and deception of intrusive polling techniques. Even discounting for lassitude, by refusing even to vote, some Americans are forfeiting their sovereignty in protest.

Nowhere is the nexus among special interests, their lobbyists, elected officials, and political parties more visible than in the current system of campaign finance, a sophisticated form of legalized corruption. In the 2000 national elections in America, more than $1 billion was raised by parties and candidates for national office, more than $800 million on behalf of congressional candidates, and at least $250 million for presidential candidates. This amount represents a 42 percent increase in spending over the previous national election just two years before. Even among these staggering figures, most astonishing is the continued explosion of "soft," or unregulated, funds:

> The largest percentage increases for both [major] parties continue to be in non-federal, or "soft money" (funds raised outside the limitations and prohibitions of the Federal Election Campaign Act). Republicans have raised nearly $211 million, an increase of 74 percent over the same period in 1995–96, the last presidential cycle, while Democrats raised almost $199 million, a[n] 85 percent increase. Soft money now represents 42 percent of all National Republican Party financial activity and 53 percent of Democratic National Party fundraising.[14]

It is difficult to imagine a factor more corrosive to public trust in a democracy than the knowledge that money, in the form of campaign contributions, buys access to public officials, including the president of the United States, not available to ordinary citizens. It is but a short step from corruptibility to corruption, a distance whose dimensions are not lost on citizens fully aware of the danger of corruption always lurking in the corridors of power.

According to Robert Putnam, "By virtually every conceivable measure, social capital has eroded steadily and sometimes dramatically over the past two generations. The quantitative evidence is overwhelming, yet most Americans did not need to see charts and graphs to know that something bad had been happening in their communities and in their country. Americans have had a growing sense at some visceral level of disintegrating social bonds."[15] The current low participation level of Americans in the minimal exercise of voting in national elections is in stark contrast to Jefferson's notion of republicanism as "government by its citizens in mass, acting directly and personally, according to rules established by the majority."

Sensitivity to corruptibility, by comparison, is now so widespread that it breeds cynicism. Indeed, that sensitivity is so acute that it sees corruptibility (if not outright corruption) everywhere, and yet, it is so deadened by an erosion of traditional standards against abuse of the public trust that it is unable to generate sufficient outrage to demand therapeutic correction. Healthy skepticism based on suspicion of corruptibility by proximity to power easily becomes a cynicism that assumes power has corrupted. Further, widespread focus on the venial takes place at the expense of concern for the venal. Classic republican theory "took corruption to be the great enemy of virtue, for it leads to the neglect of one's duty as a citizen. Corruption could take the passive form of shirking one's civic duties in favor of personal pleasures, such as indolence or the pursuit of luxury, or it could take the active form of advancing one's personal interests at the expense of the common interest when ambition and avarice—the overweening desire for power and wealth—tempted a citizen to overthrow the rule of law and install a tyranny in its place."[16] American citizens routinely and repeatedly give the access to power by special interests, Jefferson's "gamblers in corruption," as a principal reason for their nonparticipation.

Early twenty-first-century America is not a nation overly concerned with asserting, beyond the perimeters of the public school classrooms, the value of civic virtue. National leadership does not find it congenial to raise the banner of the nobility of public service. Indeed, at the close of the twentieth century, government itself was demonized. Traditional social and political values of progressivism, improvability, and concern for injustice were replaced by the values of political individualism and material acquisitiveness. To uphold the worthiness of public life and the claim of republican society on the time and energy of its citizens was assumed to reflect an unhealthy fondness for government.[17] This neolibertarianism does not, in fact, stand against government; it stands against republican government based upon genuine civic virtue. As it favors the privatization of public services, it also favors the privatization of politics. If the functions of government are privatized, the opportunity for participation and the exercise of civic virtue are thus restricted. It is only a short distance from a policy of privatization to a social philosophy of privatism. Privatization then becomes the means to *reduce*—in the sense of medieval siege—the republic. The citizen today has surrendered his civic virtue and "let his power be wrested from him" with far greater ease than letting "the heart be torn from his body."

This leads to the fourth quality of classic republicanism—dedication to a form of liberty as noninterference, nondomination, or a related refinement. This quality is alive and well both procedurally and substantively in early twenty-first-century America. The complication arises from a reading of negative liberty as freedom from public responsibility, obligation, and duty. It is a short leap from "don't tread on me" to "leave me alone." The temper of the times permits a sensitivity to corruptibility to become a presumption of corruption everywhere and therefore an argument for abrogation of civic duty in the name of liberty as noninterference. This narrow view of liberty as being left alone thus becomes the enemy of civic virtue. It is at this vital point—the nature of liberty—that America-as-republic becomes problematic.

The central question is whether a mass participatory democracy at rest, at peace, powerful, economically expansive, and fundamentally conservative can awaken to the importance of republican principles and ideals. If early twenty-first-century America only approximates republican values, and that more procedurally than substantively, are there prospects that might lead to the reconsideration of a more classic republic, an authentic republic?

Globalization, the transnational integration of capital, markets, trade, and finance, might have an important impact. The World Trade Organization protests in Seattle, Washington, D.C., and elsewhere, involving a potpourri of workers, environmentalists, and antiglobalists, might portend the rise of opposition to the loss of popular sovereignty. There are a variety of additional indicators of the stirrings of a latent populism.[18] Populism is not republicanism. But populism or its more refined variant, progressivism, can sow the seeds of a reform era, which might feature popular sovereignty, new constraints on corruptibility, the restoration of civic virtue, a definition of liberty that extends beyond noninterference, and thus a restoration of classic republican values.[19]

Robert Putnam affirms this argument by comparing the Gilded Age of the late nineteenth century and the Progressive Era of the early twentieth century to the late twentieth and early twenty-first centuries in America and the equivalent possibilities for economic and political reform:

> As a political movement, the Progressives were responsible for the most thoroughgoing renovation of public policies and institutions in American history, rivaled only by the New Deal. The secret ballot (1888, Kentucky); popular initiative and referendum (1898, South Dakota); presidential primary elections (1900, Minnesota); the city manager system (1903, Galveston, Texas); the direct election of senators (1913); women's suffrage

(1893, Colorado; 1920 in the Constitution)—in a few short decades all these fundamental features in our political process
were introduced into state and local politics and then gradually
were diffused nationwide. Quite apart from these basic political
reforms, this was also the most intense period of local administrative reform in our history.[20]

Citing a lengthy list of national initiatives, Putnam concludes, "Hardly an
area of public policy was left untouched by the Progressive avalanche of
policy initiatives. Typically, innovation began with experimental reforms
in state and local communities, then gathered strength as it thundered
toward Washington."[21]

Martin van Creveld writes: "The devil's bargain that was struck in the
seventeenth century, and in which the state offered its citizens much
improved day-to-day security in return for their willingness to sacrifice
themselves on its behalf if called upon, may be coming to an end."[22] If
he is correct, then the combination of global economics and the erosion
of nation-state authority could create a political vacuum in which a revisitation of Jefferson's theory of the radical, democratic ward or elementary
republic might occur. Citizens concerned with their loss of voice in economic decisions that directly affect their lives and even more concerned
with the decline of a corrupted nation-state might seek to resurrect popular sovereignty at the community level. They might demonstrate their
sensitivity to corruptibility by participating in local government. They
might restore the values of civic virtue by identifying with the common
good and the commonwealth. And they might come once again to conceive of liberty as the freedom to participate in public affairs.

According to Hannah Arendt, "Political freedom, generally speaking,
means the right 'to be a participator in government,' or it means nothing."[23] In theory, Americans have the right to participate in government.
But, in practice, what right does the virtuous citizen have to participate
in a government deemed to be corrupt, remote, and dominated by special
interests? Such a right can be considered only theoretical (or procedural)
at best. The liberty guaranteed by an authentic republic, however, is the
liberty to participate not only in the selection of representatives who make
the laws (that guarantee noninterference) but also to participate in the
debate over laws that affect the qualities of a life that is free, including

its education, its welfare, and its security. The debate between liberalism and republicanism does not have to be resolved in order to argue that the autonomy and individuality of traditional liberalism is best protected and perfected in a republic deemed authentic, a republic in which the autonomous individual can and should demonstrate civic virtue by participating in the governing functions that guarantee liberty and the social qualities that make it worthwhile.

According to John Rawls, classical republicanism encourages "widespread participation in democratic politics by a vigorous and informed citizen body" and resists a "general retreat into private life."[24] William Galston makes much the same point negatively: "The liberal citizen is not the same as the civic-republican citizen. In a liberal polity there is no duty to participate actively in politics, no requirement to place the public above the private and to subordinate personal interest to the common good systematically, no commitment to accept collective determination of personal choices."[25] Quentin Skinner draws a closer connection between liberty and participation in republican thought: "In a manner that contrasts sharply with modern liberal individualism, [republicans] not only connect social freedom with self-government, but also link the idea of personal liberty with that of virtuous public service."[26]

Thus, an argument is made here for what J. G. A. Pocock describes as "a *vita activa* which is specifically a *vivere civile*—a way of life given over to civic concerns and the (ultimately political) activity of citizenship."[27] Pocock contrasts Aristotelian theory, which states that the many possess sufficient knowledge based on experience to make them "capable of electing their superiors and exercising a judgment of policies," with the more active Machiavellian participation: "By basing the popular republic on the *virtú* of the armed citizen, Machiavelli had transformed the problem of popular participation from one of knowledge to one of will."[28] In less subtle terms, the former requires qualities of judgment while the latter requires qualities of sacrifice, including potentially the loss of one's life in defense of the commonwealth, the ultimate in civic virtue.

Here the original question recurs. In a mass participatory democracy of the twenty-first century, what kind of republic permits the virtuous citizen to exercise her will by participating in the political processes that guarantee her liberty and the qualities of social life that give that liberty meaning? Such a republic must be substantive and authentic rather than merely procedural.

The Constitutional guarantee of a republican form of government to the States neither guarantees nor denies a republican form of government to lesser units. Using the parameters set out above, an authentic twenty-first-century republic must affirm popular sovereignty. It must be sensitive to corruptibility. It must assert the value of civic virtue. And it must uphold a view of liberty as nondomination. Doubt has been cast on the degree to which the extended republic of America is meeting or can meet these standards. But the extended republic of America, the procedural republic, can guarantee a republican form of government to the authentic ward or township republics that constitute it.

Restoration of the authentic republic in the twenty-first century presumes there are those for whom popular sovereignty, incorruptibility, civic virtue, and a sophisticated form of democratic liberty are important, indeed vital. Without citizens who insist on asserting and exercising their sovereignty, who demand a legislative and executive process uncorrupted by money, who require liberty as, and even beyond, noninterference—the liberty to participate in the governing of their public affairs—republicanism is hollow. Without virtue, republicanism in any meaningful form perishes.

According to Joyce Appleby, "Classical republicanism offers late-twentieth-century men and women an attractive alternative to liberalism and socialism. . . . Standing outside the liberal field of imagination, it has become a vantage point for assessing that field. Like a magnet, republicanism has drawn to it the filings of contemporary discontents with American politics and culture. Unlike Marxism, it has done this by establishing its origins before Independence and hence establishing authentic American roots."[29] Assuming this attraction, or at least the possibility for it, how then might an authentic republic in twenty-first-century America be constituted?

"It is in the nature of a republic to have only a small territory, otherwise it can scarcely continue to exist," argues Montesquieu.[30] But then the issue of stability and security arises, and he admits, "If a republic is small, it is destroyed by a foreign force; if it is large, it is destroyed by an internal vice."[31] As noted earlier, Montesquieu suggests a possible solution to the conundrum of a small republic for virtue and a larger republic for strength, that is, small republics forming a federal system: "It is against the nature of the thing for one confederated state under a federal constitution to conquer another, as we have seen among the Swiss in our own time."[32]

Article IV, section 4, of the U.S. Constitution neither guarantees nor denies a republican form of government to any lesser units of government. The Constitution being silent on the point, the new economic, social, and political realities of the twenty-first century may open the possibility for the activation of small republics under the protection of the great republic of the United States. These new realities include the globalization of economics and finance, new information and communications technologies disintegrating old networks and integrating new ones, pluralism compounded by mass migrations, and the consequent demand by citizens and communities for greater control of those aspects of their collective lives and their societies that are within their purview to manage, namely, schools, welfare, local security, and a variety of other public activities.

The final portion of this work describes in concrete terms how federated elementary or ward republics might function under the aegis of a national republic. Montesquieu offered, in the form of the Swiss, one model of federated republics, a model not unlike that proposed by Thomas Jefferson. Though the Jeffersonian model was proposed more than two centuries ago, and therefore can be considered old, it was never implemented and therefore, in practical terms, can be considered new. Pocock writes that Jeffersonian republicans feared a future when "the reservoir of land must be exhausted and the expansion of virtue will no longer keep ahead of the progress of commerce." "When that point is reached," he continues, "the process of corruption must be resumed; men will become dependent upon each other in a market economy and dependent on government in great cities."[33]

For Jefferson, there was a remedy: innovation, experimentation, and progress: "I know also, that laws and institutions must go hand in hand with the progress of the human mind. As that becomes more developed, more enlightened, as new discoveries are made, new truths disclosed, and manners and opinions change with the change of circumstances, institutions must advance also, and keep pace with the times. We might as well require a man to wear still the coat which fitted him when a boy, as civilized society to remain under the regimen of their barbarous ancestors."[34] Arguably, the most radically democratic proposal for the advance of human law and institutions was the township or authentic republic:

> Divide the counties into wards of such size as that every citizen
> can attend, when called on, and act in person. Ascribe to them
> the government of their wards in all things related to them-
> selves exclusively . . . and by making every citizen an acting
> member of the government, and in the offices nearest and
> most interesting to him, will attach him by his strongest feel-
> ings to the independence of his country, and its republican
> constitution. . . . These wards, called townships in New England,
> are the vital principle of their governments, and have proved
> themselves the wisest invention ever devised by the wit of man
> for the perfect exercise of self-government, and for its preserva-
> tion.[35]

Popular sovereignty can be both preserved and promoted in such a republic. By participation in self-government, the citizen has the most effective means of maintaining sensitivity to corruptibility. The value of civic virtue is affirmed through direct and consistent participation. And the virtuous citizen exercising his sovereignty through participation in community government is the surest protection both against interference and for liberty. These are the qualities of the authentic republic and potentially the means for the restoration of republican values in twenty-first-century America.

"Pure" republicanism might also guarantee the health of the extended, or overarching, national republic. By the exercise of civic virtue and participation at the community republic level, citizens demonstrate popular sovereignty and diminish the potential for corruptibility to become actual corruption. Practice of these virtues and protection of these values might lessen the reliance of citizens on the central government for the day-to-day administration of government services, but it can only strengthen the citizens' awareness of the conduct of national affairs, including its relations with other nations and the international community. Citizens active in local affairs are much more likely to be citizens concerned with national affairs and to become citizens with proposals for their elected representatives for the solution of national challenges.

To a surprising degree, the Constitutional-era struggle over the definition of republicanism and the consequences of this struggle for the nature and structure of government resonate well more than two centuries later. There have been periods, for example in the nineteenth century when state legislatures selected members of the U.S. Senate, when John Adams's "old influential characters" played a dominant role in American public life, filling the role of "the few" in the mixed republic. The Hamiltonian commercial republic has characterized America throughout much of its life and most particularly in the second half of the twentieth century. Even more distinctly, Madison's consolidated republic, checked and balanced within its branches, has provided the persistent model for the operation of the complex American federation. Regardless of the template, however, always present behind the scenes was Jefferson's alternative, the *democratic* republic, the republic under the "direct and constant control of the citizens," the republic having more of "the element of popular election and control," pressing to be considered.

Only after leaving the presidency and reflecting back on the revolution of 1776 he had helped define and the "revolution of 1800" he had led, did he come to articulate (and possibly even understand himself) that what made his political philosophy distinctive then—and today— was his singular understanding of the republic, of the very nature of republicanism in the new nation. In 1816, "For the first time, Jefferson embraced the idea that would eventually and then everlastingly be associated with his name. What he had always called 'pure republicanism' was really 'democracy,' and what he had actually done in 'the revolution of 1800' was to restore the democratic impulse of the American Revolution after its betrayal by the Federalists."[36] The links that forged the chain of participation—anticorruption, popular sovereignty, and liberty—were the people. To give republicanism meaning and content beyond the mere negative of being that which is other than monarchy, sovereignty had to reside ultimately with the people. And the people could only exercise that sovereignty directly, and democratically, in the pure republic of the wards.

Based upon an assertion that a definable gap exists between substantive definitions of republicanism and the twenty-first-century American republic, it is left then to examine the Jeffersonian democratic republican ideal and to determine whether that ideal may now be compatible with the social, economic, and political realities of a new era.

*The Nature and Structure of Republics
according to Jefferson*

Even as one of the most prominent advocates
of the republican view, Thomas Jefferson,
when called upon by a correspondent to define
a republic, admitted, "The term republic is of
very vague application in every language."[1] For
him, the principal feature of any republic is the
direct, personal, and collective action of citizens, acting according to rules laid down by
the majority. This central proposition carries
with it profound practical implications. "Such a
government is evidently restrained," Jefferson
continued, "to very narrow limits of space and
population." The restraint of space and population—the issue of scale—is vital. Jefferson
doubted that a pure republican government
would be practicable "beyond the extent of a
New England township." Indeed, the New
England township meeting was very near
the republic in action that he envisioned. To
his famous "earth belongs to the living"
proclamation, which emphasized his belief in
generational politics, Jefferson added the restraint of time.[2] Jefferson uniquely believed

*Jeffersonian
Republicanism
and the
Restoration
of the
Republic*

3

that each generation was obliged to create its own republic virtually anew. These restraints are related but different. The restraint of scale or space reflects the need to make government accessible to all directly. The restraint of time creates a moral duty for each generation to consider its own political, and perhaps also social, values and not simply to accept them deferentially from previous generations.

"The further the departure from the direct and constant control by the citizens," Jefferson wrote, "the less has the government of the ingredient of republicanism." There was no degree of republicanism in polities such as France and Venice, where offices were hereditary, or Holland, where they were self-selected, and little degree of republicanism when the length of the elected term was extended. The longer any representative held office, even following election, the more republicanism faded. Thus, another factor, term of office, became a measure of the authenticity of republicanism.[3] "A pure republic," he wrote to another correspondent, "is a state of society in which every member, of mature and sound mind, has an equal right of participation, personally in the direction of the affairs of the society. Such a regimen is obviously impractical beyond the narrow limits of an encampment, or of a very small village."[4]

The coin of the republic has an affirmation and a resistant side. On the affirmation side are: direct citizen participation, ownership of the polity, and immediate direction of the affairs of the commonwealth. On the resistant side are restriction of the power of interests, reduction of the power of remote government, and resistance to the concentration of power. The republican coin, for Jefferson, also assumed a citizenry willing to undertake the duties of participation in the conduct of public affairs.

The emerging United States was not Athens or Thebes, however, and Jefferson knew that. He not only envisioned power distributed horizontally among citizens in the local republic, he saw power in a federal system distributed vertically as well, according to the natural functions of the levels of government in the republican pyramid:

> The way to have good and safe government, is not to trust it all
> to one, but to divide it among the many, distributing to every
> one exactly the functions he is competent to. Let the national
> government be entrusted with the defence of the nation, and
> its foreign and federal relations; the State governments with the

civil rights, laws, police and administration of what concerns the State generally; the counties with the local concerns of the counties, and each ward direct the interests within itself. It is by dividing and subdividing these republics from the great national one down through all its subordinations, until it ends in the administration of every man's farm by himself, by placing under every one what his own eye may superintend, that all will be done for the best.[5]

Once authority ascends the scale of governance, the principle of agency must apply. The practical necessities of social life and geographical reach prevent American citizens from participating in every level of government in a large and complex federal system. The idea of representation was for Jefferson the obvious solution to the preservation of democratic republicanism in the world's first modern republic. Though he drew his ideal of the republic from Aristotle, he criticized the ancient philosopher for his lack of appreciation of the innovation of representation. The classical writers, including Aristotle, proposed no idea for the structure of a government suited to protect the value of personal liberty beyond the local, pure republic: "They knew no medium between a democracy (the only pure republic, but impracticable beyond the limits of a town) and an abandonment of themselves to an aristocracy, or a tyranny independent of the people. It seems not to have occurred to them that where the citizens cannot meet to transact their business in person, they alone have the right to choose the agents who shall transact it; and that in this way a republican, or popular government of the second grade of purity, may be exercised over any extent of country."[6] Jefferson's appreciation for the importance of representation in constructing a complex new federal system testifies once again to his role apart from the Federalist-Antifederalist debate. He did not oppose a national government or a federal system based upon the principle of representation. He simply wanted to preserve a public space—the ward republic—for direct citizen participation.

Two innovations, then, made modern republicanism on a large scale possible: the ideas of federation and representation. Indeed, federation required representation. To create a federation was to create federal concerns and interests that demanded public attention. Ordinary citizens could not, as a practical matter, attend to those interests at either the State or national level. Therefore, agents or deputies chosen directly by them and accountable to them were the apparent solution. But the principle of representation in a federated system of republics exacted a price from the purity of republicanism in rough proportion to the remoteness of the level of government. Visually, Jefferson saw republicanism in shades. Thus, as authority moved from the wards or local townships to the counties, then to the States, then to the national government, the purity of the republican ideal weakened, and the "shade" of republicanism darkened.

This complex system nonetheless possessed its own positive checks on abuse. Whereas Madison assumed the inevitability of power concentrated in a national government and sought to reduce its consequent corruption by selfish interests through lateral checks and balances among the branches of the national government, Jefferson saw the emerging pyramid of governments as a vertical system of checks and balances on each other: "The elementary republics of the wards, the county republics, the State republics, and the republic of the Union, would form a gradation of its authorities, standing each on the basis of law, holding every one its delegated share of powers, and constituting truly a system of fundamental balances and checks for the government."[7]

More must be said regarding Jefferson's republican classicism on the specific issue of the scale of the republic. For that issue—scale—was at the heart of Jefferson's republicanism and his continued antagonism toward the works and beliefs of his archrival, Alexander Hamilton. In sum, the core of republicanism was civic virtue, the active and immediate involvement by the citizen in the *polis*. That participation gave every citizen a stake in the common good or the commonwealth. But the larger and more remote the locus of government became, the less the ordinary citizen could participate. The solution, one that Jefferson himself applauded as a means of establishing an extended republic, was representation. The people could directly elect their deputies or agents to represent their interests in State capitals and in the even more removed national capital. But such elected representatives were mandated to express the will of their constituents. Jefferson did not want them to have free rein. The fundamental difference between Federalists and republicans, both of whom accepted a political pyramid leading from a base in the localities to the counties, then to the States, then to the national government, was over the locus of authority in the pyramid. Would it flow to the top, as the Federalists envisioned, or would it remain at the base, as the republicans demanded?

The Jeffersonian republican ideal consisted of these elements: direct action by citizens at the township level; representation or agency as the concerns of the polity escaped local bounds; a federal system based upon representation to accommodate the functions of State and nation; a vertical system of checks and balances to prevent concentration, usurpation, or abuse of power; and shades or gradations of republicanism as representation moved up the pyramid of government and became more remote. To this were added qualifications concerning representation or agency. Heredity and self-selection were proscribed as inconsistent with authentic republicanism. But even among democratically elected representatives, terms of office were to be limited as an implicit, although not stated, hedge against careerism and courtiership. Beyond the ward republic, "The powers of the government, being divided, should be exercised by representatives chosen either *pro hac vice*, or for such short terms as should render secure the duty of expressing the will of their constituents."[8]

Yet despite the inventiveness of both federalism and representation as structural solutions to the challenges of scale occasioned by the creation of a modern extended republic and despite hedges on those inventions, such as strict accountability and limitations on terms of office, mischief still abounded in the hearts of men and could only finally be checked if the ultimate locus of power remained among the people, and that exclusively and necessarily at the primary level of government:

> Even over these representative organs [other levels of government], should they become corrupt and perverted, the division into wards constituting the people, in their wards, a regularly organized power, enables them by that organization to crush, regularly and peaceably, the usurpation of their unfaithful agents, and rescue them [the people] from the dreadful necessity of doing it insurrectionally. In this way we shall be as republican as a large society can be, and secure the continuance of purity in our government, by the salutary, peaceable, and regular control of the people.[9]

Notable in this formulation of the closing of the intricate republican circle is the reference to corruption, the classical Machiavellian nemesis of republics. Jefferson seldom mentioned corruption, but he assumed its presence everywhere outside the pure republican precincts of the ward. For Jefferson, otherwise notorious for his optimism and generosity of spirit, corruption was historic, endemic, and systemic: "No other depositories of power [than the people themselves] have ever yet been found, which did not end in converting to their own profit the earnings of those committed to their charge."[10] Madison trusted elected representatives more than he trusted those who elected them; by contrast, Jefferson trusted the people more than he did their elected representatives.

Jefferson's therapy for the inevitable abuse of power, once direct citizen participation in the ward republic is not available, is the "regularly organized power" of the people. This point is central to Jeffersonian republicanism. Once the trust relationship between the people and their government is breached, it is for the people—not a lateral branch of federal power—to remedy the offense. They must crush the usurpation of power by their unfaithful agents regularly and peacefully. Otherwise, there is always the "dreadful necessity" of insurrection (never too far from Jefferson's radical mind) to hand. The principal point is that sovereignty, ultimate political power, never leaves the people. Regardless of complex federal structures, intricate checks and balances, remedies for abuse institutionalized in the laws and the Constitution, inventive systems of representation and agency, principles of accountability and limits on official terms, political authority does not ever truly migrate upward. It remains right where it begins and where it is most safe, indeed, where it must belong in a democratic republic, with the people themselves. The people, acting through their local republics, are the ultimate legislators, executives, and judges.

Jefferson did not see a contradiction between popular sovereignty and individual rights; indeed, the former was a necessary ingredient of the latter. For him, those elected to higher levels of government were more delegates than representatives.[11] Jefferson approached national government as a Lockean and local government as an Aristotelian.

Republican Liberal, or Liberal Republican

Jefferson was the principal author of the *Declaration of Independence* and one of the foremost advocates of a bill of rights, a founder who regularly named John Locke as a dominant influence on his sophisticated understanding of the natural rights of man (though he never referred to rights within "a state of nature"). Indeed, to the degree that Jefferson remains in the political consciousness, it is as one of the most articulate advocates of human liberties rather than as a promoter of republican duty. Therefore, Jefferson's republicanism was neither simple nor primitively conceived in opposition to rights and liberties.

Locke played a central philosophical role in the drama of republicanism versus liberalism in the founding of America and, more particularly, in the thought of Thomas Jefferson. Was Jefferson a republican who became a liberal, as some have claimed?[12] Was he a liberal who became a republican, as others have claimed?[13] Or was he and did he always remain an idiosyncratic combination of both? Was it Jefferson's genius to amalgamate into a new political alloy strains of political thought and theory that others have found and still find disparate if not outright incompatible?

With the rise, in the last quarter of the twentieth century, of neorepublican analysis of America's founding, historians and political theorists have tended to divide the founders between republican Antifederalists and liberal Federalists. For some, the Jefferson of the *Declaration* was a Lockean liberal who migrated to republicanism later in life in opposition to the rise of centralized government powers. For others, Jefferson began as a rather primitive States' rights republican and made his way, over the years, to the position of a liberal defender of rights in opposition to the government that he had helped found and lead.

In contrast to these two schools of analysis, it is argued here that Jefferson, uniquely among the founders, developed a liberal-republican synthesis not fully understood in his time and not fully developed since. Put directly, Jefferson's view was that rights are inherent in the condition of humanity—"endowed by their Creator with certain unalienable rights"—although their enjoyment can only be secured through the regular exercise of civic virtue. Individual rights derive from the very nature of humanity; the rights to life, liberty, and security of property, to freedom of speech, assembly, and worship, to a jury trial by peers, to participation in the defense of these rights, and others originate in nature and are unqualified. Yet these rights are not secured in opposition to government; they are secured through government—government that, in some cases, must actively secure those rights and, in others, must simply not interfere with their exercise. The *practice* of democracy is the process by which rights are secured. But actual practice, not simple observation, is the key. To abstain from participation in government—to forgo the practice of civic virtue—is to jeopardize natural rights. Free men and women must possess and occupy government; it must belong to them and be operated by and for them. This occupation of government can best be achieved through the practice of republican principles. Civic virtue is exercised not to develop moral or psychological excellence but rather to secure the rights acquired from nature. Immediate participation in the polity is the surest guarantee that governmental powers will not be used by others to diminish, qualify, or abolish individual liberties. In the Jeffersonian view, the state can become the enemy of rights and liberties when, among other perils, it falls into the hands of interests. Thus, to care for liberty is to demand ownership of government, to make citizen-controlled government the shield of rights. Civic virtue is to be exercised as a means of protecting and constantly earning the rights granted in nature. Jefferson saw no conflict between the duties of republicanism and the rights of liberalism. They are each necessary to the other.

In his most visible departure from Locke, Jefferson, in the *Declaration*, substituted "the pursuit of happiness" for "property" among the "natural rights." Though Locke, in his *Essay on Human Understanding*, made the pursuit of happiness a central motivation of human action, he did not raise it to the status of a natural right. *The Declaration of Independence* elevated it to a right. "Reason and moral sense provided safeguards against the extravagances of individualism," according to Jefferson's biographer Merrill Peterson. "Virtue being essential to happiness, and virtue consisting in the duty to others, it was negated by mere selfishness. Because the pursuit was a public activity, in part, dependent on public well-being, all men had a stake in the *res publica* and should have a voice in its affairs. Property, on the other hand, Jefferson apparently considered a civil rather than a natural right."[14]

Classical Roots and Influences

Before returning to a more thorough analysis of this republican formulation, it is profitable to establish its roots in antiquity as well as to determine how many of its components sprang *sui generis* from Jefferson.

For most of America's founders, republicanism represented a civil religion. Some took it more seriously than others. John Adams, like Jefferson, wondered what it actually meant, since the term *republican* was so overused. If republicanism is everywhere, might this not mean that, in substance, it is nowhere? How did it happen that so many distinctly individualistic characters accepted the same frame of political reference so automatically? To the degree that the founders shared a common type of education in republican values, what forces shaped the thinking of their teachers? Are there identifiable reasons that some, like Jefferson, took republicanism more literally and more fundamentally than others? What were the characteristics and qualities of republicanism that influenced so profoundly the thought and action of those, like Jefferson, who continue to influence their political progeny so many generations later?

On the eve of revolution, America's founders had in mind not only to achieve political independence from the English monarch but also to accomplish a social revolution. They intended to found a republic on a scale hitherto unknown. Fully aware of the fate of the ancient republics in Greece and Rome and knowing the brief, unhappy fate of English republicanism, the founders of the new republic understood that the only republics on the planet in their time were "tiny, insignificant states." "All the[se] notions of liberty, equality, and public virtue were indelible sentiments already graven upon the hearts of Americans," writes historian Gordon Wood, "who realized fully the fragility of the republican polity."[15]

During the Revolution, Thomas Jefferson remarked to Benjamin Franklin that Americans "seem to have deposited the monarchical and taken up the republican government with as much ease as would have attended their throwing off an old and putting on a new suit of clothes."[16] The ease of this transition seems remarkable to Wood even today: "For republicanism after all involved the whole character of the society."[17] For Wood and other historians who have lately emphasized the power of the engine of republican ideology in shaping America's founding, the *social* revolution involved in the wholesale, and virtually unquestioned, adoption of republican principles was at least as remarkable as the *political* revolution it inspired. "Such was their enlightened faith in the comprehensive power of republican government itself that their very anxiety and apprehensions about the fitness of the American character for republicanism became in the end the most important element in their sudden determination to become republican. By 1776 republicanism had become not only a matter of suitability. It had become a matter of urgency."[18]

The republicanism of eighteenth-century America "was in every way a radical ideology—as radical for the eighteenth century as Marxism was for the nineteenth century." It replaced monarchical principles of hierarchy, patriarchy, privilege, patronage, and inequality with new values and interpretations of personal and family relationships, concepts of the state, and social culture. Indeed, "Republicanism offered nothing less than new ways of organizing society."[19] Following Adam Smith's division of all governments into monarchies and republics (monarchists loving peace and order and republicans loving liberty and independence), Jefferson divided humankind into two parties, whether Whigs or Tories, democrats or aristocrats, leftists or rightists, liberal or servile: "The sickly, weakly, timid man, fears the people, and is a Tory by nature. The healthy, strong and bold, cherishes them, [and] is formed a Whig by nature."[20]

Jefferson, perhaps more than any of the other principal founders, took his republicanism with utmost seriousness, starting in his native State of Virginia even before the formation of the revolutionary nation. In Virginia, he wrote in his *Autobiography*, he and its other political leaders intended to form "a system by which every fibre would be eradicated of ancient and future aristocracy; and a foundation laid for a government truly republican."[21]

Jefferson and other founders, schooled by teachers committed to the texts of the ancients, came by their classicism and their republicanism honestly and comprehensively. "The founders' models of personal behavior included mythological figures, Athenians and Romans. The founders met their mythological heroes in the works of Homer, Hesiod, Virgil, and Ovid. They found their Athenian heroes in Herodotus, Thucydides, Xenophon, and especially Plutarch. . . . The founders encountered their Roman heroes in the works of Polybius, Livy, Sallust, Plutarch, and Tacitus. Thomas Jefferson particularly admired Tacitus, whose moralistic Annals heaped scorn on the emperors and glorified the republic."[22] The principal Roman heroes found in the cited historical works include Cato the Younger, Brutus, Cassius, and Cicero, "statesmen who had sacrificed their lives in unsuccessful attempts to save the republic in its expiring moments."[23]

"Lord! Lord! What can I do with so much Greek?" John Adams complained at Jefferson's fondness for quoting Greek passages in his correspondence. But it was not just the classical literary allusions, the classical influences on Jefferson's (and, through him, the nation's) architecture, or the temptation to find revolutionary solace in ancient mythologies and heroes. The ancients provided the very roots of American republicanism. America's founders believed that, to make both a political and a social revolution at once, the intellectual authority found in those who first imagined republican government was required:

> The classics exerted a formative influence upon the founders, both directly and through the mediation of Whig and American perspectives. The classics supplied mixed government theory, the principal basis for the U.S. Constitution. The classics contributed a great deal to the founders' conception of human nature, their understanding of the nature and purpose of virtue, and their appreciation of society's essential role in its production. The classics offered the founders companionship and solace, emotional resources necessary for coping with the deaths and disasters so common in their era. The classics provided the founders with a sense of identity and purpose, assuring them that their exertions were part of a grand universal scheme. The struggles of the Revolutionary and Constitutional periods gave the founders a sense of kinship with the ancients, a thrill of excitement at the opportunity to match their classical heroes' struggles against tyranny and their sage construction of durable republics.[24]

In *The Ideological Origins of the American Revolution*, Bernard Bailyn finds the influence of the ancients pervasive, if not always based on thorough scholarship: "Knowledge of classical authors was universal among colonists with any degree of education, and references to them and their works abound in the literature. From the grammar schools, from the colleges, from private tutors and independent reading came a general familiarity with the habit of reference to the ancient authors and the heroic personalities and events of the ancient world." According to Bailyn, "Homer, Sophocles, Plato, Euripides, Herodotus, Thucydides, Xenophon, Aristotle, Strabo, Lucian, Dio, Polybius, Plutarch, and Epictetus, among the Greeks; and Cicero, Horace, Vergil, Tacitus, Lucan, Seneca, Livy, Nepos, Aurelius, Petronius, Suetonius, Caesar, the lawyers Ulpian and Gaius, and Justinian, among the Romans—all are cited in the Revolutionary literature; many are directly quoted." The learning behind this, according to Bailyn, was among many politicians of the day often superficial and misappropriated, yet Jefferson "was a careful reader of the classics" and one of the "thorough reader[s] of the texts."[25] Though references to classical times were sweeping and often indiscriminate, the founders' most insistent focus was upon writings covering the period of the Roman republic's civil wars in the early first century B.C. through the establishment of the empire on the republic's ruins at the end of the first century A.D. For these accounts, they relied heavily on Plutarch and Livy but primarily on Cicero, Sallust, and Tacitus, "writers who had lived either when the republic was being fundamentally challenged or when its greatest days were already past and its moral and political virtues decayed. They had hated and feared the trends of their own time, and in their writing had contrasted the present with a better past, which they endowed with qualities absent from their own, corrupt era. The earlier age had been full of virtue: simplicity, patriotism, integrity, a love of justice and of liberty; the present was venal, cynical, and oppressive."[26] The contrast between the true republic of virtue and the corrupt and corrupting empire was, in the founders' minds, stark, dramatic, and powerful. According to Gordon Wood, none of the ancient republics familiar to the founders—Athens, Sparta, Thebes—was as critical to their thinking as was the Roman republic. Through the Roman writers Cicero, Virgil, Sallust, and Tacitus, republican political and social values and ideals made their way to and were revitalized by the Italian Renaissance, especially through Machiavelli, and then, with the appellation of "civic humanism," to seventeenth-and eighteenth-century English and Scottish Enlightenment thinking, which "was thoroughly infused with these classical values and to that extent at least was republicanized."[27]

The American Republic in the Context of History

With the extraordinary range of personalities the founders represented, something more than the mere recitation of ancient texts was at work, something more intense and more immediate than worship of antiquity for its own sake, something more intensely political. For one of the most influential of recent political historians, J. G. A. Pocock, the American

Revolution had its roots in the Aristotelian and Machiavellian traditions as shaped and formed by English opposition thought. It represented a distinctive view of history and especially a view focused on the corruptibility of government and the state, which was nothing less than "an early form of the quarrel with modernity." For Pocock, the American revolutionary experience was the most recent and powerful exposition of "the Machiavellian moment," the historic confrontation of political humans with the corrosive and corrupting forces of time on human political institutions:

> A political culture took shape in the eighteenth-century colonies which possessed all the characteristics of neo-Harringtonian civic humanism. . . . The Whig canon and the neo-Harringtonians, Milton, Harrington and Sidney, Trenchard, Gordon, and Bolingbroke, together with the Greek, Roman, and Renaissance masters of the tradition as far as Montesquieu, formed the authoritative literature of this culture; and its values and concepts were those with which we have grown familiar—a civic and patriot[ic] ideal in which the personality was founded in property, perfected in citizenship but perpetually threatened by corruption; government figuring paradoxically as the principal source of corruption and operating through such means as patronage, faction, standing armies (as opposed to the ideal of the militia), established churches (as opposed to the Puritan and deist modes of American religion) and promotion of a monied interest. . . . A neoclassical politics provided both the ethos of the elites and the rhetoric of the upwardly mobile, and accounts for the singular cultural and intellectual homogeneity of the Founding Fathers and their generation. Not all Americans were schooled in this tradition, but there was (it would almost appear) no alternative tradition in which to be schooled.[28]

The homogeneous culture of neoclassical politics provided a convenient, common frame of reference and a forum in which the founders could work their revolution along lines of common understanding. Yet, for those like Jefferson, who took this culture and its history seriously, a troublesome legacy of decay and human corruptibility underlay the endeavor and colored their perspectives. The American Revolution offered the means to overthrow the monarchy and establish the republic. It was also doomed, they believed, to follow the fate of previous republics, from the Greek and Roman periods up through the English experience, which had foundered on the shoals of the inevitable human lust for power, wealth, influence, interest, and access, that is, unless means could be found in the structuring of republican institutions to defeat the forces of time, history, and human nature so corrosive to the republican ideal. The republics of history offered the ideal. But the republics of history had all fallen prey to the fallible humans who inhabited them.

Those founders most heavily influenced by the republics of antiquity also appreciated the issue of scale. Republics had decayed by corruption from within. They had also been overthrown by superior military force from without—either other Greek republics or the might of Alexander. This historical recognition led Jefferson to understand the need for a federation to replace the more fragile early confederation. It is among a number of reasons for his refusal to side wholeheartedly with the Antifederalists. But, unlike the Federalists, he did not see the interests of union as antithetical to those of the preservation of republican values, thus his distinctive formulation making ward republics the base of the federal structure.

Madison, at least to the extent that he was sympathetic to Jefferson's concerns, found his solution in the remedy of checks and balances, a government so mixed and divided in its powers that it could withstand the inexorable will of the majority to tyrannize dissenting or nonconforming minorities. For the Jeffersonian republicans, however, the forces of corruption would inevitably find their way around any conceivable combination of legislative and administrative institutions in a government so large and remote as to be inaccessible to the people directly.[29] The remedy for historic corruptibility could only be found in the people themselves who, through the exercise of civic virtue, would defeat the forces of interest and corruption. But the people could only participate in a government accessible to them, a polity on a scale where citizenship—and virtue—could be exercised immediately and consistently.

There is every evidence that Jefferson saw himself in the Aristotelian tradition, that he saw humans more in the context of society, civic association, and the *polis* than in the state of nature enshrined by Rousseau, and that the nature of humankind could be exercised fully only in active participation in the achievement of the common good. "It is clear that the city-state is a natural growth, and that man is by nature a political animal," Aristotle wrote, and Jefferson accepted this on conviction and experience.[30] From Aristotle he also acquired his strongly held belief that forms of government are inseparable from forms of property ownership and that private property ownership, in the context of a belief in the common good, was necessary to the proper functioning of a republic. For Aristotle, the city-state was a community, and a community owned things in common: "To have nothing in common is clearly impossible; for the state is essentially a form of community, and it must at any rate have a common locality: a single city occupies a single site, and a single city belongs to its citizens in common."[31] But for Aristotle, and Jefferson, common ownership had its own limits in human nature: "Property that is common to the greatest number of owners receives the least attention; men care most for their private possessions, and for what they own in common less, or only so far as it falls to their own individual share." Citizens, wrote Aristotle, "should not only possess enough [property] to meet their requirements in civic life, but also to encounter the perils that face them from outside."[32] For Jefferson, property ownership, particularly land, was not an objective in and of itself, a product of greed and self-aggrandizement, but more appropriately was the means by which a citizen might achieve the self-sufficiency required for participation in civic affairs. This led Jefferson to propose the distribution of undeveloped land within the original States and on the frontier to landless citizens.

Following Aristotle in Jefferson's pantheon is Cicero, whose writings on the republic and the laws would have appealed to Jefferson if for no other reason than Cicero's assertion in his *De Re Publica* that "there is no other occupation in which human virtue approaches more closely the august function of the gods than that of founding new States or preserving those already in existence."[33] Scipio, who filled a Socratic role for Cicero, echoes Aristotle in *De Re Publica*: "A commonwealth is the property of the people." And further: "For what is a State except an association or partnership in justice?"[34] Jefferson found in the wisdom of Cicero not necessarily a form of government, the mixed republic, but a way of thinking about governance. Cicero finds a "balanced combination" among kingship, aristocracy, and democracy, but Jefferson would have found in Cicero an even more resonant balance along functional lines: "Unless there is in the State an even balance of rights, duties, and functions, so that magistrates have enough power, the counsels of the eminent citizens enough influence, and the people enough liberty, this kind of government cannot be safe from revolution."[35] Thus, a Ciceronian balance of duties between a powerful executive and an influential parliament was necessary to protect the rights of a free people, but democratic liberties also provided a balance against kingship and aristocracy. Jefferson must also have found sympathy for his antagonism toward traders in money in Scipio's contrast between virtue and wealth:

> For when, on account of this mistaken notion of the common people [that the best leaders are rich, prosperous, or born of famous families], the State begins to be ruled by riches, instead of the virtue, of a few men, these rulers tenaciously retain the title, though they do not possess the character of the "best." For riches, name, and power, when they lack wisdom and the knowledge of how to live and to rule over others, are full of dishonor and insolent pride, nor is there any more depraved type of State than that in which the richest are accounted the best. But what can be nobler than the government of the State by virtue?[36]

With a reading of Cicero came a confirmation of the Aristotelian principles of the republic as a partnership; the godlike responsibility (and honor) of founding a state; the superiority of republican governors; the triumph of virtue over "riches, names, and power"; the balance of rights, duties, and functions; the inseparability of personal happiness from the common good and life in a well-constituted commonwealth; and the duties of civic participation. "I believe that those who rule such cities by wise counsel and authority," claimed Cicero, "are to be deemed far superior, even in wisdom, to those who take no part at all in the business of government."[37]

Though not in Jefferson's canon of republican works, his eclectic scholarship could well have encompassed *Utopia* (1516), in which Sir Thomas More advocated a federated republic as a means of accommodating the participation of large populations, or Milton's tract more than a century later which advocated that "every county in the land" should become "a kinde of subordinate Commonaltie."[38] Though Jefferson had little use for Machiavelli, he would not have quarreled with the Florentine's thought: "It is not the pursuit of individual good but of the common good that makes cities great, and it is beyond doubt that the common good is never considered except in republics."[39]

Jefferson further considered the iconoclastic, radical republican Algernon Sidney as an heir to the Aristotelian tradition. He especially appreciated Sidney's almost rabid antimonarchical stance: "As monarchy is in itself an irrational, evil government, unless over those who are naturally beasts and slaves, the worst of monarchies is that which is hereditary."[40] Sidney saw himself as an heir of Aristotle. "Aristotle well resembles the constitution of a body politic to a body natural, that is, a society of men to one man. Both direct their actions to some end. Both desire to preserve themselves and enjoy what is respectively good for both."[41] Jefferson would also have been attracted to Sidney's understanding of the roots of Rome's collapse—a constitution dependent on continued conquest for the satisfaction of its citizens until that conquest replaced discipline and virtue with power, luxury, and pride.[42]

Sidney's vigorous seventeenth-century arguments against monarchy after the restoration of Charles II and even against Cromwell's monarchical tendencies and his strong defense of both political and religious liberty would have brought him to Jefferson's attentions a century later. Although Sidney's contemporary James Harrington receives much more prominent scholarly attention as an heir to the Aristotelian and Machiavellian republican tradition, Jefferson himself rarely made reference to Harrington. It may have been that Sidney's death in 1683, as a martyr to the cause of parliamentary government following his rumored involvement in Whig plots to organize an uprising against the king, gave him an iconic status in the mind of revolutionary America. Employing the dialogistic style of Aristotle and Cicero, Sidney also understood, with them, the dependence of republicanism on civic virtue:

I know not any word more abused than that of policy or politics. The mistake will be discovered by the etymology of it. A *polis* signifies a city, and politeia is nothing but the art of constituting and governing cities or civil societies. And he that rightly understands and exercises that art is a politic man. These societies are constituted that men in them may live happily. We need seek no other definition of a happy human life in relation to this world than that set down by Aristotle as the end of civil societies, namely, that men may in them enjoy vita beata secundum virtutem ["a happy and honorable life," Aristotle *Politics* III]. For as there is no happiness without liberty ... there is neither liberty, nor happiness, where there is not virtue.[43]

On March 4, 1825, near the end of his life, in a resolution passed by the Board of Visitors at the University of Virginia (which he founded), Jefferson provided this endorsement: "As to the general principles of liberty and the rights of man, in nature and in society, the doctrines of Locke, in his 'Essay concerning the true original extent and end of civil government,' and of Sidney in his 'Discourses on government,' may be considered as those generally approved by our fellow citizens of this [Virginia] and the United States."[44] Also near the end of his life, Jefferson provided the sources for the natural law theories contained in the *Declaration of Independence*: "All its authority rests, then, on the harmonizing sentiments of the day, whether expressed in conversation, in letters, in printed essays, or in the elementary books of public rights [such] as Aristotle, Cicero, Locke, Sidney, etc."[45]

The classical sources, political philosophers such as Aristotle, orators and politicians such as Cicero, and historians such as Tacitus and Thucydides, place the attributes of the republican *polis*—virtue, happiness, and the good life—in the collective concern for the common good. They also warn of the dangers inherent in concentrated power and wealth, citizen detachment, corruption of the *polis* by commerce, the replacement of virtue by interest, and the corrosion of the republic as individual autonomy replaces concern for the commonwealth. Jefferson saw this contrast and the dangers inherent in the erosion of the republican ideal more starkly than others, and he emerged, even in those times when he was not physically present for the debates (most particularly the Constitutional debate), as the preeminent voice for the republican cause. Though he could support the principle of representation as one of the great political inventions of all time, he did so with great caution and profound reservation. His concern always was that the further away from direct participation by the people that government becomes, the less it is republican.

Brilliant schemes of representative government and national sovereignty can be adopted, he seemed to be saying, but do not pretend that what results is pure republicanism.

The Scale of the Republic and
Its Implications for Democracy

Jefferson's preoccupation with the *scale* of the republic—his scheme of wards or township governance—was not simply a literalistic tribute to the ancients. It was central to his political philosophy and perhaps even to his view of human nature. Concentration of power in a centralized state invited—indeed bred—corruption, preference, and interest. As that centralized government became the home of interests (*interest* referring to access and preference), its concerns inevitably became commercial. By the second half of the eighteenth century, commerce encompassed large-scale trade among nations. Far-flung commercial interests were strongly inclined, especially when struggling, to seek the support of national finance, in the form of central banks, credit, legislated subsidies, and national power, including, quite often, power in the form of a military establishment. To finance large-scale commercial enterprises and military forces to protect them, national governments issued paper to raise capital. This led both to national debt and to speculation in the government paper. The military establishment, in turn, had to include, at the very least, naval assets for such cases as suppression of the Barbary pirates or an expeditionary force of credible capacity. Both naval and expeditionary capabilities cost money to maintain. Ordinary taxpayers, whether they benefited from the commercial undertaking or not, were required to support the cost of the military assets maintained to protect the commercial interests, that support measured in both tax revenues and the lives of their sons. Therefore, the issue of the maintenance of a standing army—and, where maritime trade was at issue, a navy—wove its way through the history of republican thought (nowhere more vividly than in the writings of Machiavelli and the English Country opposition) and into the center of the Constitutional debate during America's founding era.

Scale has implications, implications that are economic, political, and social. The grand commercial republic, espoused most vigorously by Alexander Hamilton, George Washington's secretary of the Treasury, would concentrate wealth in the nation's capital. That wealth would attract interests, those whose motives were commercial not patriotic and whose concerns were with private wealth not the commonwealth. Interested parties, financiers and speculators alike, would become courtiers and would inhabit the corridors of power, seeking advantage and position. Government officials, in turn, both administrators and legislators, would constantly be courted for financial favors, perquisites, subsidies, and advantages, which they might grant. This concentration of wealth and power would, inevitably, create a governing class, remote from common citizens, preoccupied with its own perpetuation, composed of courtiers, lobbyists, and other representatives of special interests elbowing each other for access to the public trough, factionalized, selfish, and largely immune from public accountability. Few ordinary citizens could participate in such a government, and fewer still would want to. As if to mock the Antifederalists' concerns for corruption, Hamilton seemed eager to make early U.S. fiscal policy the handmaiden of wealth creation (which is of concern in a democracy only if one is among the vast majority without access to this process of wealth creation).

Though many of Jefferson's republican colleagues saw this government of concentrated wealth and power as a giant step back to monarchy, Jefferson saw it as a form of monarchy itself. He often referred in his voluminous correspondence to a "federalist monarchy." To preside over such a distinctly nonrepublican government, a president would not have to be a king, but he would surely assume kingly powers and preside over the kind of monarchical court so opposed by Bolingbroke's Country party in Walpole's England. For the early American republicans, a "monarchy" did not require a king to achieve its antirepublican purposes. For the purpose of protecting its prerogatives, it was sufficient to make government remote from public participation. For Jefferson, the issues of scale, distribution and dispersal of power among the people in their local republics, became central to his political thought.

How could the disparate collection of personalities who founded America agree so overwhelmingly on the theory of republicanism in the abstract and divide so deeply over its concrete application? This division had to do less with commitment to the ideal of the republic in the abstract and more to do with divergent understandings of the nature of democracy in the concrete. The Hamiltonian Federalists distrusted "the people" and saw them as incapable of self-governance, or at the very least requiring the guidance and direction of a superior ruling class, and dangerously prone to imprudent action. Jeffersonian republicans, though recognizing a natural aristocracy of talent and virtue, saw the local republics as the venue of democracy—direct citizen participation in decisions involving the public's shared concerns and the governance of the commonwealth. Jefferson's theory of democratic governance was directly dependent on "the common sense and good judgement of the American people." At its core this philosophical and political debate was about different views of human nature.

For the Federalists, an understanding of basic rights and liberties might be common to all, but government was "a complicated science, and requires abilities and knowledge, of a variety of subjects, to understand it." The most talented people (men) would be drawn to the new national government, but the States and local governments would suffer "till our old influential characters acquire confidence and authority."[46] Or, as historian Gordon Wood puts it: "Only if the respected and worthy [Adams's 'old influential characters'] lent their natural intellectual ability and their natural social influence to political authority could governmental order be maintained" and, by implication, the dangers of mobocracy be tempered.[47] In sum, the unspoken conflict was over the issue of popular sovereignty and the related question of the role of the state.

Among the Federalists, John Adams carried much of the argumentative burden for the elite groups in opposition to Jefferson's radical democratic views. "God Almighty has decreed," Adams declared, "in the creation of human nature an eternal aristocracy among men. The world is, always has been, and ever will be governed by it."[48] Adams believed in a mixed constitution that granted sufficient powers to a strong executive and an upper legislative house, composed of the natural elite of "the rich, the wellborn, and the able," which must be "separated from the mass" to guard against the excesses of mass democracy. "It was his solution [to the locus of power in society] that marked him as an aristocrat, for Adams's cure . . . was to create what America had never had: institutions giving permanent political power to an assigned group, 'standing bodies' as he called them."[49] Such views created deep divisions in postrevolutionary America, divisions that divided "parties," in the sense of contested points of view and eventually "parties" in the partisan, ideological, and institutional sense as well. "The line of division was again drawn," Jefferson wrote to Adams late in life, reviewing the organization of the new U.S. government, "into two parties, each wishing to give a different direction to the government; the one to strengthen the most popular branch [Congress], the other the more permanent branches [the presidency and the Senate], and to extend their permanence. Here you and I separated for the first time."[50] The stakes were high not only for the distribution of power but also for the nation's own self-image. Are we a new nation and a new people, the founders asked and wrote, believing in ourselves sufficiently to create a new consensual public trust that all shall govern all? Or are we, when all is said and done, transplanted Europeans subject to the interests of elites and the corrupting influences of power and history and so ultimately fallible that elaborate checks, especially against popular sovereignty, must be erected against unstable and inflammable public opinion?

In the years following Jefferson's presidency from 1801 to 1809, and up to and beyond his death in 1826, conservative opinion increasingly coalesced behind the view that Jefferson and his ideas represented a dangerous radicalism. "The web of conservative thought was spun out from the core principle that American government, rightly conceived, was republican [mixed and class driven] rather than democratic. The form of the distinction varied, but the meaning was consistent: American government was a genetic growth from English institutions, and it established sovereignty in the permanent Constitutional order of the state."[51] One prominent pamphleteer, in opposition to the continuing and corrupting Jeffersonian influence, made Jefferson's election the true American revolution: "From that moment [1800], the history of the American republic has presented the singular spectacle of a republican Constitution, imposing salutary checks on the popular will . . . and yet, the popular will in the shape of a dynasty of opinion, has habitually triumphed over these provisions. The government has been republican in form, but democratic in fact; and the rising element of democracy has been constantly increasing in power and influence."[52]

In other words, the continuing American struggle has been less over whether America would be a republic—there was general consensus on that—and more over to whom the republic belonged, where sovereignty would reside (with "the old influential characters" or with the people), and what would be the role and authority of the state. It was not an easily resolved question, indeed, it constituted a genuine dilemma. The historian Bernard Bailyn summed up the troubling conflict succinctly:

> "Democracy"—this was the point. "Republic" and "democracy" were words closely associated in the colonialists' minds; often they were used synonymously; and they evoked a mixed response of enthusiasm and foreboding. For if "republic" conjured up for many the positive features of the Commonwealth era and marked the triumph of virtue and reason, "democracy"— a word that denoted the lowest order of society as well as the form of government in which the commons ruled—was generally associated with the threat of civil disorder and the early assumption of power by a dictator.[53]

Knowing that ordinary citizens, "the people," could not collectively organize and participate in a distant national government, Jefferson instead insisted that the government had to come to the people in the form of the ward republic. For him, sovereignty belonged always with the people and not with a remote oligarchy, but this power was always under classic republican conditions, dependent on the exercise of civic virtue, duty, and participation, as well as on preeminent attention to the common good and the commonwealth. These conditions were the checks against demagoguery, irresponsibility, and majority tyranny and were the guarantors of true democratic republicanism.

The American Paradox; or,
The Paradoxical Americans

"Settlers of New England were by inheritance suspicious of power in the hands of kings, aristocrats, priests, and churches," writes historian Michael Kammen, "but they were equally suspicious of power in the hands of the people."[54] This contradiction produced both "democratic elitism" and "aristocratic liberalism." Compounding this philosophical confusion and political paradox was the early nation's search for legitimacy. Legitimacy in a democracy arises from the will of a majority, but legitimacy erodes if the majority becomes despotic. Jefferson, committed to the ideal of the republic as well as to the principles of democracy—and radically so, in both cases—could find no way to resolve the paradox, to make the republic democratic, except by founding it at the grassroots level, the local or ward republic. He believed that the ward republic was both the best political forum, or *polis*, for the protection of natural rights, and it was the only form of republic that could also be truly democratic. The distant national republic might meet the mechanical test of republicanism, but only the local republic, where every citizen could exercise her civic virtue through participation, could be truly democratic. "Jefferson's plan for small ward republics in which citizens regularly participate, along with that system of representation which grows out of local democracy and is characterized by a natural aristocracy of wisdom and virtue, was a classical conception of democracy, adapted to the vast American continent."[55]

With the exception of James Madison, few American founders sought to resolve this paradox of popular sovereignty and representative government. As a follower of Jefferson, Madison sought to do so but reached a different conclusion. In the *Federalist*, Madison defined a republic as "a government which derives all its powers directly or indirectly from the great body of the people, and is administered by persons holding their offices during pleasure, for a limited period, or during good behavior. It is essential to such a government that it be derived from the great body of society, not from an inconsiderable portion, or a favored class of it."[56] Like Jefferson and unlike Adams, Madison feared corruption of the republic by interested elites—and constructed Constitutional checks and balances against it—and therefore, at least in theory, located ultimate sovereignty in the people. Accepting both Hamilton's centralized government structures and Jefferson's concerns about the corruption of them, he sought to resolve the paradox by having each branch of the central government check the others. In the nearest recognition he gave to Jefferson's notion of periodic revolution, he strengthened his commitment to popular sovereignty: "All power is originally vested in, and consequently derived from, the people," he wrote in introducing a bill of rights to the new Constitution. He continued, "That government is instituted and ought to be exercised for the benefit of the people . . . and . . . the people have an indubitable and indefeasible right to reform or change their Government, whenever it is found adverse or inadequate to the purposes of its institution."[57] Although both men shared a fear of the historic forces of corruption, Madison accepted centralization and sought to restrict governmental powers horizontally; Jefferson resisted concentrated political power and sought to restrict it vertically. "Madison's 'compound republic of America' . . . was an imposing conception—a kinetic theory of politics—such a crumbling of political and social interests, such an atomization of authority, such a parceling of power, not only in the governmental institutions but in the extended sphere of society itself, creating such a multiplicity and scattering of designs and passions, so many checks, that no combination of parts could hold, no group of evil interests could long cohere. Yet out of the clashing and checking of this diversity Madison believed the public good, the true perfection of the whole, would somehow arise."[58] Addressing Jefferson's concerns about corruption of the republic by checking the power of the various elements in the Hamiltonian central government, Madison could draft a Constitution that, after travail, would be adopted for an infant and unformed nation, a Constitution that would demonstrate enormous resilience over time and be more effective than it was efficient. But he did not thereby manage to resolve the great paradox between a large republic with power concentrated in a national government and mass participatory democracy. "The American republic was influenced from the start by problems of legitimacy and unstable pluralism which, in turn, produced syzygy—'the conjunction of two organisms without loss of identity, a pair of correlative things, a paradoxical coupling of opposites'—also called biformities."[59]

Individualism and Humanism: Rights, Responsibilities, and the Role of Property

Having identified the ward republic as Jefferson's solution to the paradox of creating a new hybrid of republicanism and democracy, a further word must be said concerning the second paradox, the role of the local republic in the reconciliation of liberal individualism with civic humanism. To a certain degree, exploration of this paradox leads to consideration (among other factors) of the role of property in governance. Do people form governments to protect their rights in property, or is property ownership a means by which people become free to participate in government?

According to J. G. A. Pocock, republican civic humanism founded on the notion of virtue is in conflict with liberal individualism, which ac-

knowledges the impact of fortune (*Fortuna*) and its most vivid formulation, corruption, in the actual practice of governance in human history
(or what he calls "secular time").[60] Pocock posits a thesis regarding American political society that combines an Aristotelian notion of human nature as civic with the Machiavellian contradiction that the virtue required
by civic duty is always subject to the corruption brought on by time and
history. This thesis is posited in contradistinction to the traditional view
that the American republic was founded on a Lockean paradigm of human's need to form societies and governments to protect their rights in
property.[61]

In the second *Treatise*, Locke offers, then answers, his own explicit
question: If man in the state of nature is free and under no one's control,
what could compel him to "give up this Empire" of natural freedom?
Quite simply, Locke posits, because of the unsafeness, insecurities, and
dangers to his enjoyment of his freedom and property and its vulnerability
to "the Invasion of others," "he seeks out, and is willing to joyn in Society
with others who are already united, or have a mind to unite for the mutual
Preservation of their Lives, Liberties and Estates, which I call by the general name, Property. The great and chief end therefore, of Men's uniting
into Commonwealths, and putting themselves under Government, is the
Preservation of their Property."[62] By individual and common consent, people divest themselves of their absolute natural liberty in order to unite
into a community and form a commonwealth subject to the will of a
majority. They create a government of laws, which holds its powers in
trust for those who created it.

In contrast to the narrower Lockean view that men form commonwealths at the cost of unrestrained liberty principally to protect property,
Jefferson followed the classic Aristotelian model of the *polis* as the forum
for the exercise of virtue. "The state cannot be defined merely as a community dwelling in the same place and promoting the exchange of goods
and services," according to Aristotle, rather, "a city is a partnership of free
men. . . . All those . . . who are concerned about good government do take
civic virtue and vice into their purview. . . . any state that is truly so called
and is not a state merely in name must pay attention to virtue; for otherwise the community becomes merely an alliance." Aristotle held that
virtue was not implanted in man by nature but rather that it was achieved
through citizenship, social involvement, and action (*energia*), such action

being demonstrated in the *polis* and engendering "a certain character in the citizens and making them good and disposed to perform noble actions."[63]

"In contrast to Locke's conception of the state as limited to preserving individual rights, the ancients [for example, Aristotle] conceived of politics as cultivating man's highest faculties and establishing a polity of virtue and purpose."[64] Further, civic action for most citizens must take place in a polity whose scale permits participation in the public affairs of the day. "A citizen is in general one who has a share both in ruling and in being ruled with a view of life that is in accordance with goodness." How else can this be done except in a democratic republic whose public institutions and processes, in short, whose government is accessible to all? "In order to give decisions on matters of justice and for the purpose of distributing offices in accordance with the work of the applicants, it is necessary that the citizens should know each other and know what kind of people they are."[65]

Locke exercised a heavy influence on Jefferson's philosophy of rights, especially as that philosophy is embodied in the *Declaration of Independence*. The seeds of Locke's ideas would find fertile soil in the New World once firmly planted in the American consciousness by Thomas Jefferson. Yet Jefferson, the student, would find greater uses and purposes for government than would his master Locke.

During his presidency, Jefferson invented the phrase "Americanism" and meant it to encompass an economic, social, and political alternative to aristocracy, the last vestige of European feudalism.[66] In his *Autobiography*, he referred to his lifelong effort to create a system of laws "by which every fibre would be eradicated of ancient and future aristocracy." The great ideological divide, indeed the point of friction between entire social and economic structures, focused on one principal issue: ownership of property. On this question, Jefferson anticipated Marx. An aristocratic concentration of land ownership was incompatible with both individual freedom, which required economic self-sufficiency, and civic virtue, which required the participation in government of equal citizens. In this respect, Jefferson followed both Aristotle and Rousseau in identifying the incompatibility of republicanism with substantial economic inequality.[67] To Madison, Jefferson wrote: "Legislators cannot invent too many devices for subdividing property," and he further advocated a progressive tax scheme for large landholdings, which exempted small holdings from its effect: "Another means of silently lessening the inequality of property is to exempt all from taxation below a certain point, and to tax the higher portions of property in geometrical progression as they rise."[68]

Taken together, Jefferson's views on property ownership, systematically delivered over four decades, and his connection of economic independence with individual political freedom expressed through civic virtue in the local republic, constituted a comprehensive political philosophy.[69] Locke's commonwealth by consent might be formed to secure men in their property, but property was the means toward, not the ends of, Jefferson's participatory democratic republic. For Locke, government by representation was created for the purpose of enacting laws to protect the individual's rights in property. For Jefferson, the individual's rights in property provided the economic means by which he could participate directly and democratically in local republican government. "Governments," Jefferson insisted, "did not exist to protect property but rather to promote access to property or, more broadly speaking, opportunity."[70]

Together with Bacon and Newton, Locke was a third of the trinity at the apex of the pantheon of intellectual influences on Jefferson ("the wisest men who ever lived"). Locke's influence on *The Declaration of Independence* especially has been exhaustively documented. In the *Declaration*, Jefferson repeatedly lifted whole phrases from the second *Treatise* or slightly altered them: all men are created "equal and independent," "preservation of life and liberty," "consent of those who make up the community" (consent of the governed), "the people (mankind) who are more disposed to suffer," and "a long train of abuses" subjecting the people to "arbitrary power." More important, the *Declaration*'s assumptions concerning the natural rights of man to equality and independence, the role of consensually formed government in securing these rights, and the citizens' right and duty to replace that government when it no longer fulfills this function—all are founded in Locke.[71] But, by definition, the *Declaration* was a claim of right as a foundation for revolution, not a conceptual framework for a government to be built on that foundation. When Jefferson turned his mind to the draft of a *Constitution for the Commonwealth of Virginia* (1776), to the process of formation of a union of States, to consideration of a constitution for that union, and to processes for resisting Federalist centralization of national power by institutionalizing local democracy, his innate republicanism came to dominate his thinking and writing.

So central was the issue of land ownership to Jefferson's political economics that he pursued, with considerable consistency, two sweeping real-property distribution measures in the forum of his native State, the commonwealth of Virginia. In a 1777 session of the State legislature, Jefferson proposed "to abolish the law of primogeniture, and to make real estate descendible [*sic*] in parcenary [equal distribution] to the next of kin, as personal property is by the statute of distribution" and, later, "the repeal of the laws of entail [to] prevent the accumulation and perpetuation of wealth in select families."[72] By these measures he sought to fracture the backbone of feudal landholding, those measures that assured passage of land ownership undisturbed and undivided to the oldest surviving male heir. The second measure regarding land distribution proposed to extend the franchise to all landowners and to expand land ownership by dividing into fifty-acre plots all unoccupied land in the commonwealth. He drafted three versions of a constitution for the State of Virginia, each of which provided for the fifty-acre distribution to every male not then a landowner. The right of suffrage being connected to land ownership, "This grant assures the citizen not only of economic but also of political freedom."[73] Even beyond these measures, the distinctive historic character of Jefferson's presidency has much to do with the opening and expansion of the American frontier, through both the Louisiana Purchase and the Lewis and Clark expedition. In these cases, as well as in his strong opposition to frontier land speculation, his central stated purpose was to expand the pool of land available for citizen entrepreneurs concerned with establishing their economic independence. He wrote to Marbois in 1817, "My hope of its [the republic's] duration is built on the enlargement of the resources of life [land] going hand in hand with the enlargement of the territory, and the belief that men are disposed to live honestly, if the means of doing so are open to them."[74] Jefferson believed, *contra* Pocock, that expansion in space could overcome corruption by time.[75]

The centrality of property ownership in the form of land in Jefferson's political economics is difficult to overemphasize. Land provided individual economic stability and independence, which in turn enabled the independent and self-sufficient landowner to participate in the governance of local affairs and to achieve the common good. In turn, the task of the republican ward was politically to liberate the individual's full potential and to achieve human flourishing. Writing to Dupont de Nemours in 1816, Jefferson, having substituted "the pursuit of happiness" in the *Declaration of Independence* for Locke's triumvirate of life, liberty, and "property," nonetheless makes a right to property a "natural" right: "A right to property is founded in our natural wants, in the means with which we are endowed to satisfy those wants, and the right to what we acquire by those means without violating the similar rights of other sensible beings."[76] Jefferson the revolutionary had sought throughout much of his public life to overturn the feudal practices of Europe whereby "kings, hereditary nobles, and priests" constrained "the brute forces of the people" by "forces physical and moral, wielded over them by authorities independent of their will," keeping them, in the words of one commentator, in "hard labor, poverty, and ignorance." At the nation's founding convention, Jefferson wrote, his party was composed of "the landed and the laboring interests of the country," and he believed that "man was a rational animal, endowed by nature with rights, and with an innate sense of justice; and that he could be restrained from wrong and protected in right by moderate powers, confided to persons of his own choice, and held to their duties by dependence on his own will."[77] Whereas traditional economic theory had placed the mass of people outside the realm of citizenship due to their economic and political dependence upon the will of the higher orders, Jefferson "unmasked the self-fulfilling prophecy in that formulation" and reversed its logic. He sought to "use Constitutional and statutory measures to make the poor independent [in large part through land ownership]. Here his environmentalism merged imperceptibly into his convictions about the basic human endowment. What today would appear as social engineering presented itself to Jefferson as a liberation of those natural forces long held in check by the Old World artifices of monarchy, nobility, and established religion."[78]

For Jefferson, the natural right to property and the individual freedom that right, once secured, conveyed were the foundation on which the civic humanism of the true republic is based. That right opened up both the freedom to participate in government and the responsibility for self-governance that accompanied full citizenship. Though not particularly given to irony, Jefferson fully understood the irony of property—in at least two of its forms—in republican thought. Property is simultaneously the guarantor of liberty and, when wielded as political and economic influence, a source of corruption. This is the reason that "real" property—land—was more compatible with republican ideals than was paper wealth. The former was identified with virtuous labor, while the latter was an instrument of speculation and manipulation. Jefferson held paper wealth, a form of property, in contempt.[79] Economic expansion by financial speculation was material progress at the expense of civic virtue. The values of this form of capitalism were incompatible with those of republicanism. Laboring in the earth, however, was the essence of republican citizenship from its earliest days.[80]

The Relationship of the Small to the Large Republic: The Issue of Scale

In American Constitutional literature, Montesquieu is the touchstone for the small republic. He is cited more than any other source in Jefferson's *Commonplace Book*. In the Constitutional debates, particular attention was given to Montesquieu's observations on the scale of republics:

> It is in the nature of a republic to have only a small territory; otherwise, it can scarcely continue to exist. In a large republic, there are large fortunes, and consequently little moderation in spirits; the depositories are too large to put into the hands of a citizen; interests become particularized; at first a man feels he can be happy, great and glorious without his homeland; and soon, that he can be great only on the ruins of his homeland. In a large republic, the common good is sacrificed to a thousand considerations; it is subordinated to exceptions; it depends upon accidents. In a small one, the public good is better felt, better known, lies nearer to each citizen; abuses are less extensive there and consequently less protected.[81]

Another pertinent observation by Montesquieu on the matter of scale relates to issues of the security of republics and might be called the Montesquieu corollary: "If a republic is small, it is destroyed by a foreign force; if it is large, it is destroyed by an internal vice." Given these realities, people would have been consigned to live perpetually under "the government of one alone" if they had not devised a constitution that combined the advantages of republicanism with the strength of monarchy. "This form of government is an agreement by which many political bodies consent to become citizens of the larger state that they may want to form [to resist destruction by a foreign force]." This new creation is "a society of societies that make a new one, which can be enlarged by new associates that unite with it." "I speak," Montesquieu wrote, "of the federal republic."[82]

Strongly influenced by Montesquieu as early in his public life as the time of his attendance at the first Continental Congress in 1774 (at the age of thirty-one), Jefferson, demonstrating the capacity to alter intellectual course that so intrigued his supporters and excited his enemies, came later to marginalize Montesquieu's influence on his own republican thinking.[83] Ten years later, well before his principal works on ward republics, Jefferson wrote: "I suspect that the doctrine, that small States alone are fitted to be republics, will be exploded by experience [together] with some other brilliant fallacies accredited by Montesquieu."[84] Later in life Jefferson's attentions were more strongly drawn to the French philosopher Antoine Louis Claude Destutt de Tracy's *Commentary and Review of Montesquieu's Spirit of the Laws*, translating it into English after he left the presidency and referring to it in later correspondence as "the best elementary book [in the world] on the principles of government."[85] On the complex question of small republics and their relationship to larger ones, Jefferson would find this observation in de Tracy:

> Representation, or representative government, may be considered as a new invention, unknown in Montesquieu's time; it was almost impossible to put it into practice before the invention of printing, which so much facilitates the communication between the constituents and the representative, and renders it so easy for the former to control, and the latter to account for his conduct; and above all, which averts those sudden storms, so often excited by the force of an impassioned and popular eloquence.[86]

Seeking to work out his own notions of scale in republicanism, Jefferson wrote in 1807, in favor of larger republics: "It seems that the smaller the society the bitterer the dissensions into which it breaks. Perhaps this observation answers all the objections by Mr. Adams from the small republic of Italy. I believe ours is to owe its permanence to its great extent, and the smaller portion comparatively, which can ever be convulsed at one time by local passions."[87]

Thus, the reconciliation of the small or democratic republic with the large or representative republic was never, for Jefferson, a simple task. He was never so naive as to think that the new nation would merely be a collection of isolated local community governments. If for no other reason than that the thirteen original colonies, having become States, reserved for themselves all powers under the federal Constitution not explicitly granted to the U.S. government, attention had to be given in actual practice to the complex structure of relationships between the States and the new national government. This task, together with the definition of the powers of the government of the United States, preoccupied the attentions of the negotiators at the Constitutional convention. Antifederalists, struggling always against concentration of power in the national government, found their principal success in two Constitutional measures, the Article IV provision that "the United States shall guarantee to every State in this Union a Republican form of government," and, more explicitly later in the Tenth Amendment to the Constitution: "The Powers not delegated to the United States by the Constitution, nor prohibited by it to the States, are reserved to the States respectively, or to the people." The prerogative of the States, properly protected, to govern their own affairs would play a substantial role in lessening the concentration of power in the national government. Even so, State governments were, by the measure of the day, themselves remote entities and scarcely accessible to ordinary citizens. Therefore, the only institution in which the individual citizen could exercise his right of self-government remained the local or "pure" republic.

Montesquieu's federative principle helped reconcile Jefferson's various definitions of republicanism and was well adapted to American needs and experiences. Federated State republics could form the Union, and federated local republics could form the States. This pyramid of republics would be "more or less republican" as it moved from the local, directly democratic republic to the remote, representative republic at the national level. So long as it was understood that ultimate sovereignty remained with the people, this new and complex scheme could resist the ravages of corruption and despotism. The key to representative republicanism for Jefferson was the ability of the people to choose their representatives immediately and directly and to remove or recall those representatives, hence direct accountability. In a letter to Dupont de Nemours, he reconciles direct with representative democracy by introducing the element of competence: "We [Americans] think experience has proved it safer, for the mass of individuals composing society, to reserve to themselves personally the exercise of all rightful powers to which they are competent, and to delegate those to which they are not competent to deputies named, and removable for unfaithful conduct, by themselves immediately." Logically, citizens are most competent regarding matters directly to hand, local issues and problems that they know immediately. Likewise, they are least competent regarding the nation's relations to other nations, its conduct of international affairs, or matters arising in distant regions of the large republic. Jefferson thus concludes his views on the relationship of small to large republics succinctly: "That action by the citizens in person in affairs within their reach and competence, and in all others by representatives, chosen immediately and removable by themselves, constitutes the essence of a republic; . . . all governments are more or less republican in proportion as this principle enters more or less into their composition, and . . . a government by representation is capable of extension over a greater surface of country than one of any other form."[88]

Although not distinguished for his republicanism, a half century later, in his essay "Concerning Representative Government," John Stuart Mill offered support for Jefferson's position by proposing "a division of labor" between central and local governments. Mill sounds very Jeffersonian in his view that "the ideally best form of government is that in which the sovereignty, or supreme controlling power in the last resort, is vested in the entire aggregate of the community; every citizen not only having a voice in the exercise of that ultimate sovereignty, but being, at least occasionally, called on to take an actual part in the government, by the personal discharge of some public function, local or general."[89] Mill notes the "great discouragement to an individual, and a still greater one to a class" to be left out of the constituted government, to be "reduced to plead from outside the door of the arbiters of their destiny."[90] The only government, he continues, that can satisfy the exigencies of the social state is one that includes full citizen participation, "the admission of all to a share in the sovereign power of the state." Admitting that this "ultimately desirable" government cannot operate beyond the scale of a small town, he then acknowledges the requirement of representation to reach the ideal.

Mill was critical of the British government of his day for "busying itself far too much with local affairs" and "an enormous amount of private business," instead of attending to the "small portion of the public business of a country" that is "the proper occupations of the great council of the nation." Instead, he proposed a "division of labor" whereby the central government uses its greater knowledge to develop principles of government and the local governments are involved in the details of management that require familiarity with local concerns and issues: "The authority which is most conversant with principles should be supreme over principles, while that which is most competent in details should have the details left to it. The principal business of the central authority should be to give instruction, of the local authority to apply it. Power may be localized, but knowledge, to be most useful, must be centralized."[91] For Mill, the local authority was for participation and the central authority for competence.

Like Jefferson, Mill saw synergy, not incompatibility, between central and local authority. Although he based his belief more on a pragmatic assessment of the relative competences of levels of government than did Jefferson, for whom the locus of sovereignty was paramount, they shared an appreciation for the profound relationship between participation and patriotism. Mill wrote: "Let a person have nothing to do for his country, and he will not care for it. It has been said of old, that in a despotism there is at most but one patriot, the despot himself."[92] Ultimately, for Jefferson, the conditions for extended republicanism, for republican government over large distances in remote capitals, are that citizens participate directly in the selection of their representatives, that those representatives operate primarily as delegates carrying out the direct will of the people, that the delegates be strictly and directly accountable to the electorate, that they attend primarily to those matters regarding which the people are least competent to judge directly, and that the people retain the right of recall if the delegate proves faithless or self-interested.

The Jeffersonian republic in its purest form is small and local, much like the New England town meeting, but it can also operate through representatives, under conditions strictly established and followed, over extended territories, such as the expanding United States.

Summary

A restatement of Jefferson's alternative political vision includes these fundamental propositions: the earth belongs to the living; laws and constitutions must keep pace with the progress of the human mind; concentrated and centralized wealth and power are conducive to corruption; widespread distribution of land offers the best hope for independent citizens in pursuit of happiness; and the local republic is the only *polis* able to found, and promote, authentic democracy.

His political philosophy contains these elements: all people are created equal; people are political and social beings inclined naturally to participate in the life of the *polis*; nature has given human beings the inalienable right to life, liberty, and the pursuit of happiness; civic virtue and the duties of citizenship are the best protectors of these rights; sovereignty exercised by remote governments, instead of by the people themselves, is susceptible to corruption; and democratic equality and popular sovereignty are best exercised in and promoted by local republican governments.

Thus, the ward republic is the means by which classic republican civic virtue can be reconciled with the liberal value of nondomination by the state. Only through direct citizen participation in the *polis* and control of local governmental affairs can individual liberty be reconciled with civic duty. Jefferson did not envision the recreation of a classic city-state but rather the creation of a new democratic *polis* of civic virtue, whose responsibility it is to protect individual rights and liberties. Jefferson produced the most sweeping declaration of civil liberties in the modern age, yet he was a radical republican. His thesis was simple: rights must be protected by civic virtue. He saw no contradiction between rights and duties.

Hamilton's republic was that of a merchant court and Adams's that of an old aristocratic few. Jefferson introduced the notion of a truly democratic republic. At least one recent scholar, Joyce Appleby, concludes, "The presence of [this kind of] republicanism in America's past has provided roots at last for a genuine alternative to the world view of liberal capitalism."[93]

Jefferson's Republican Ideal in the Context of the Constitutional Debate

Thomas Jefferson's complex ideal of the republic was not presented to the delegates to the Constitutional convention in Philadelphia in 1787. Indeed, it was not fully spelled out, even in Jefferson's own mind, until almost twenty-five years later, after his retirement to Monticello following his presidential terms. Thus, the Jeffersonian pyramid of republics founded on the wards or "pure" republics never became an alternative model for the founders and framers of the American federal republic. The delegates to the Constitutional convention had before them for deliberation James Madison's proposal for a union or federation of State republics, favored, more or less, by the Federalists, and the alternative of the continuation of the loose confederation of States favored, more or less, by the Antifederalists. The former created a new centralized national government with legislative, executive, and judicial powers balanced among and checked by each other. The latter sought refuge from a dominant, centralized, national government in the *status quo*. The Constitution neither acknowledged, created, nor rejected a public space for the township republic.

Jefferson did not choose to absent himself from this debate. He had been delegated to Paris as the new nation's second minister to France, replacing Benjamin Franklin. He followed the Constitutional debates as intensely as one could, given dependence on transatlantic, glacial correspondence. He sought to counsel Madison and others, also by correspondence, especially on three matters: the need for a bill of rights, limits on presidential terms, and the dangers of a judiciary too independent and too powerful. Otherwise, though suspicious of Hamiltonian Federalist ambitions, believing them to be antirepublican, Jefferson was a remote observer of the Union's founding and relatively unprovoked by the heat of the Antifederalist cause.

Jefferson's mature republicanism was the product of his early Enlightenment studies, his role in the founding of the State of Virginia, his revolutionary antipathy toward the British monarchy, his diplomatic years in France (1784–1789), his service as secretary of state, his combat with the Federalists in the revolutionary election of 1800, his two terms as president, and his reflective years in semiretirement from the public arena. But much of his thought on the subject flowed from the critical definition given to the new republic in the Constitutional era and his efforts to reconcile their inconsistencies two and a half decades later. The new Constitution was a bundle of compromises and, like all compromises, it satisfied no one, including its principal author, Madison. To Jefferson he wrote: "The plan should it be adopted will neither effectually answer its national object nor prevent the local mischiefs which every where excite distrust against the state governments."[94] Alexander Hamilton, who created "Publius" with Madison and John Jay in authoring *The Federalist*, the most comprehensive defense of the draft Constitution, found it, as a strong Federalist, wanting: "I never expect to see a perfect work from imperfect man." Nevertheless, he wrote, "I am persuaded that it is the best which our political situation, habits, and opinions will admit, and superior to any the revolution has produced."[95]

Madison laid down the arguments for a written constitution at once strongly federative and republican by drawing a sharp distinction between a "pure democracy" and a republic. "A pure democracy, by which I mean a society consisting of a small number of citizens, who assemble and administer the government in person, can admit of no cure for the mischiefs of a faction. . . . Such democracies have ever been spectacles of turbulence and contention; have ever been found incompatible with personal security or the rights of property; and have in general been as short in their lives as they have been violent in their deaths."[96] What Jefferson many years later would describe as ward republics thus, to Madison, were "pure democracies" historically riddled with factionalism, turmoil, and disruption. By contrast, "A republic, by which I mean a government in which the scheme of representation takes place, opens a different prospect and promises the cure for which we are seeking." Already the troubles brought on by the failure of a common definition of *republic* make their appearance. For Jefferson, a republic was elementary, democratic, participatory, and immediate. For Madison, a republic was representative, delegable, and at least once removed. Ironically, each believed his ideal of the republic the best hedge against chaos. It is an interesting question whether, if Jefferson had produced his theory of ward republics more explicitly earlier and presented it in the Constitutional debates, Madison might have been inclined to consider it, at least as a compromise answer to the Antifederalists.

For Madison, "The two great points of difference between a democracy and a republic are: first, the delegation of the government, in the latter, to a small number of citizens elected by the rest; secondly, the greater number of citizens and greater sphere of country over which the latter may be extended." Madison wanted the tasks of government to be delegated. Jefferson wanted them to be exercised, to the degree practicable, by citizens locally. More important, Madison saw delegation as the only means to extend the republic over a wider scale than the local arena. Jefferson saw direct participation in the wards as the means by which political issues affecting the township could be resolved without handing them off to a higher political authority. Madison feared turbulence at the local level. Jefferson feared "interest" and corruption at the higher level. Madison believed that "public views" or issues were best passed through the medium of a wise, patriotic, and just "chosen body of people" as a means of ensuring that "the public voice, pronounced by the representatives of the people, will be more consonant to the public good than if pronounced by the people themselves, convened for that purpose." Here, at the basic level of human nature, was the true difference between the two political theorists. Madison trusted the detached judgment of a "chosen body." Jefferson, though a believer in a natural aristocracy for conducting certain levels of public affairs involving the nation as a whole, nevertheless trusted "the common sense and good judgment of the people" for the conduct of the day-to-day public duties of immediate and common interest to the community.

Even though Jefferson was not available to force this debate in the way that Antifederalists were, the crucial matter of the scale of the republic emerged as central to Madison's Constitutional arguments. "The question resulting," he wrote in *Federalist* number 10, "is whether small or extensive republics are most favorable to the election of proper guardians of the public weal; and it is clearly decided in favor of the latter by two obvious considerations." First, he said, the pool of "fit characters" for elective public service would be proportionately greater in a large republic. Second, given a larger voter base in the greater republic, it would be more difficult for "untrustworthy candidates" to practice the "vicious arts" of deceptive politics on the larger stage. Ever conscious of the need for balance, Madison found it in the proposed constitution's dependence on representatives both knowledgeable of local events and capable of grasping "great and national objects." "The federal Constitution," he wrote, "forms a happy combination in this respect; the great and aggregate interests being referred to the national, the local and particular[ly] to the State legislators." This is not too far from Jefferson's republican pyramid. Jefferson, trusting the people themselves to combat the evils of faction at the local level, saw the "pure democracy" of the ward republic as the proper forum for the "local and particular" objects and the base of the pyramid of republics. On the theme of faction, Madison contended that the greater number of citizens and larger territory of the republican (representative) government, more than the democratic (participatory) government, were the best bulwark of resistance to the tendency of small groups of people in small majorities "to concert and exercise their plans of oppression." This same principle applied, he argued, to the relationship between the Union and the State governments: "The same advantage which a republic has over a democracy in controlling the effects of faction is enjoyed by a large over a small republic—is enjoyed by the Union over the States composing it." Thus, in Madison's mind, there are always cabals or factions, present or waiting to be formed, capable of arising to oppress. These cabals can most easily form in a small ("democratic") arena. Therefore, the best remedy against such machinations is to expand the arena and raise its level.

The advantage that the extended (representative) republic has over the smaller (participatory) democracy encompassed also the superiority of "enlightened and virtuous" representatives over "local prejudices" and "schemes of injustice," which characterize local democracies. The larger number of parties in a representative republic provided security against one party arising to outnumber and oppress the rest as might well occur in a smaller venue. The larger union presented a greater obstacle to "an unjust and interested majority" imposing its secret wishes on the unsuspecting minority. Throughout the framing of the complex federation of the union and his arguments in support of its ratification, James Madison was conditioned by a Humean view of man as inclined toward faction tending toward oppression when opportunity arose, and untrustworthy as either a dominant majority or an unchecked minority. These negative characteristics of man in society could only be checked by the superior enlightenment and virtue of representatives to a more extended national government. "In the extent and proper structure of the Union," he concluded as "Publius," "we behold a republican remedy for the diseases most incident to republican government." Thus, the principal argument for the Constitution from its principal draftsman was not the need for a strong central government to conduct the affairs of the United States in the world, but rather the need to protect against the propensity of democratic man to form oppressive factions within the domestic venue.

Employing rhetoric considerably more flamboyant than his fellow "Publius" Madison, Alexander Hamilton nevertheless pursued a similar tack regarding the scale of the new republic. To respond to those founders resting their case on Montesquieu's argument for small republics, Hamilton assessed the risk of "splitting ourselves into an infinity of little, jealous, clashing, tumultuous commonwealths, the wretched nurseries of unceasing discord and the miserable objects of universal pity or contempt" and found it high.[97] The great innovation in the science of politics where republics were concerned, Hamilton claimed, was in the "enlargement of the Orbit within which such systems are to revolve." Then he noted the further observation of Montesquieu in this regard, conveniently overlooked by the Antifederalist forces: "So far are the suggestions of Montesquieu from standing in opposition to a general Union of the States that he explicitly treats of a Confederate Republic as the expedient for extending the sphere of popular government and reconciling the advantages of monarchy with those of republicanism."[98]

Hamilton notes that the States retain their separate identities as parts of the national sovereignty, as shown by their direct selection of representatives to the proposed Senate of the union and the reservation to them of certain important and exclusive sovereign powers. "So long as the separate organizations of the members [States] be not abolished; so long as it exists, by a Constitutional necessity, for local purposes; though it should be in perfect subordination to the general authority of the union, it would still be, in fact and in theory, an association of states, or a confederacy." Madison and other Federalists did not go so far as to propose "perfect subordination," the reddest of flags to the Antifederalists.

The Antifederalists active in the Constitutional debate drew a sharp distinction between the confederacy claimed by the Federalists as their objective and a "consolidated government," which the Antifederalists claimed to be the Federalists' true objective. According to Patrick Henry, speaking before the Virginia ratifying convention on June 5, 1788, the question is whether the proponents of the Constitution had in mind a compact among the States, in which case it would be a confederation, or a consolidated government. "The question turns, Sir, on that poor little thing—the expression, We, the people, instead of the States of America."[99] The principles of the proposed union, he said, would lead to a monarchy patterned after the compact between the English king and his subjects rather than to the kind of confederacy obtained in Holland by an association of independent States, each retaining individual sovereignty. "It is not a democracy," he claimed, in any case, "wherein the people retain all their rights securely. Had these principles been adhered to, we should not have been brought to this alarming transition, from a Confederacy to a consolidated Government."[100] Citing the provisions having to do with amendments to the proposed Constitution, themselves requiring elaborate processes involving supermajorities in State or federal legislatures, Henry noted how far they varied from the republican declarations in such documents as the Virginia Bill of Rights: "whenever any Government shall be found inadequate, or contrary to these purposes, a majority of the community hath, an undubitable, unalienable and indefeasible right to reform, alter, or abolish it, in such manner as shall be judged most conducive to the public weal."

"This, Sir," Henry asserted, "is the language of democracy; that a majority of the community have a right to alter their Government when found to be oppressive."[101] The true purpose of this plan, for Henry and others who opposed it, was consolidation of the States as a stepping-stone to empire: "The American spirit, assisted by the ropes and chains of consolidation, is about to convert this country to a powerful and mighty empire: If you make the citizens of this country agree to become the subjects of one great consolidated empire of America, your Government will not have sufficient energy to keep them together: Such a Government is incompatible with the genius of republicanism."[102]

Thus, Federalists feared faction and oppression from below, and Antifederalists feared consolidation, empire, building, and oppression from above. Both claimed republican principles to make their case. From his distant outpost in Paris, Jefferson could only urge the inclusion in the new Constitution of a bill of rights to protect Americans from oppression by their own new government. He did not engage, at this point, in a debate with Madison on the importance to the complex federal republic of citizens' participation in their local townships, councils, and wards as a republican foundation for the republics of the States confederated or consolidated into the grand republic.

So fearful was Madison of democratic chaos at the local level that he seemed never seriously to have considered a meaningful role for a township republic. He considered significant citizen involvement in daily governance a threat to the proposed new union of States. For Madison, republicanism was based upon the principle of representation. A participatory republic in which citizens deliberated over the issues affecting their daily lives was, therefore, an oxymoron. Such a creature was not a republic; it was a democracy.

The Jefferson theory of township or pure republicanism was presented neither to the Constitutional convention nor directly to the people during the ratification debate. How Madison might have responded to his mentor had Jefferson been present for the debate and had he sufficiently developed his theory by that time will never be known. By extrapolation from the arguments Madison did make on behalf of a balanced and checked federal union, however, his principle objections can be rendered: local democracy is open to oppression of the minority by a willful majority or of a lethargic majority by a willful minority faction; factions pursuing narrow interests form most easily in small venues; factionalism leads to friction, confusion, and eventual chaos; the most enlightened and virtuous citizens are most inclined to participate in larger issues at higher levels of government; such citizens will avoid involvement in faction-ridden local politics; the result of leaving too much authority in the hands of democratic masses is social and political destabilization; and ordinary citizens are not especially qualified to manage public affairs.

Though Madison and Jefferson shared a similar background in the enlightened Virginian landowning aristocracy and shared similar political philosophies throughout their lives, in the instance of their respective views on the trustworthiness of democratic citizens to participate in republican government, they diverged widely at this crucial crossroad of early U.S. history.

Slavery and the Jeffersonian Republic

"I tremble for my country when I reflect that God is just."[103] These words of Jefferson, carved into the walls of his monument in Washington, reflect his most immediate sense of the immorality of slavery. They are reconcilable with his most famous declaration—"All men are created equal"— but not with the fact that he was himself an owner of slaves throughout his life. Any effort to transpose Jefferson's ideal of the republic to the present age must at least acknowledge this irreconcilable contradiction.

As students of the classics, especially classical republican texts, Jefferson and other American founders were well aware that ancient Greek and Roman republican societies were slave-owning societies. "Epictetus, Terence, and Phaedrus were slaves," Jefferson noted. Though this fact might offer some solace, it was rarely if ever used as a rationalization for slave ownership. The acceptance of slavery in the southern colonies was based upon pragmatism not theory. The plantation economy of the southern colonies and eventual States was largely based upon slave labor, though some slave ownership persisted in many sectors of colonial society.[104] Even Jefferson's most conciliatory biographers concede that he could have maintained Monticello and the lifestyle it represented only with the labor of the slaves he inherited.

Throughout his life, Jefferson was plagued by the political and moral consequences of slavery and the inequality of the races, seeking to deal with it on some occasions biologically, on some occasions sociologically, on some politically, and, with most consistency, morally. One of democracy's most ardent apostles could hardly ignore an unjust condition so blatantly apparent in almost every waking moment. His most consistent attempt to resolve this injustice was to propose nationalism, colonialism, and segregation. That is to say, he favored a separate nation for African slaves, preferably back in Africa. He held out little, if any, hope of peaceful integration, and he readily and repeatedly admitted that the issue would continue to plague the new nation as long as it remained unresolved. He even forecast the Civil War as the inevitable outcome.

But Jefferson did not deal with slavery and racial inequality in formulating his scheme of ward republics as the basis for a pyramid of republics. He accepted exclusively white, male suffrage as a given. His lengthy and often contradictory writings over more than five decades on the subject of race were quite separate from his commentaries on republican theory. He never attempted to deal with the question of the role of enslaved African Americans in the elementary republics of the wards. His assumption seemed to be that the slavery issue was separate and apart from the structure of government and the locus of sovereignty. Jefferson never attempted to insert the slavery issue into or abstract it from his ideal of the republic. His formulation of republican theory was not used as a means to avoid the issue. His republican formulation was what it was, and the slavery issue was separate from it.

On this basis, had Jefferson's scheme of elementary republics been accepted and implemented, it is likely that racial segregation and discrimination would have existed in the small republics even as they did in the larger ones of the States and the nation. Would Jefferson have permitted individual local republics to outlaw slavery? Because he permitted the larger republics of the States that option, one can presume that Jefferson's scheme would have permitted the existence of both slave and nonslave ward republics.[105]

Although a detailed analysis of Jefferson's complex attitudes toward slavery is well beyond the scope of this volume, certain critical observations may be made. As a young, first-term member of the Virginia colonial assembly, Jefferson joined with Richard Bland, one of the assembly's senior members, to seek amelioration of the slaves' condition and possibly even manumission of slaves.[106] Further, Jefferson's original draft of the *Declaration of Independence*, presented to the Second Continental Congress in Philadelphia in late June 1776, contained a lengthy, angry, stinging indictment of King George III for "cruel war against human nature itself" by the traffic in slaves permitted by his government and the royal vetoes of the Virginia colony's legislative efforts to ban the slave trade. Of these efforts, he wrote in his *Notes on the State of Virginia*: "In the very first session held under the republican government, the [Virginia] Assembly passed a law for the perpetual prohibition of the importation of slaves. This will in some measure stop the increase of this great political and moral evil, while the minds of our citizens may be ripening for a complete emancipation of human nature."[107] Sensing its own hypocrisy in its collaboration in this traffic, Congress, at the behest of Georgia and South Carolina, struck this language from the draft *Declaration*.[108] Jefferson's draft of a proposed constitution for the state of Virginia prohibited the enslavement of any new person entering the country. In 1784, Jefferson proposed an ordinance that would prohibit the expansion of slavery into the western territories. And in his *Notes*, published in 1785, he proposed a plan for the gradual emancipation of slaves. Indeed, it was in the *Notes* that he stated his fear of God's justice and produced the moral basis for his opposition to slavery—that it both corrupts the master and debases the slave: "The whole commerce between master and slave is a perpetual exercise of the most boisterous passions, the most unremitting despotism on the one part, and degrading submission on the other. . . . The man must be a prodigy who can retain his manners and morals undepraved by such circumstances."[109]

"Jefferson consistently denounced the institution of slavery, calling it an 'abominable crime,' a 'political and moral evil,' and a 'hideous blot' on the American republic, prompted by 'avarice and greed.' "[110] In 1786, he wrote to Edward Coles: "My sentiments on the subject of slavery of negroes have long since been in possession of the public, and time has only served to give them stronger root. The love of justice and the love of country plead equally the cause of these people, and it is a moral reproach to us that they should have pleaded it so long in vain, and should have produced not a single effort, nay I fear not much serious willingness to relieve them and ourselves from our present condition of moral and political reprobation."[111]

While president, Jefferson called for the abolition of the slave trade. In his annual message to Congress on December 2, 1806, he called attention to the impending expiration of the twenty-year Constitutional moratorium prohibiting congressional action against slave trading and urged Congress "to withdraw the citizens of the United States from all further participation in those violations of human rights which have been so long continued on the unoffending inhabitants of Africa, and which the morality, the reputation, and the best interests of our country, have long been eager to proscribe."[112]

More than a dozen years later, he wrote to J. P. Brissot DeWarville: "You know that nobody wishes more ardently to see an abolition, not only of the trade, but of the condition of slavery; and certainly nobody will be more willing to encounter every sacrifice for that object."[113] Yet the institution of slavery and the common belief in his own milieu that slaves were merely a form of property led Jefferson to despair that his generation would ever adopt his policy of gradual emancipation and colonization. His strong belief in the improvement of the human mind along generational lines, however, led him to hope that future Americans would elevate themselves above the narrow thinking of his own generation. In 1814, he wrote: "I had always hoped that the younger generation, receiving their early impressions after the flame of liberty had been kindled in every breast, and had become, as it were, the vital spirit of every American, that the generous temperament of youth, analogous to the motion of their blood and above the suggestions of avarice, would have sympathized with oppression wherever found, and proved the love of liberty beyond their own share in it." This hope produced in Jefferson tragic disappointment, and indeed, events produced the opposite results: divisions over slavery deepened and led a half century later to the bloody Civil War.

Two weeks before his death, he wrote his last sentiment on the subject that plagued him like no other: "Persuasion, perseverance, and patience are the best advocates on questions depending on the will of others. The revolution in public opinion which this cause [slavery] requires, is not expected in a day, or perhaps even an age; but time, which outlives all things, will outlive this evil also. My sentiments have been forty years before the public. . . . Although I shall not live to see them consummated, they will not die with me; for living or dying, they will ever be in my most fervent prayer."[114]

Jefferson readily understood the irony, if not also the hypocrisy, of a nation dedicated to human liberty that was also composed of states that practiced slavery. In response to inquiries made by the encyclopedist Jean Nicolas Demeunier, Jefferson wrote:

What a stupendous, what an incomprehensible machine is man! Who can endure toil, famine, stripes, imprisonment & death itself in vindication of his own liberty, and the next moment be deaf to all those motives whose power supported him thro' his trial, and inflict on his fellow men a bondage, one hour of which is fraught with more misery than ages of that which he rose in rebellion to oppose. But we must await with patience the workings of an overruling providence, & hope that that is preparing the deliverance of these, our suffering brethren. When the measure of their tears shall be full, when their

groans shall have involved heaven itself in darkness, doubtless
a god of justice will awaken to their distress, and by diffusing
light & liberality among their oppressors, or at length by his ex-
terminating thunder, manifest his attention to the things of
this world, and that they are not left to the guidance of a blind
fatality.[115]

Jefferson "believed black Americans should eventually enjoy the natural rights enumerated in the Declaration of Independence, but in Africa
or the Caribbean, not the United States."[116] Intellectually, Jefferson managed the plague of slavery with one hand and the structure of the republic
with the other. Emancipation of slaves would not lead to creation of the
elementary republics of the wards. Nor would creation of the ward republics cure the cancer of slavery. His hope that slavery would eventually
become unprofitable, and thus economically liberate the republic from its
burdens, was unfulfilled and further justified his most noted conclusion
on this inherent paradox of American democracy: "We have the wolf by
the ears; and we can neither hold him, nor safely let him go. Justice is
in one scale, and self-preservation in the other."[117]

The Mature Jefferson and the Radical Republic

Following his retirement from public life, a number of factors led Jefferson to revisit and sharpen his theory of republicanism and his emphasis
on the wards. Most obviously, as a private gentleman farmer at Monticello, he now had the luxury of time—largely unavailable in public life—
to place political issues in more historical, theoretical, and philosophical
frameworks. With but few exceptions, his five diplomatic years in Paris,
his four years as secretary of State, his following four years as Adams's
vice president, his intense involvement in the controversies leading up to
the "revolution of 1800," and his eight years as president—all left little
time for reflection or theorizing.

When not trying to satisfy his substantial personal indebtedness, he
used this period in retirement from public duties to revisit the favorite
classical writers: "I wish at length to indulge myself in more favorite
readings, in Tacitus and Horace and the writers of that philosophy which

is the old man's consolation and preparation for what is to come." He claimed now to know more of "the heroes of Troy, of the wars of Lacedaemon and Athens, of Pompey and Caesar, and of Augustus" than of the affairs of the day.[118] To this personal period of reflection was added the frequent visitation of domestic and foreign thinkers of the day: "Monticello was a country philosophical hall."

Additionally, Jefferson now had the opportunity to further his intellectual pursuits by promoting other authors. During 1810 and 1811, in the guise of an unnamed Frenchman, he undertook the translation and publication of Destutt de Tracy's *Commentary and Review of Montesquieu's Spirit of the Laws*. De Tracy's work could not be published in France due to its criticism of prevailing conventional political wisdom concerning Montesquieu, and he sought, with Jefferson's help, to release the work in English in America and then have it republished in his native land. Jefferson found de Tracy's critique of Montesquieu much needed and "the most valuable political work of the present age." The experience caused Jefferson to reevaluate republican theory and to radicalize his own republicanism.

A third factor in Jefferson's renewed republicanism was the rise of nationalism and new public interest in the heroic revolutionary era in the aftermath of the invasion by Great Britain during the War of 1812. By now Jefferson and Adams had become patriarchs of the American Revolution, and they were sought out to restate the fervor and idealism of the founding era to the generation just coming of age, which had no direct experience of that uniting time now thirty-six years before. Jefferson's contribution to this nationalistic revival came less in the form of polemics and more in the form of profiles and vignettes of the great leaders, such as Washington, Franklin, and others now passed. The exercise revived in him the idealism and the motivating theories, including that of classic republicanism, that had stimulated him toward a leading role in the Revolution.

Fourth, perhaps more than any other factor, the recovery of the Adams-Jefferson friendship and, with the help of intermediaries, the restoration of a flourishing correspondence, much of it ideological in nature, caused Jefferson to recapture the ideas that had so energized his political theories during the founding era. Adams inaugurated the exchange with the classic admonition, "You and I ought not to die, before we have explained ourselves to each other." Among other familiar topics, one of the most serious was their divergence in views over the nature of aristocracy. Adams, as before, thought it an inevitable circumstance of every polity and recommended a separate deliberative body for the social aristocracy. Jefferson thought the true aristocracy to be a natural one, an aristocracy of merit, enlightenment, and talent, distinguishable by the people themselves. Yet again, he recommended that the people, through the exercise of the democratic franchise, separate "the [natural] aristoi from the [hereditary] pseudo-aristoi, the wheat from the chaff. In general they will elect the really good and wise." After years of practical politics, exchanges such as these sharpened Jefferson's thinking about his original republicanism and, in the process, radicalized it further.

A fifth influence on Jefferson's revitalized republicanism resulted from his revisitation of his religious and moral principles. Once in retirement, Jefferson undertook a review of his opinions of Christianity in fulfillment of a commitment made to his friend Benjamin Rush on the eve of Jefferson's presidency. Some fourteen years later, Jefferson honored the commitment by surveying his religious philosophy at considerable extent for Rush, who believed that Christianity laid the groundwork for republicanism. His restatement went to such lengths that he eventually excerpted the teachings of Jesus into a syllabus, which came to be known as the "Jefferson Bible." According to Peterson, "He did not even accept Jesus on his own terms, for Jesus was a spiritualist by the grace of God and he a materialist by the grace of science. But he had brought the morals of Jesus, above all the love of man, within the perimeters of the older faith of the Enlightenment. The simple precepts of Jesus infused a universal ethic founded on the natural rights of man."[119] He who made us, Jefferson wrote, "has formed us as moral agents . . . that we may promote the happiness of those with whom he has placed us in society, by acting honestly towards all, benevolently to those who fall within our way, respecting sacredly their rights bodily and mental, and cherishing especially their freedom of conscience, as we value our own."[120] In his theology and religious beliefs, Jefferson claimed to be a sect to himself. More than perhaps any of his other mature writings, this exploration of moral and religious foundational beliefs reveals Jefferson's social philosophy and its relation to the scale of government. Individual citizens cannot delegate their moral conscience or social commitments to others. Elected representatives may, or may not, reflect the deeply held beliefs of the represented about man's responsibility to man. Benevolence does not always translate upward into the heady realm of national politics. Only in the forum of the township and the polity of the ward can every citizen do unto every other citizen, in social and political terms, as he would have done unto himself. What today is called social justice or welfare was very much part of the scope of responsibility of the pure republic for Jefferson.

Sixth, Jefferson's retirement gave him time for his favorite cause, that of public education. As before, this cause was intimately intertwined with his theory of the republic. In his later years he spent more time creating and establishing the University of Virginia than in any other pursuit. This effort would continue until his death. But more broadly he addressed his lifelong concern for education generally, believing as before that it was the rock upon which democracy in America had to be founded. To be accessible to all, schools necessarily had to be local. But, being local, they had to be the responsibility of local citizens concerned with their maintenance and functioning. The best means of assuring citizen participation in the educational function of a republican society was to provide for a true republic in which the educational functions, among others, could be exercised by responsible local citizens: "The wards, or hundreds, while associated with primary education, would be miniature republics, drawing every citizen immediately into the administration of local affairs and voicing the will of the people through all the expanding circles—county, state, and federal—of Jefferson's concentric commonwealth."[121] Both proposals—wards and general education—traced back to Jefferson's *Bill for the More General Diffusion of Knowledge* in Virginia in 1778: "The crucial defeat of his young years, he hoped it might ripen into the triumph of his old age." Education, the heart of republicanism, was for Jefferson a "holy cause."[122]

These factors—time and distance for reflection and revisitation of the political classics, revitalized public interest in the ideals of the founding revolutionary era, translation and publication of de Tracy's critique of Montesquieu's republicanism, restored communications with John Adams and the calmer reiteration of their contending political philosophies, elaboration of his moral, ethical, and religious principles, and circling back to the cause of public education as the prime guarantor of the true republic—all influenced Jefferson in refining the nature of his republican philosophy and in sinking its roots in the township republic.

Jefferson singled out the New England township as one model for the scale of the local republic. Unlike Tocqueville, however, Jefferson's fascination with the township may have been tempered by strong Federalist sentiment in New England generally and Massachusetts particularly and by the fact that his focus on republican scale came at least a quarter century after his almost 1,000-mile journey through New England in 1791. Yet, he would have been at least generally knowledgeable of the strength of conviction concerning local self-government in that region. "There the mistrust of any central authority, legislative or magisterial, was most pervasive. New Englanders, particularly in the western areas, in fact considered their towns, and not the [representative] legislature, as the real loci of authority and objects of concern." One frightened pamphleteer in 1778 described the people of the region as "now erecting little democracies."[123] Indeed, one scholar "finds the explanation for Americans' embrace of republicanism partly in their practice of self-government on the small scale," which he compares with the practices of ancient Greece: "What predisposed so many colonists to choose some form of republicanism as the basis for their new country? Though surely not the whole answer, perhaps part of it lies in the fact that in 1776 the overwhelming majority of Americans still lived in the kind of small-scaled community whose life and values we have seen were essentially stable since the Greeks."[124] Prerevolutionary Connecticut towns had reached such a semiautonomous stage of development that they were referred to as "independent republics."[125]

Though Jefferson found resonance for the ideal of the American local republic in the autonomy of the early New England township, that region's resistance to his republican movement would have diminished somewhat his enthusiasm for making that region's history of local government the predominant model for the ward republic he had in mind.

The Role of the Ward Republic in
the Life of the Citizen

In a letter to Samuel Kercheval in 1816, Jefferson outlined what he thought should be the scope of the local republic's authority. He held forth at some length on the roles of the various levels of government, criticizing the performance of national and State governments against the standards of fundamental republican principles, arguing for strict adherence to representation in proportion to population ("a government is republican in proportion as every member composing it has his equal voice in the directions of its concerns"), and coming finally to assess the role of the counties, the subdivisions of the States:

> Divide the counties into wards of such size as that every citizen can attend, when called on, and act in person. Ascribe to them the government of their wards in all things relating to themselves exclusively. A justice, chosen by themselves, in each, a constable, a military [militia] company, a patrol, a school, the care of their own poor, their own portion of the public roads, the choice of one or more jurors to serve in some court, and the delivery, within their own wards, of their own votes for all elective officers of higher sphere, will relieve the county administration of nearly all its business, will have it better done, and by making every citizen an acting member of the government, and in the offices nearest and most interesting to him, will attach him by his strongest feelings to the independence of his country, and its republican constitution.[126]

The range of government functions and services is wide: an elected "justice" or judge; a constable or officer of the peace; a military or citizen militia company; a "patrol" or constable; a school; a welfare system for the care of the local poor; maintenance of local roads within the jurisdiction of the ward; jurors to judge the facts as required in judicial proceedings; and a process for the conduct of elections for higher office. The net effect of the proper conduct of these functions is to relieve the next higher level of government, the county, of virtually all of its duties, to carry out these functions in a more competent manner, and, more important, to make every citizen an officeholder, thereby instilling a republican sense of duty and responsibility and providing an immediate sense of ownership of the government not presently available in societies where power is concentrated in remote capitals.

Long before the Kercheval letter, just over a year after leaving the presidency, Jefferson expressed many of the same opinions, in particular linking education to the flourishing of the local republic:

I have indeed two great measures at heart, without which no republic can maintain itself in strength. 1. That of general education, to enable every man to judge for himself what will secure or endanger his freedom. 2. To divide every county into hundreds, of such size that all the children of each will be within reach of a central school in it. But this division looks to many other fundamental provisions. Every hundred, besides a school, should have a justice of the peace, a constable and a captain of militia. These officers, or some others within the hundred, should be a corporation to manage all its concerns, to take care of its roads, its poor, and its police by patrols &c. (As the select men of the Eastern townships).[127]

He added provisions, which will also occur in later formulations, for selection of jurors for jury trials and for the conduct of elections for higher office: "These little republics would be the main strength of the great one. We owe to them the vigor given our revolution in its commencement in the Eastern States." He may here have been referring to the minutemen of revolutionary legend and folklore, for he continued to describe mobilization procedures: "General orders are given out from a centre to the foreman of every hundred, as to the sergeants of an army, and the whole nation is thrown into energetic action, in the same direction in one instant and as one man, and becomes absolutely irresistible."[128]

A few years later, in the context of a long dissertation sent to John Adams on the perfidies of wealth and aristocracy, Jefferson refers to his successful efforts in Virginia to repeal the laws of primogeniture and entail and then once again relates his theories on public education to his ideal of "little republics":

This [bill in the legislature] proposed to divide every county into wards of five or six miles square, like your townships; . . . My proposition had, for a further object, to impart to these wards those portions of self-government for which they are best qualified, by confiding to them the care of the poor, their roads, police, elections, the nomination of jurors, administration of justice in small cases, elementary exercises of militia; in short, to have made them little republics, with a warden at the head of each, for all those concerns which, being under their eye, they would better manage than the larger republics of the county or State.[129]

Thus, in each of these formulations, Jefferson fostered education, care of the poor, and organization of the local defense as among the principal functions of the local republics.

For purposes of understanding more clearly Jefferson's intentions as to the practical operation of the ward republics, more detailed analysis will be made of these three specific, local governmental functions: education (the local school), welfare (care of the poor), and local security (the militia).

Ward Republics and Public Schools

In his Bill for the More General Diffusion of Knowledge in Virginia in 1778, Jefferson proposed "to establish in each ward a free school for reading, writing, and common arithmetic; to provide for the annual selection of the best subjects [students] from these schools, who might receive, at the public expense, a higher degree of education at a district school; and from these district schools to select a certain number of the most promising subjects, to be completed at a University, where all the useful sciences should be taught. Worth and genius would thus have been sought out from every condition of life, and completely prepared by education for defeating the competition of wealth and birth for public trusts."[130]

Education for Jefferson was both the most important function of democratic government and its means of survival. Democratic citizens required education to enable them to participate in government, and educated citizens needed to participate in government to preserve and promote democracy. "If a nation expects to be ignorant and free, in a state of civilization," he said in one of his most famous pronouncements, "it expects what never was and what never will be."[131] Uneducated citizens, unequipped to understand and deal with the issues of the day, could not adequately manage self-government in the local republic and thus might provide proof to democracy's critics, the aristocratic elite, who believed the great mass of people incapable of self-government. "Every government degenerates when trusted to the rulers," Jefferson said. "The people themselves therefore are its only safe depositories. And to render even them safe, their minds must be improved."[132]

The notion of tying popular education to the proper functioning and flourishing of the republic has roots in Enlightenment thought. In *The Commonwealth of Oceana*, James Harrington held: "The formation of a citizen in the womb of the common-wealth is his education. . . . That which is proposed for the erecting and endowing of schools throughout the tribes capable of all the children of the same, and able to give unto the poor the education of theirs *gratis*, is only [a] matter of direction in the case of very great charity, as easing the needy of the charge of the children from the ninth to the fifteenth year of their age."[133] In his *Commonplace Book*, Jefferson took note of Montesquieu's view that civic virtue was the "energetic principle" of a democratic republic and that every government should make this energetic principle "the object of the education of its youth." He was referring to this specific passage in *The Spirit of the Laws*:

> It is in a republican government that the whole power of education is required. The fear of despotic governments naturally arises of itself amidst threats and punishments; the honor of monarchies is favored by the passions, and favors them in its turn; but virtue is a self-renunciation, which is ever arduous and painful. This virtue may be defined as the love of the laws and of our country. As such love requires a constant preference of public to private interest, it is the source of all private virtues; for they are nothing more than this very preference itself. This love is peculiar to democracies. In these alone the government is entrusted to private citizens. Now, a government is like everything else: to preserve it we must love it.[134]

The genuinely *public* nature of Jefferson's education system and thus its democratic character is important to note. He had in mind that all (free) children and young people would receive three years of tuition-free education and education at private expense for such unspecified further period of time as their parents might choose. In his Bill for the More General Diffusion of Knowledge for the state of Virginia, local education is specifically proposed for "free children, male and female." But in his more general description of education in the context of the ward republic there is no restriction of education to "free" children, and there is no three-year limitation on free tuition. In the broader context of the ward republic, education was central to both republican theory and democratic practice. It was the means by which citizens prepared themselves for self-government and through which citizens and leaders alike learned civic virtue and the qualities of citizenship. The ward-based education system was inseparable from republican government, and thus it was not accidental that the boundaries of the school district were also the boundaries of the ward republic. "My partiality for that division [wards] is not founded in views of education solely," Jefferson wrote, "but infinitely more as the means of a better administration of our government, and the eternal preservation of its republican principles."[135]

Jefferson and other Antifederalist republicans were seeking to create a political system based upon merit, a system open to the elevation of talent and a natural aristocracy and closed to a traditional aristocracy of inherited wealth, power, and privilege. This accounts in large part both for Jefferson's persistent opposition to primogeniture and entail laws, which guarantee the descent of estates intact, and for his insistence on a broadly based public education system as the political greenhouse for talent and merit. "It was widely believed that equality of opportunity would necessarily result in a rough equality of station," according to Gordon Wood, "that as long as the social channels of ascent and descent were kept open it would be impossible for any artificial aristocrats or overgrown rich men to maintain themselves for long. . . . And projected public educational systems would open up the advantages of learning and advancement for all."[136]

For most of Jefferson's notions on education, his native State of Virginia was the laboratory. He studied educational institutions in other countries, interviewed those experts in educational theories and methods whom he could find, paid particular attention, as an Enlightenment thinker, to the exposure of students to the sciences, and delivered recommendations to the trustees of the University of Virginia and other State officials. His hierarchy of educational institutions was based upon the elementary schools (the ward schools) for both "the laboring and the learned." The former would receive "the first grade of education" to prepare them for their pursuits and duties, with the latter receiving "a foundation for further requirements." Following elementary schooling the "laboring" students would proceed to general schools teaching agricultural studies or providing apprenticeships in useful arts and crafts, and the "learned" students, "destined to the pursuits of science," would proceed to either a general college or a professional school. These students could prepare for one of the "learned professions" or for productive lives in the private or public sectors by receiving instruction in all "the higher branches of science." These were to be arranged into three departments: language, mathematics, and philosophy. Language includes, in Jefferson's scheme, languages and history (ancient and modern), grammar, belles lettres, rhetoric, and oratory; mathematics includes pure mathematics, "physico-mathematics," physics, chemistry, natural history, mineralogy, botany, zoology, anatomy, and the theory of medicine; and philosophy includes ideology, ethics, "the law of nature and nations," government, and political economy. Jefferson proceeded to break each of these subjects into further subcategories.[137] At the apex of the educational hierarchy stood the professional schools encompassing theology, law, medicine (including surgery and pharmacy), architecture, the military, "technical philosophy," rural economy, and fine arts.

This elaborate construction had equally elaborate objectives. For the primary schools, their purpose was to provide a citizen with the information necessary to carry out her own private pursuits, to make necessary mathematical calculations, to write and speak clearly, to become sufficiently literate to improve "morals and faculties," and, perhaps most important for citizens of a republic, to "understand his duties to his neighbors and country," to know his rights, "to exercise with order and justice those he retains; to choose with discretion the fiduciary of those he delegates; and to notice their conduct with diligence, with candor, and judgment." For Jefferson, the whole purpose of basic public education was "to instruct the mass of our citizens in these, their rights, interests, and duties, as men and citizens," and the purpose of higher education was to form the statesmen, legislators, and judges necessary to manage public affairs and to understand the principles and structure of laws and government, which would help banish "all arbitrary and unnecessary restraint on individual action" and "leave us free to do whatever does not violate the equal rights of another."[138]

Education, for Jefferson, performs a socializing as well as a purely instructive function. It generates habits of "order and love of virtue," it alters human nature, engrafting "a new man on the native stock," it advances the knowledge and well-being of humanity, it helps harness the elements of nature to the advancement of life's comforts, and it dispels the supposition that each generation is locked into blind veneration of previous ones, treading "with awful reverence in the footsteps of our fathers," a doctrine which is "the genuine fruit of the alliance between Church and State." But, for Jefferson, the overwhelming advantage and purpose of broad-based education is to raise up "able counsellors" to administer all of the affairs of government in all of its departments "and to bear their proper share in the councils of our national government," since "nothing more than education [will] advanc[e] the prosperity, the power, and the happiness of a nation."[139]

Jefferson's faith in democratic republicanism was based upon the people having sufficient information to make intelligent judgments concerning the public matters affecting their lives. He wrote from Paris: "Wherever the people are well informed they can be trusted with their own government," and "whenever things get so far wrong as to attract their notice, they may be relied on to set them to rights."[140] Education was also to supply the judgment necessary to make profitable use of any information gained: "If we think [the people] not enlightened enough to exercise their control with a wholesome discretion, the remedy is not to take it from them, but to inform their discretion by education."[141] Jefferson certainly saw the economic advantage of better-educated citizens but, unlike Hamilton, economic productivity was not education's primary role: "Where Jefferson looks forward to educating a new generation of children so that they can take their place as citizens, Hamilton cannot wait to enroll them into the labor force 'at a very tender age.' "[142]

Jefferson readily stated and believed the truism that knowledge is power, that education is the most democratic form of empowerment. In the context of criticizing the slowness of his own State of Virginia to get on with educational advancement, especially in contrast to more progressive States, such as Massachusetts, he argued: "All the States but our own are sensible that knowledge is power. The Missouri question [regarding the terms for admission of Missouri to the union] is for power. The efforts now generally making through the States to advance their science, is for power; and [mean]while we are sinking into the barbarism of our Indian Aborigines, and expect, like them, to oppose by ignorance the overwhelming mass of light and science by which we shall be surrounded. It is a comfort that I am not to live to see this."[143]

The ultimate empowerment that flowed from education was that exercised in popular, democratic, local community government, in the ward republic. "The anxiety Jefferson manifested in his educational projects to ensure the spread of knowledge to every small, however remote, locale in America," writes Adrienne Koch, "is elevated into a political principle of the first magnitude in the concept of wards."[144] Education is also central to Jefferson's theory of rights. For of what use are the right of free speech if a citizen has nothing to say, or the right of assembly if a citizen has nothing to share, or the right to a free press if a citizen cannot read or form judgments? Unlike his Federalist opponents, for whom information, knowledge, judgment, and discretion were within the province of an oligarchic elite of wealth, power, and privilege, Jefferson saw education as the liberating force in a democracy, as indeed the only means by which a true democracy could be achieved. By implication, education was a right, a right meant to be adapted to individual capacity but necessary for economic independence and therefore required for participation in self-government. "Jefferson's theory [of rights] implies the right to be free from inadequate education, degrading poverty, and bureaucratic fiat."[145]

The Militia, Community Security, and the Ward Republic

Few issues divided Americans of the Constitutional era more than that of a militia versus a standing army. This is not surprising given that this issue, raised in earliest republican Greece, was central to the nature of the republic. Also unsurprisingly, the voice of Thomas Jefferson on this question became a prominent one. Since "the supreme power is ever possessed by those who have arms in their hands and are disciplined to the use of them," Jefferson wrote in his *Summary View of the Rights of British Americans* (1774), the danger to liberty lay in the supremacy "of a veteran army making the civil subordinate to the military instead of subjecting the military to the civil power." In a clear return to the English Country-versus-Court debate less than a century before, Jefferson here and after became a powerful defender of the Country position. As expansion of the standing army began for the early 1790s Indian campaign, Jefferson deplored it: "Every rag of an Indian depredation will . . . serve as a ground to raise troops with those who think a standing army and a public debt necessary for the happiness of the United States and we shall never be permitted to get rid of either." In his first inaugural address, Jefferson counted among the principles forming "the bright constellation which has gone before us, and guided our steps through an age of revolution and reformation . . . a well-disciplined militia, our best reliance in peace, and for the first moments of war, till regulars may relieve them."[146] Jefferson saw defense as exactly that, a military capable of repelling attack but not of attacking anyone else. Thus, he stands modern defense on its head—the militia will hold off the invaders until the regulars arrive.[147] Jefferson believed that a citizenry trained and organized in arms would enable the standing army to be abolished. A universal military-training obligation would be instituted, and the natural aristocracy of talent and virtue would serve as the officers of the armed citizens.[148]

Given the deep divisions this debate inspired in revolutionary America and the centrality of the militia issue to the nature of American and, more specifically, Jeffersonian republicanism, attention must be given to the historical and ideological origins of this debate.

It is significant that in every description or explication of his notion of ward republics, Jefferson included the citizen militia. Next to public education, the cause of the citizen defender seemed most important. There were, as ever, powerful roots in reason and experience for his views. The notion of the citizen-soldier has a tradition strongly based in colonial, prerevolutionary America and, in more ancient times, in the Greek city-state and later Roman republic. In revolutionary America, the minuteman—a young, mobile, citizen-guerrilla—took on heroic qualities that eventually assumed mythic proportions. Having fought in every American war, as an individual he was never an instrument of the state but rather was the guarantor of his own freedom in the manner envisioned by Jefferson.

The early Americans resisted central authority in military matters as well as in other aspects of public life. Strongly motivated by radical Whig ideology, which depicted standing armies as instruments of tyranny, they saw the militia as the proper recourse for republican citizens seeking to defend their political liberties, their property, and ultimately their freedom.[149] Provincial soldiers, whether volunteer or conscript, were citizens first and soldiers second.[150]

Resentment by provincial soldiers toward central authority, whether represented by colonial governments or the British army, contributed to the highly local character of prerevolutionary society. In military affairs, soldiers identified closely with local units and officers and insisted on explicit contractual recognition of their personal rights. Rather than endorsing the view of a mythological, Turnerian, frontier citizen-soldiery, transformed by contact with Native Americans and the New World's forests, modern historians examining prerevolutionary America have found a complex military system with institutional similarities to the English militia, which itself was closely tied to town and country life. In this system, the militia fulfilled social and political functions as well as military needs. By 1700, the militia had become an established colonial institution. Virtually all colonies required some type of universal military training and service for eligible men. Militiamen were also required to arm and equip themselves,[151] thus, the controversial Second Amendment to the U.S. Constitution.

Although time, economic exigencies, and the Revolution itself eroded the purity of the militia ideal, the militia principle became well established in American society. On the eve of the Revolution, Americans carried with them more than a century and a half of military experience, which began with a universal military obligation eventually modified by economic necessity and political opposition. An inclusive militia system that imposed service on all classes in the colonies had given way to a system that preferred the use of "marginal men" whenever possible. But radical Whig republicanism reemerged as the Revolution approached and reasserted a universal military requirement for loyal citizens. Nevertheless, the legacy of colonial history stressed "the new-born states as the focal point of mobilization, a distrust of central authority and strong preference for local control, a deep distaste for military conscription, and a military informality resistant to strict discipline, stark separation of officers and men, and professionalism generally."[152]

From whence did ideas such as civic duty, citizen-soldiers, the militia principle, and local military control originally arise? Seventeenth- and eighteenth-century English militia traditions and radical Whig republicanism have already been suggested as early influences. But these traditions and principles had deeper roots in the ancient Greek *polis*, the city-state from which the Roman, Renaissance, Enlightenment, and modern republics spring.

In many Greek city-states, ownership of land was a prerequisite for full citizenship, and full citizenship involved frequent military service. Therefore, a close connection developed between agriculture and warfare, the farmer and the warrior. The fourth-century B.C. general and military historian Xenophon quotes Socrates as responding to a question concerning what arts or skills are most important: "Well, should we be ashamed to imitate the king of the Persians? For they say that he considers that the noblest and most necessary arts are those of farming and warfare and he practices both assiduously."

The Roman experience was similar to that of the Greeks, if less pronounced. The transformation of Rome from early republic to mature empire was accompanied by a parallel transformation of its army. As Rome evolved from the fourth century B.C. to the fourth century A.D., complex interrelationships developed among military service, land ownership, social mobility, and the civilian and military worlds. In its earliest republican years, Rome's military was small, family-based, and relatively unstratified. Early republican political, and especially military, leaders of the fifth and fourth centuries B.C. were characterized more by their resistance to public office than by their lust for it. Lucius Quinctius Cincinnatus, having been elected consul of Rome, had to be brought, shedding tears, from behind his plow on "his little farm" to govern the republic. By the time of the late republic, and on the eve of empire, the rustic republican military originally led by citizen-soldiers such as Cincinnatus had been transformed into a much larger, more cohesive, and more professional army of conquest.[153] Paralleling the evolution from citizen to professional army was, significantly, the political evolution that accompanied it. In the early to middle Roman republic, the same procedures were used to assemble the people to vote on war as were used to marshal the army. The Roman people assembled (the *comitia centuriata*) in the Campus Martius to vote on issues of war and peace. If the assembly voted for war, the same venue was then used to organize the military forces. Thus, the ideological link between membership in the citizen body and membership in the militia forces became clear and would be used two millennia later by Jefferson in his theory of the ward republic. Octavian, as Augustus, replaced the old citizen militia with a new professional army of legions, funding the transition with new tax levies. "In the fifth century A.D. the Roman army disappears from view in the West" and is replaced totally by mercenaries. "The Roman state soon follows."[154]

In the Roman republic the sturdiest link of citizen to public affairs was forged by service in its defense. Once that link was weakened, then broken, citizens had little concern for or interest in affairs on the borders of the empire. This early division between imperial power and *res publica* prefigured the English Court-versus-Country and American Federalist-versus-Antifederalist debates. Brief note must be made, however, of that important transition figure, the Florentine Machiavelli, for his role in framing this debate. In the service of the republican ideal, no more ardent disciple of the militia principle than Machiavelli exists. In his repeated and protracted recourse to this issue, Machiavelli could not divorce the role of citizen from the responsibility for defense of the republic. Service in the militia became, for him, the essence of civic virtue. The "well-ordered republic" is his description of a polis governed by a just prince—combining the fierceness of the lion to frighten away the wolves with the shrewdness of the fox in avoiding the snares—and citizens who place the common good at least equal to, if not before, self-interest. A well-ordered republic is both well-trained and well-armed, and therefore its character is unchangeable and not dependent on the whims of Fortune. The quality of being well-ordered is not simply one of organization; it connotes a republican society that neither despairs in adversity nor becomes arrogant in victory. The well-ordered republic is composed of those willing to dedicate their lives, if necessary, in combat to its preservation.

In analyzing Machiavelli's *Art of War* (*Arte della guerra*), one scholar claims that his debt to the militia tradition in Florentine theory, plus his experience in actually organizing a militia unit, led him to connect citizenship and military virtue to the point where citizenship actually becomes the product of military service. Resorting to the early Roman republican ideal, Machiavelli believed that the citizen should be trained by civic religion and military discipline to devote himself to the *patria* (the nation) and also trained to carry this spirit over into civic affairs. Machiavelli combines his notion of virtue (*virtù*) with Aristotle's ideal of citizen attentiveness to the common good: "The mercenary soldier is a mere instrument in another man's hand; but the citizen-warrior is more than an instrument in the public hand, since his *virtù* is his own and he fights out of knowledge of what he fights for."[155] The citizen-soldier should be what he was in republican Rome where, according to Machiavelli, "the captain, content with triumph, returned to private life with desire; and those who were soldiers put [their] arms down with greater desire than they had picked them up, and each one returned to his trade around which he had arranged [his] life." Here, he clearly had republican leaders such as Cincinnatus in mind.

Unable to separate citizenship from service in a civilian army or citizen militia, Machiavelli went further. He believed that citizens would fight well only if the city was kept in good order and had just laws, therefore to commit oneself to a citizen army was necessarily to commit oneself to good laws and a just city. Machiavelli, who hated and distrusted mercenaries, argued with considerable consistency that only a part-time citizen-soldier could be trusted to make full-scale war: "A citizen called to arms, with a home and an occupation of his own, will wish to end the war and go home, where a mercenary, glad rather than sorry if war drags on indefinitely, will make no attempt to win it." Machiavelli thought that the individual who devoted himself and his energy only to his own business, craft, or trade and not at all to public issues and affairs was less than a citizen and was a weak link in the social chain that bound the *polis* together. Participation in public affairs necessarily and centrally included defense of the city. But one who "makes war his art" (the *condottiere*) is not merely neglecting the good of the city, he is antisocial and makes the duties of citizenship a profession for which he is paid. In the preface to *The Art of War*, Machiavelli wrote: "And if, in every other institution of city-states and kingdoms, the greatest care is taken to keep men loyal, peaceable, and full of the fear of God, in the military this care should really be doubled. For in what man can the commonwealth seek greater loyalty than who has promised to die for her? In whom should there be more love of peace than in him who can only be harmed by war? In what man should there be more fear of God than in him who, submitting himself to countless dangers, has greatest need of Him?" Machiavelli is important on the subject of citizen-soldiery not simply because he has been near the center of the political debate in the West for five hundred years, but because he helped revive the ideal of citizen participation in governance. This ideal held citizenship to contain duties and responsibilities, the most vital of which was the defense of the *patria*. Professional armies remove this duty, thus weakening society and making it more subject to both tyranny and conquest. In *The Prince*, Machiavelli wrote: "The arms of another man [mercenary] either slide off your back, weigh you down, or tie you up." A citizen willing to surrender his most important responsibility to a mercenary was likely also to surrender his liberty and freedom. That this question is neither idle nor superfluous, but indeed is central to the very meaning of republican government, is shown by the fact that it has recurred in virtually every debate over the nature of republics—including the American Constitutional debate—that has taken place down to the present day.

For American Whigs, the question of citizen-versus-professional soldier had already been framed by English political debate a century before. The English Civil War of 1642 had provoked a great dispute between the House of Commons and Charles I over, among other things, control of the county militia, which the Commons was claiming. Led by Cromwell, the antiroyalist leaders created the New Model Army, which featured, for the first time, the opportunity for commoners to earn commissions through battlefield valor and the institutionalization of discipline and pay. The New Model Army was the first army that belonged to the Commons and thus to the people. Perversely, however, at the same time, "a military . . . dependency was engrafted upon the commons." For an army, once created, searches incessantly for a branch of government to maintain it. "The professional officer is the cause as well as the effect of this corruption, and his capacity to act in this baneful way arises from the fact that his decision to become a professional has rendered him the lifelong dependent of the state that can employ him."[156] Englishmen saw military force under Cromwell interfere at least six times—usually in the form of the abolition of one Parliament or another—in the processes of civil government. Eventually, the New Model Army's excesses—for example, its slaughter of the Irish garrisons at Drogheda and at Wexford—planted the seeds of a haunting fear of standing armies as a political force and became one of the strongest arguments for the militia system. By the late seventeenth century, the militia came to be seen in England as a means to avoid the corruption of position and centralized power and the instrument for the restoration of freedom, independence, and virtue.

Largely in response to the corruption of the Cromwell protectorate, only a few years later James Harrington wrote *The Commonwealth of Oceana*, the utopian political tract that, among other things, revived Machiavellian republicanism. Harrington resurrected the interrelationship between citizenship and public service in a militia but with a new dimension. It was crucial, said Harrington, that the citizen-soldier also be a landowner, not merely a tenant or a vassal: "[Land ownership] determined whether a man's sword was his lord's or his own and the commonwealth's; and the function of free proprietorship became the liberation of arms, and consequently of the personality, for free public action and civic virtue."[157] If a citizen would fight harder for a just commonwealth than would a mercenary, that citizen would fight harder still if he had a material stake—his own land—in the outcome. The strength of feeling on this issue is shown by Shaftesburean political writers, after Harrington, who regularly coupled a standing army with corruption and privilege: "A standing Parliament and a standing Army are like those Twins that have their lower parts united, and are divided only above the Navel; they were born together and cannot long outlive each other. The same might be said concerning the only Ancient and true Strength of the Nation, the Legal Militia, and a Standing Army. The Militia must, and can never be otherwise than for English Liberty, because else it does destroy itself; but a standing Force can be for nothing but Prerogative."[158]

In England in the later decades of the seventeenth century, the citizen militia became a potent symbol of independent freeholders, republican government, anticorruption, and civic virtue. Following the Revolution of 1688, and the emergence of Britannia as a commercial, military, and imperial power, the division between Court and Country became pronounced, a division presaging the American Constitutional debate a century later. In simplified terms, the Court represented centralized power, the great barons, landed nobility, courtiers and rentiers, the extension of credit for imperial enterprise, and a permanent standing army. The Country, in equally general terms, stood for freeholding citizens; local authority; resistance to credit, materialism, and luxury; and a citizen militia. In the mind of the Country, the Court represented corruption, and the Country represented civic virtue.

Largely from this dispute sprang basic principles such as "separation of powers," later to play such a crucial role in the formation of the American republic. The central point of the issue in seventeenth-century England was that the party of the Court represented patronage, the promise of office, position, and pensions for many members of Parliament, thus making them courtiers, suborning them to the executive, or the Crown, and corrupting their independent judgment. The Country party, composed largely of independent freeholders, sought to counter this pattern of corruption by proscribing officeholders of the Crown (so-called place-men) from serving also in the Commons and by demanding short parlia-ments, thus requiring members to remain dependent on their constitu-encies rather than on the Court. For the Country party, corruption and centralized power, if backed by a standing army, was the greatest danger to liberty and independence.

The Country argument was well stated at the turn of the eighteenth century by the Scot Andrew Fletcher (described as "a patriot ideologue of high intellectual attainments who would have made an admirable contem-porary of Patrick Henry and Richard H. Lee"). Anticipating Jefferson, Fletcher was torn between the ideal of an agrarian world of self-sufficient farming warriors and the need for commercial development in impover-ished Scotland. He struggled with, but failed to create, a civic morality for market men but prescribed instead military training for all freeholders as a means of education in civic virtue. Fletcher then, after Harrington, added yet another dimension to the mosaic of the predemocratic republic: the citizen-soldier–property owner who is educated in civic virtue. This combination of qualities came to describe the American yeoman, who is often associated with, but not claimed by, Jefferson.

As the Court-versus-Country struggle continued into eighteenth-century England, other military movements were at work in Europe. Fred-erick the Great of Prussia, often called the father of the modern army, "pushed warfare in the prevailing code to the limits of acceptable ruth-lessness." He was ruthless and rational in his approach to warmaking, in keeping with the spirit of the Age of Reason. Because of his profession-alization of the Prussian military and the degree to which he made it an instrument of state power—anticipating both Bonaparte and Clausewitz—his Prussian armies established a standard that other nations strove to match well into the twentieth century.

By the early eighteenth century in England, Fletcher, like Harrington before and Jefferson after, was being made to seem bucolic at best and irrelevant at worst by the rise of the imperial-commercial-colonial state in the form of Great Britain. For, if a nation has empire and commercial domination on its mind, it will first create elaborate, centralized systems of credit, finance, and taxation to provide for the needs of capital and entrepreneurship, and it will form a professional standing army to protect those economic interests and its empire (precisely Hamilton's argument, which would appear later in the American founding debates). It will then require a system of taxation even more, because a standing army is an expensive enterprise. The subject of taxation and the British army and navy that it supported leads to the doorstep of the American Revolution.

One of the many ironies of that Revolution was that the militia—a British import from earliest colonial times—was part of the force that defeated the British. This militia heritage, together with the sense of military insecurity and the inability of the economically poor colonies to maintain an expensive professional army, combined to transplant the Elizabethan militia into the North American wilderness. Throughout the revolutionary war, the Continental army was constantly augmented by colonial militia, thus establishing the "two army" tradition in America. The decentralized nature of the militia democratized and nationalized warfare: "Military authority no longer resided in a sovereign, but in the people and their chosen representatives."[159]

Having successfully prosecuted a war with England using a Continental army in part based upon and substantially supported by citizen militias, the founders of the republic and the drafters of the Constitution were forced to face a dilemma as ancient as the republican ideal itself: Shall we have a standing army or a citizen militia and, if a standing army, what is its mission? As Pocock states:

> The Second Amendment to the Constitution, apparently drafted
> to reassure men's minds against the fact that the federal gov-
> ernment would maintain something in the nature of a profes-
> sional army, affirms the relation between a popular militia and
> popular freedom in language descended from that of Machia-
> velli, which remains a potent ritual in the United States to this
> day. The new republic feared corruption by a professional
> army, even while—like England a century before—it saw no al-
> ternative to establishing one; and the implications of the rheto-
> ric employed in this context were to be fully worked out in the
> debates and journalism of the first great conflict between
> American parties.[160]

Among those whose views affected preconstitutional thinking in colonial America was the legal scholar William Blackstone, who wrote: "In free states . . . no man should take up arms but with a view to defend his country and its laws; he puts not off the citizen when he enters the camp; but it is because he is a citizen, and would wish to continue so, that he makes for a while a soldier."[161] George Washington proposed a three-tiered land force: a regular army, a ready reserve similar to the volunteer militia, and an improved common militia.[162] Not surprisingly, the leading Federalist supporter of a substantial, professional, standing army was Alexander Hamilton. His arguments, principally contained in *Federalist* numbers 24, 25, 26, and 28, were founded much more strongly on the need to protect America's anticipated far-flung international commercial interests than on the need to defend its borders from acquisitive European powers. "If we mean to be a commercial people," he wrote, "or even to be secure on our Atlantic side, we must endeavor, as soon as possible, to have a navy. To this purpose there must be dockyards and arsenals; and for the defense of these, fortifications, and probably garrisons." It was a short step from assuming far-flung interests in peaceful commerce to establishing a network of military bases and forces to defend them.

Hamilton, for the eventual majority opinion, placed great stress on the proposed Constitutional power of the Congress to constrain and regulate standing armies, especially in times of peace: "To the powers proposed to be conferred upon the federal government, in respect to the creation and direction of the national force, I have met with but one specific objection, which . . . is that, proper provision has not been made against the existence of standing armies in time of peace."[163] Hamilton's response to this objection was simple, assertive, and dismissive: "Restraints upon the discretion of the legislature in respect to military establishments would be improper to be imposed, and if imposed, from the necessities of society, would be unlikely to be observed."

The classic republican argument against standing armies had already been raised in State Constitutional debates. North Carolina and Pennsylvania included this interdiction in their constitutions: "As standing armies in time of peace are dangerous to liberty, they ought not to be kept." The bills of rights of at least four other States—New Hampshire, Delaware, Massachusetts, and Maryland—contained a clause to this effect: "Standing armies are dangerous to liberty, and ought not to be kept without the consent of the [State] legislature." The principle of legislative consent to a standing army derived historically from William of Orange's defeat of

James II in the English Revolution of 1688. In response to the dangerous authority represented by the thirty thousand troops kept under arms by James II, the resulting Declaration of Rights required that the consent of Parliament be given to raising or maintaining a standing army in peacetime.

The depth and breadth of the fear of standing armies throughout revolutionary America is a strong theme in the nation's military history. The fear of standing military forces—brought to America from England with the earliest settlers—looms large in the history of the militia. Behind it was the even greater fear of arbitrary, highly centralized government, which, with a force armed to compel obedience to it, became even more dangerous to liberty. Because of the dual State-federal control under which it functioned, the militia seemed to many Americans the best security against that which they feared.[164]

As reasonable and balanced as Federalists' arguments might seem today, Antifederalist passions were aroused more by Congress's power, under Article I, section 8, "to raise and support armies" than by any other federal power. Historian Bernard Bailyn claims that it is difficult to over-estimate the volume and fervor of the Antifederalists' denunciation of this provision. It revived for them both a general fear of military power and the specific danger of standing armies, "a peculiar and distinctive threat to liberty that had been formulated for all time, they believed, in England in the 1690s, and had been carried forward intact to the colonies."[165] None was more passionate in opposition to the permanent standing army of the Federalists than Patrick Henry. "A standing army we shall also have," he thundered sarcastically, "to execute the execrable commands of tyranny. . . . Some way or other we must be a great and mighty empire; we must have an army, and a navy, and a number of things."[166] "Brutus," the anonymous and collective voice of the Antifederalists, raised similar arguments from Roman and English history. In Rome, the writer argued:

> The liberties of the commonwealth was [sic] destroyed, and the
> constitution overturned, by an army led by Julius Caesar, who
> was appointed to the command by the Constitutional authority
> of the commonwealth. He changed it from a free republic . . .
> into that of the most absolute despotism. A standing army ef-
> fected this change, and a standing army supported it through a

succession of ages, which are marked in the annals of history, with the most horrid cruelties, bloodshed, and carnage . . . that ever punished or disgraced human nature. . . . The same army, that in Britain, vindicated the liberties of that people from the encroachments of despotism of a tyrant king, assisted Cromwell, their General, in wresting from the people, that liberty they had so clearly earned.[167]

The Antifederalists believed quite simply that a standing army, once established, would be a constant drain on tax revenues and an instrument of despotism in the hands of centralized power.[168]

More than a strictly military question, at issue were two different visions of the new America. One was of a commercial and political power whose strong central government could make treaties, collect taxes, form capital through a national bank, finance national "improvements" through government borrowing, and enforce its will through a standing army—in short, something that looked to Antifederalist republicans like an imperial, and therefore inevitably corrupt, state power. The other vision, based upon classical theory, radical Whig ideology, and republican idealism, was of a new nation of yeoman landowners controlling their own destinies and capable, as citizen-soldiers, of protecting their individual and collective rights and interests. The Federalists' hopes for commercial growth and international prestige were, to the Antifederalists, only the lust of ambitious men for a "splendid empire," which, according to the patterns of history, would burden the people with taxes, conscription, and military campaigns.[169]

According to military historian Russell Weigley, Jefferson believed that a citizenry trained and organized in arms would enable the standing army to be abolished. A universal military obligation should be practiced, and the natural aristocracy of talent and virtue should serve as the officers of the armed citizens.[170]

The cause of the standing army in peacetime was not strengthened by the widespread knowledge that its principal proponent was Alexander Hamilton, who managed personally to embody all of the Caesarean qualities so frightening, if not loathsome, to republican idealists. Hamilton's ambition to increase the republic's permanent military strength, and the widespread suspicion that he hoped to head that strength himself, confirmed his critics in their belief that rule by a strong executive, supported by the interests of concentrated wealth, would lead inevitably to rule by a standing army that would be both authoritarian and corrupt.[171] To curb Hamiltonian-Federalist ambition, the Antifederalists proposed their own amendment to the Constitution on July 27, 1788: "That the people have a right to keep and bear arms; that a well-regulated militia, composed of the body of the people trained to arms, is the proper, natural, and safe defense of a free state; that standing armies, in time of peace, are dangerous to liberty; and therefore ought to be avoided, as far as the circumstances and protection of the community will admit; and that, in all cases, the military should be under strict subordination to, and governed by, the civil power."[172] Only the first part of this proposal was to survive in the form of the controversial Second Amendment.

Not unexpectedly, it fell to James Madison to negotiate a resolution of the standing army–militia dispute. He did so by coming down on the Federalist side but without raising the personal animosity and suspicion that Hamilton did. In the context of a discussion in *The Federalist Papers* of the stability and autonomy of state governments under the shadow of what many considered to be an oppressive national government, Madison addressed the "visionary supposition" that the federal government would accumulate a military force either to repress the States or to undertake foreign expeditions. Assume, he wrote, using Jeffersonian mathematical logic, that the national government formed the largest army it could from the postrevolutionary population of approximately three million people. Standard calculations of the day held that the maximum permanent force any nation's population and resources could support was one that was one-hundredth of the entire population or one-twenty-fifth of all those (men) able to bear arms. This, he calculated, would yield a federal army no larger than twenty-five or thirty thousand men under arms. "The State governments with the people on their side," he argued, "would be able to repel the danger" for, against the federal forces "would be opposed a militia amounting to near half a million citizens with arms in their hands." Thus, Madison assumed full-strength local militias made up of one in six of all American citizens.[173]

Within a half century Alexis de Tocqueville arrived to assess what the Americans had wrought. He brought with him what might be called a pragmatic-republican prism through which he viewed life in the new union and the military role as part of it. "A large army amongst a democratic people will always be a great danger; the most effectual means of diminishing that danger would be to reduce the army, but this is a remedy which all nations are not able to apply," he wrote. But then he took note of America's strongest defense, geography: "Fortune, which has conferred so many peculiar benefits upon the inhabitants of the United States, has placed them in the middle of a wilderness, where they have, so to speak, no neighbors; a few thousand soldiers are sufficient for their wants; but this is peculiar to America, not democracy."[174] He might also have credited Fortune with making the United States, strategically, an island. Tocqueville showed more interest in the sociology of democratic armies, however, than in the merits of the republican arguments surrounding them. He observed that the equality of conditions characterizing democracies did not exempt them from the need for armies, and those armies "always exercise a powerful influence over their fate." He particularly noted the difference between "aristocratic armies" in which the officers exercise a conservative and therefore restraining influence because they alone "have retained a strict connection with civil society and never forego [sic] their purpose of resuming their place in it sooner or later," and "democratic armies" in which private soldiers "stand in this position, and from the same cause."[175] He believed strongly that recruits in democratic armies mirrored the qualities and values of the communities from which they came: "If that community is enlightened and energetic, the community itself will keep them within the bounds of order." Tocqueville saw a direct relation between civil and military principles: "Teach the citizens to be educated, orderly, firm, and free and the soldiers will be disciplined and obedient."[176] Thus, he believed, "The remedy for the vices of the army is not to be found in the army itself, but in the country."[177] Matters become more complicated for democracies, according to Tocqueville, when they move from structuring their forces to actual war fighting: "If democratic nations are naturally prone to peace from their interests and propensities, they are constantly drawn to war and revolutions by their armies." Tocqueville believed that war developed in otherwise peaceful men the propensity for violence and despotism: "All those who seek to destroy the liberties of a democratic nation ought to know that war is the shortest and surest means to accomplish it. This is the first axiom of the science." He is caught in the paradox of armed democracies. They require at least some military institutions—a standing army and the means to equip it—for their defense and security. If the soldiers for this force are drawn from a stable, well-ordered, and educated civil society, they will reflect these values. But the more professional and institutionalized these military forces become, the more inclined they are toward conflict, which educates the soldiers in the codes of despotism and violence and undermines the very democracies they are meant to secure. For this conundrum Tocqueville could find no resolution, except in this aphorism: "There are two things that a democratic people will find most difficult, to begin a war and to end it."

Jefferson saw the inevitable competition between the costs of financing the military and domestic needs, especially education of the people. In his sixth annual message to the Congress and the people in 1806, as president, he propounded a "national establishment for education," possibly to be funded with income from a new trust of federal lands, which would have the advantage of being "independent on war," that is, immune from the military's demands for resources. "Were armies to be raised whenever a speck of war is visible on the horizon," he wrote, "we never should be without them. Our resources would have been exhausted on dangers which have never happened, instead of reserved for what is really to take place." To protect limited resources necessary for education and the improvement of the lives of the people, he added: "A militia so organized that its effective portions can be called to any point in the Union, or volunteers instead of them to serve a sufficient time, are means which may always be ready yet never preying on our resources until actually called into use." On fiscal grounds alone, a citizen reserve force is much less costly than a professional standing force.[178] In his eighth and final annual message, he revisited the national defense question in light of possible resumed hostilities with the British over the trade embargo he had succeeded in enacting: "For a people who are free, and who mean to remain so, a well-organized and armed militia is their best security. It is, therefore, incumbent on us, at every meeting, to revise the conditions of the militia, and to ask ourselves if it is prepared to repel a powerful enemy at every point of our territories exposed to invasion."[179]

For Jefferson, the militia principle was at once a matter of frugality in the public expense, a denial of military forces to centralized authority, the most practical and effective means for the defense of national borders, a means of strengthening local republican resolve, a form of and opportunity for the exercise of civic virtue, and most of all consistent with the theory and practice of republicanism. By definition a militia company was locally manned and locally based. It provided resources for the national defense, but it also represented security for the ward republic.

For the twenty-five hundred or more years of republican history leading up to the founding of the United States, virtually any consideration of the nature of a republic involved, sooner or later, serious concern over the role of the military in civil society. More often than not this debate was central to the nature of the republic. The instinctive and informed belief of political thinkers over time, repeatedly confirmed by experiences that began with the Romans, was of a direct correlation between standing armies and imperial aspirations. Rarely did a nation at peace require a professional army except to further its ambitions for political power, commercial advantage, or both abroad. For the theorists of the republican ideal, standing armies inevitably became symbols of political corruption, commercial enterprise, centralized authority, concentrated wealth, power, influence, prerogative, and the Court over the Country.

Confronted, as they believed, by persistent British, French, and Spanish colonial ambitions in the New World, as well as by Native American hostilities, sometimes more imagined than real, on the frontier, moderate Federalists of the Madisonian persuasion prevailed in the Federalist-Antifederalist debate and convinced a majority of their colleagues to authorize a modest standing army, with the proviso that Congress could authorize expenditures for it no further than two years into the future. This spending limitation, together with overwhelming numbers of citizens armed and at large, were believed to be sufficient to counterbalance military ambition.

Along with many other perpetually perplexing paradoxes left unresolved in the Constitutional debate, the legal and political relationships between the standing federal army created by Article I, section 8, clause 12, of the Constitution and the State militia authorized in clause 16 of the same section were largely left for time and experience to work out. For more than two hundred years, this paradoxical relationship has had a rough and uneasy life, which has persisted into the twenty-first century. For the second half of the twentieth century, America was Franklin Roosevelt's "great arsenal of democracy." Before and during that period, the battle going on *inside* the arsenal often gave off as much heat, if not bloodshed, as the battles going on outside. New twenty-first-century realities (discussed more thoroughly in chapter 4) offer a resolution of this conflict.

A Fundamental Right to Labor the Earth: Social Justice in the Ward Republic

"More than any other figure in his generation Jefferson integrated a program of economic development and a policy for nation-building into a radical moral theory," according to Joyce Appleby. This, she claims, emanates from "a fairly coherent theory" of the kind of economic base necessary to support a democratic republic.[180] Central to this economic theory is property, more specifically real property, as widely distributed as possible. Economic deprivation and dependency resulted from the lack of land of sufficient dimensions to produce sufficient economic independence to enable political participation.

Impressed by the poverty he saw while traveling as American ambassador to France in late eighteenth-century Europe, Jefferson's lifelong beliefs about the direct relationship between property (particularly land) ownership and independence were only strengthened by the experience. "Jefferson's sobering contact with the landless poor in Europe made him all the more anxious to prevent the development of a similar class in America."[181] Property-less people inevitably were people dependent on the wealthy for employment or on the state for charity. Dependent people were not people capable of full political participation. During a trip through southern France and northern Italy in 1787, Jefferson noted "women and children carrying heavy burdens, and laboring with a hoe. This is an unequivocal indication of extreme poverty. Men, in a civilized country, never expose their wives and children to labor above their force and sex, as long as their own labor can protect them from it."[182] In a letter written from Fontainebleau two years earlier, Jefferson recalled an encounter with a poor woman while walking outside of town. Moved by the account of her plight, he gave her an amount triple her normal daily earnings, which reduced her to tears and Jefferson to this observation: "This little *attendrissement* . . . led me into a train of reflection on that unequal division of property which occasions the numberless instances of wretchedness which I had observed in this country and is to be observed all over Europe. The property of this country is absolutely concentrated in a very few hands." He then wrote one of his more important statements on property distribution: "I am conscious that an equal division of property is impracticable, but the consequences of this enormous inequality producing so much misery to the bulk of mankind, legislators cannot invent too many devices for subdividing property, only care to let their subdividings go hand in hand with the natural affections of the human mind." He then mentions specifically the descent of property to all children in a family, not merely the eldest son, the exemption of small portions of property from taxation, and graduated taxation as sizes of landholdings escalate. He then continues:

> Whenever there are in any country uncultivated lands and un-
> employed poor, it is clear that the laws of property have been
> so far extended as to violate natural rights. The earth is given
> as a common stock for man to labor and live on. If for the en-
> couragement of industry we allow it to be appropriated, we
> must take care that other employment be provided to those ex-
> cluded from the appropriation. If we do not, the fundamental
> right to labor the earth returns to the unemployed. It is too
> soon yet in our country to say that every man who cannot find
> employment, but who can find uncultivated land, shall be at
> liberty to cultivate it, paying a moderate rent. But it is not too
> soon to provide by every possible means that as few as possible
> shall be without a little portion of land. The small landholders
> are the most precious part of a state.[183]

Here Jefferson makes several startling, but related, propositions: laws permitting maldistribution of land (uncultivated land and the unemployed poor) violate natural rights; if land is provided to stimulate industry, "we" (society or the state) must provide employment to those not sharing in the appropriation; there is a "fundamental right to labor the earth"; that right supersedes the appropriation of land for industry; at some point, unemployed people ("men") may have the right to cultivate undeveloped land, paying reasonable rent; and finally, every effort should be made to provide some portion of land to as many people as possible. Thus, Jefferson's radical social policy was premised on a "fundamental right to labor the earth," which should be honored by every means possible through distribution of sufficient land to provide a stable living, whether through ownership or rent, as a means not only of reducing poverty but also as a major step toward social equity, fair distribution of wealth (or at least the means to wealth), and the creation of an independent citizenry capable of participation in the local republic.

Three years before his death, Jefferson wrote an extraordinary letter to Justice William Johnson, which described the fundamentally differing views of the political world in Constitutional-era America. One view, a Hobbesian view, which he describes as "European" or of "the old countries," held that men were brutal, disorderly, and unjust and that they therefore required restraint physically and morally by "authorities independent of their will." The "brute force of the people" had to be kept down by "hard labor, poverty, and ignorance." The authorities over them were monarchs, hereditary nobles, and priests, who treated the people as "bees," profiting from their labor and leaving them only enough for the barest subsistence. The earnings of the people, wrote Jefferson (sounding much like Machiavelli), were used by the privileged classes to sustain their idleness and to awe the miserable multitudes into believing that they, the nobles, were superior by divine right. According to Jefferson, a sufficient number of his contemporaries had proceeded down this road that the threat of recreating an equally unjust society seriously existed in the Constitutional era, and it had taken another revolution, that of his election to the presidency in 1800, to reverse this dangerous tendency.

By contrast, he wrote, republicans believe humans to be rational, endowed with rights and an innate sense of justice, and capable of self-governance directly or through the agency of elected representatives accountable to them. They further believed that all men should receive by right the "full fruits of their own industry" and thus be immune from economic, political, and social dependency on an unelected elite. "The cherishment of the people then was our principle, the fear and distrust [and servitude] of them, that of the other party." The republicans, he said, were the party of "the landed and laboring interests" of the country, in contrast to the monied, industrial, urban Federalists.[184] These two contrasting views of human nature thus divided the nation and the parties from that day to this. And from these drastically different perspectives flowed sharply contrasting views of human rights and social justice. Joyce

Appleby summarizes Jefferson's enlightened philosophy this way: "As early as 1784, Jefferson had charted a different course: use Constitutional and statutory measures to make the poor independent. Here his environmentalism merged imperceptibly into his convictions about the basic human endowment. What today would appear as social engineering presented itself to Jefferson as a liberation of those natural forces long held in check by the Old World artifices of monarchy, nobility, and established religion."[185]

In the arena of social justice as elsewhere, Jefferson's beliefs were accompanied by actions. His resistance to what he saw as both the remnants and roots of feudal aristocracy in Virginia was demonstrated by his efforts to abolish the laws of entail and primogeniture, his bill for broadly based education, his statute for religious freedom in Virginia, his consistent advocacy of republican ideals, his equally consistent belief in the wisdom and common sense of the people and in their capacity for self-government, and, perhaps most important, his determination to distribute land, including public land on the emerging frontier, to those who had no land.[186] In his letter to Maria Cosway, the famous "Heart and Head" debate, his Heart summarized his social philosophy succinctly: "Though we cannot relieve all the distressed, we should relieve as many as we can."[187]

The common thread throughout this social philosophy was land distribution. Property ownership was a guarantee against both economic oppression and government tyranny. It provided individual freedom and encouraged the civic virtue central to republicanism. It was, for Jefferson, always more than simply an economic proposition. It was central to his view of humanity: "This justification of property rests, in the last analysis, on the right to life at a more than animal level: freedom from coerced labor and arbitrary government are held to be part of what is meant by a fully human life. At the same time this justification is an assertion of the right to the means of labor: the whole point is that by working on his own land or other productive resources a man can be independent and uncoerced."[188] People without land were by definition dependent, dependent either on the wealthy and propertied for employment (and therefore beholden) or on society for relief. The greater the distribution of property, the less the need for social welfare.

Among the functions of the ward republics, Jefferson included "care

of their poor." Though he could report in response to a foreign interloc-
utor, in his *Notes on the State of Virginia*, that "I never yet saw a native
American begging in the streets or highways" (those who do beg are "in
the larger towns" and "usually foreigners") and that "a subsistence is
easily gained here," he did understand that there were those in need of
care, through poverty, illness, or age, and through no cause of their own.
These were supported through locally collected (ward) revenues distributed by community leaders ("usually the most discrete farmers"). For
those who have some but insufficient means, their meager earnings or
savings are supplemented, and they live in their own accommodations.
The destitute are boarded in local homes and subsidized by the community. Those with neither property nor vocation, but able, are placed in
workhouses where they are "well cloathed [sic], fed, lodged, and made to
labor." Wherever possible, the sick are taken in by "the family of a good
farmer" where, with the help of others in the community, they are fed,
cared for, and nursed to health. "Nature and kind nursing save a much
greater proportion in our plain way, at a smaller expense, and with less
abuse."[189] Jefferson's vision of social welfare "differs substantially from
both contemporary . . . national welfare programs and the local private
charities which existed throughout America prior to the New Deal. And,
while not as technologically sophisticated as the former, they seem rather
closer in humanitarianism to the latter, while still being publicly supported."[190]

Jefferson's social views as related to property were distinctly Aristotelian in that too little property led to dependency and too much led to
oligarchy and domination: "The citizen[s] should not only possess enough
[property] to meet their requirements in civic life, but also to encounter
the perils that face them from outside; hence they should possess neither
so large an amount of wealth that it will be coveted by their neighbors
and by stronger states while its possessors will be unable to repel their
assailants, nor yet so small an amount as not to be capable of sustaining
a war even against equal and similar states."[191] Like Aristotle, Jefferson
managed to promote, protect, and celebrate the liberal individualism of
the *Declaration of Independence* while recognizing humans to be political
animals, whom function in communities and who therefore must organize their activities in collaboration with their fellow citizens. Since those
fellow citizens inevitably will include those less well off, accommodation

to this reality requires policies of support and maintenance for those unable to care for themselves and the distribution of assets required for self-sufficiency to those capable of labor. At least in Jefferson's time, the principal asset was land. It remains to be explored whether a modern-day equivalent of land exists for those claiming their fundamental right to labor in the earth.

THE CLASSICAL ROOTS of Thomas Jefferson's republicanism have been explored, his political economics and philosophy summarized, and his reconciliation of individual rights with civic duties considered. His highly individual view of the scale of the republic, both in the context of the Constitutional debate and in his more mature reflections, has been discussed, and an analysis of the education, welfare, and security functions of the ward republic has been set forth. Before that, we considered the new economic, social, and political realities of the twenty-first century and whether these new realities may overcome the original objections to Jeffersonian republicanism and render it worthy of reconsideration. Consideration has also been given as to whether twenty-first-century America is still a republic and, if so, the nature of the republic it has become.

It now remains to be considered whether the small scale or "pure" republic—the Jeffersonian ideal—is relevant to America in the current age.

GIVEN THE NEW REALITIES of the expanding impact of global economics and international finance on every society, the contracting authority of the nation-state, and the erosion of ideological cohesion, how should government be organized to realize the democratic values of social justice and equality and to encourage the republican values of civic duty and popular sovereignty? The Jeffersonian pyramid of republics— a national representative republic composed of a federation of States based upon democratic, participatory, assembly republics—offers one potential solution.

Applying Jefferson's model to America in the current age, the national government would continue to be entrusted with defense against threats to the national security, with the conduct of foreign relations, and with "federal relations." Federal relations would include responsibility for all matters relating to the common good of all the citizens of the nation ("provide for the ... general Welfare of the United States" and "make all Laws necessary and proper for carrying into Execution the foregoing Powers," as set forth in Article I, sec. 8, of the Constitution) and for harmonizing the actions of the various States as they affect each

The Jeffersonian Republic in the Current Age

4

other and the rights of citizens generally. The present elaborate network of interstate communications and transportation, protection of the environment, health and safety, federal support for education, social security and assistance, and other such laws and regulations would be maintained and overseen by federal officials as contemplated under the Constitution.

Acting at least to the degree that it does at present through the various State governments, however, the national government could, over reasonable time, cede authority to local communities to administer those programs of greatest interest to the community and within the particular competence of the community. Under this proposed structure, the national government would be responsible for two comprehensive domestic functions: first, it would establish baseline performance standards for local government programs, such as education, health, and social welfare; and second, it would provide financial resources to communities in the form of shared revenues required to meet those standards. These standards would represent a uniform, national, common good where basic social goals are concerned, and federally administered income distribution would help local communities achieve that common good. National standards for local school performance would be uniform throughout the nation but could be adapted to local circumstances—for example, greater emphasis on languages in one case or on technical training in another—only as provided in federal authorizing legislation. This is standard practice for virtually all federal laws affecting local communities. The rights of those in permanent racial, ethnic, religious, or other minorities in communities large and small would continue to be protected under the universal application of federal civil rights and other equal protection laws.

No argument is made here for the overall diminution of federal authority to legislate or regulate in the national interest as provided for in the Constitution. National governmental authority, it is argued here, is in much greater jeopardy from trends toward internationalization and privatization than it would be as a result of the restoration of local republicanism. For democratic republicanism to flourish and to assume greater influence in citizen self-governance, it is not required for federal authority to diminish. It simply requires citizens, in their local communities, to assume much greater authority over and responsibility for local issues of common concern and for the administration of federally mandated programs for social equity and well-being, including education, health, environment, transportation, and welfare.

For their part, the various States could augment the revenues provided by the federal government to local communities, through technical support and expertise assist those communities in greatest need of assistance to meet national standards, and advise communities concerning the most effective investment of federal revenues. Federal and State revenues distributed to less well-off local republican governments would be required to be spent for the purposes for which they were distributed, including public schools, health care facilities, and other public functions subject to federal regulation. A clear case in point is the local security provided by the National Guard. The Guard, Constitutionally a creature of the State, accepts its training and equipment budget from the Department of Defense and is required to use its funds as directed by federal authority. Most federal revenue-sharing social programs operate similarly. Local discretion over the expenditure of federal funds is permissible only as prescribed by federal statute.

Under the allocation of political authority discussed here, it would be for the local republics to operate the public schools and training centers, the hospitals and clinics, the social welfare agencies, the local environmental protection agencies, the public safety services, the public transport systems, and other such agencies within their jurisdiction and competence. Most important, regular town meetings would enable all citizens to participate in the decisions regarding the matters of common good that affect their lives. Closed-circuit community television or even Internet broadcasts may make such town meetings "virtual" before long. At least, modern means of communication can convey meeting notices, agendas, and background support materials. Robert Putnam believes that the key is to find ways in which Internet technologies can reinforce rather than supplant enduring social networks:

> Computer-mediated communications also open opportunities
> for hitherto unthinkable forms of democratic deliberation and
> community building—like citywide citizens' debates about local
> issues or joint exploration of local history or even announce-
> ments of a local ultimate Frisbee tournament. Several early

studies of well-wired communities suggest—tentatively, but hopefully—that residents who have easy access to local computer-based communications use that new tool to strengthen, not supplant, face-to-face ties with their neighbors and that some of them become more actively involved in community life, precisely as we social-capitalists would wish.[1]

Against the idea of empowerment of local republics will be heard an argument concerning fragmentation, an argument that says that the more government is dispersed, the less efficient it is. But this argument comes too late. Fragmentation of government in the United States has already occurred. And Jeffersonian republicanism, rather than exacerbating fragmentation, can help cure it. Richard Dagger, for one, has documented both geographical and functional fragmentation in American government, even as national power consolidated in Washington, D.C. Geographical fragmentation occurred as the result of the growth of suburban America in the second half of the twentieth century. Each major metropolis now is surrounded by dozens, sometimes scores, of suburbs, each with its own government, and many are now overlaid, for coordination purposes, by regional councils of government. Functional fragmentation has occurred largely within metropolises. Special districts, often led by unelected professional managers, have assumed many government functions in a manner often invisible to public—voter and taxpayer—scrutiny. Many similar quasi-governmental entities have sprung up to administer an increasingly vast area of federal government programs mandated to be administered by State and local authorities, and many such entities possess little competence to do so. According to Dagger:

> The consequences of this twofold fragmentation are readily apparent. Superimposed on the layer of municipal governments in the metropolis are a number of other jurisdictions—school districts, police and fire protection districts, sewer districts, cultural districts, transit districts, port authorities, metropolitan councils, and so on. According to the 1977 Census of Governments, the 272 Standard Metropolitan Statistical Areas (SMSAs) in the United States had a total of 25,869 "local governments," or an average of 95.1 each. In the 35 SMSAs with populations of a million or more, the average was 293.3. Metropolitan Chi-

cago led the way with 1,214 local governments, including school districts, counties, municipalities, townships, and special districts.[2]

Rather than increase citizens' confusion and sense of lack of control, the Jeffersonian republic might help reduce them. The local republic could become the unit of government that consolidates these diverse functions under one accountable roof. It might provide the single forum in which citizens gather to discuss and resolve virtually all issues of local common concern. No claim for this role is made here; that would be much too ambitious for this study. However, the possibility is raised as an antidote to the argument that local republican government would add confusion where none presently exists. Confusion abounds, even without the ward republic. The possibility is simply here raised that the ward republic might be its solution rather than its cause.

An argument must also be addressed concerning the need for equity in national policy, an argument with its historical roots in the Fourteenth Amendment to the Constitution ensuring "equal protection of the laws" to all citizens. According to this argument, greater community self-governance invites disparity of treatment of citizens living in poorer or less civically minded communities or mistreatment of minorities by powerful majorities. In response, it must be restated that nothing in the Jeffersonian republican argument made here diminishes the responsibility of the federal government *under the Constitution* for ensuring the equitable treatment of its citizens regardless of the community in which they happen to live. The Constitution permits no inconsistency in enactment or administration of federal policy. There is nothing in Jefferson or this study that contemplates resort to authentic republicanism as a means of creating pockets of discrimination or avoidance of responsibility. Indeed, the republican case is based strongly upon the enhancement of citizens' responsibility not merely toward themselves, as neolibertarians would have it, but also toward all those within their communities. If power is to devolve to the community, it is to be in the arena of policy initiative and administration not in the enactment or enforcement of national standards. Local republics would be required to operate within the federal Constitutional and legal framework, a framework that guarantees, *inter alia*, against majorities coercing minorities. The distinction is between ends and means. The ends of justice, equity, and fairness can and should enable a variety of means to achieve them. The issue is the role of the citizen in achieving justice, equity, and fairness in her community. Any suggestion that empowerment of citizens is a threat to federal authority is a suggestion both of a distrust of democracy and of a vulnerability in the federal structure requiring considerable attention.

This proposal raises many questions, some dealt with in greater detail below and some outside the scope of this book, which is a work (as set forth in the introduction) of political theory not of political science. The local republic of the classical age, the Renaissance, and the American Revolution offers the ideal. Application of the ideal to twenty-first-century America would require observance of an extensive body of Supreme Court opinions and statutory law regarding the relationship not only of federal to State governments but also the relationship of both to municipal and local governments. Two centuries of legislative action and judicial interpretation provide a rich legal and political context in which this proposal must be considered. For example, within the pluralistic American society, special consideration has been given within the Constitutional framework to the protection of the rights of special communities, such as the Amish and other religious sects. Though rare, these cases do offer an instance of the myriad kinds of issues raised by a proposal to reawaken republican values through local community empowerment. Resolution of these issues must be the task of another work.

The republican proposal made here, it must be emphasized, does not vary greatly in form from the present structure of federal, State, and local governments. But it varies a great deal in substance. Local citizens, citizens of an authentic republic in which they play a decisive role, would achieve much greater empowerment and responsibility. They would have a greater immediate sense of matters affecting the quality of their community's life, including the quality of teaching, education performance results, causes of both temporary and persistent dependency on public assistance, the pay scale of nurses, identification of those responsible for local environmental damage, the condition of the elderly, problems of criminal justice, and the causes and consequences of unemployment. Even more important, citizens would have a much greater immediate sense of responsibility, under the mandate of federal standards, for alleviating conditions adversely affecting their community's life. And, with federal and State financial assistance where necessary, they would have the resources to take steps to solve their community's problems. Overall, establishment of republican government in local communities could fundamentally alter the role of the citizen in mass society and could, therefore, alter the society itself. In Jefferson's words, "By placing under every one what his own eye may superintend . . . all will be done for the best."

This belief was based upon an even stronger belief that resistance to tyranny is greatest among those who have responsibility for self-government. "Where every man is a sharer in the direction of his ward-republic, or of some of the higher ones, and feels that he is a participator in the government of affairs, not merely at an election one day in the year, but every day; when there shall not be a man in the State who will not be a member of some one of its councils, great or small," then there would not be a citizen who would not lay down his life rather than surrender the control of it to a tyrant.[3] This theme was directly echoed by Tocqueville: "The most powerful way, and perhaps the only remaining way, in which to interest men in their country's fate, is to make them take a share in its government."[4] This might today be called a theory of "ownership" (in Tocqueville's construction, coercive ownership) of public affairs and responsibilities.

The revolutionary character of Jefferson's insistence on a space for genuine democratic participatory government can best be understood by reference to the absence of such space in the U.S. Constitution, where every concern was expressed for the relationship between national and State governments and none for the township as the true repository of the republicanism so proclaimed by every founder at every turn. Hannah Arendt noted this great oversight and attributed it to the profound conservatism of the "revolutionary" founders, whose concern for a stable union and fear of an unstable "democracy" far outweighed any regard for the revolutionary spirit of future generations. She finds it significant that "only Jefferson among the men of the American Revolution ever asked himself the obvious question of how to preserve the revolutionary spirit once the revolution had come to an end."[5] For him, the notions of generational revolution (each generation adopting its own laws and reconsidering its inherited constitution) and of the ward republic, township, or council were the best means of providing to all citizens and each generation the means for keeping the revolutionary spirit alive. The basic assumption of Jefferson's township republics, wrote Arendt, "was that no one could be called happy without his share in public happiness, that no one could be called free without his experience in public freedom, and that no one could be called either happy or free without participating, and having a share, in public power."[6] Even within the context of revolutionary America these notions were revolutionary; they sought to institutionalize both the memory of and capability for revolution in case it might ever again be required.

The merit and value of the restoration of township or authentic republics cannot be weighed on the scales of conventional political science, measured by the language of efficiency, nor judged by concerns for the disruption of established power-sharing arrangements. Restoration of republican values has much more to do with the restoration of civic virtue, resistance to corruption, the sovereignty of the people, and the establishment of a *polis* in which citizens participate in self-governance, in short, with the very nature of the character of citizenship among free people.

Since not all functions of the township *polis* can or need be characterized in detail to demonstrate this idea, three particular matters of immediate public concern will receive consideration: the public education system, the provision of social welfare, and the renewed demands of homeland security. The locally controlled public education system is one of the most persistent legacies of Thomas Jefferson. Here the discussion will focus upon education as an entitlement, as a possible new form of property, and as central to a concept of equality (in the context of equal opportunity). In the twentieth century, welfare has been considered principally a responsibility of the national state. Can it better be administered and can social justice be better achieved in the authentic republic of the township? Can there be a "right to work"? Is poverty incompatible with liberty? Finally, following a century of nation-state wars, the threat and the reality of terrorism has brought warfare to the neighborhood. That being the case, are the local militias (National Guards) maintained by the various States the first line of defense and security? The demands of homeland defense may offer the most vivid opportunity for a demonstration of civic virtue by local citizens. It is a matter of singular public immediacy, where the duties of the state to protect the citizen and the duties of the citizen to defend the *polis* coincide.

Thomas Jefferson, unique among America's founders, possessed a theory of rights based upon a theory of duties.[7] Rights and liberties, he believed, must be protected and earned by citizen participation. The state could not be the enemy of rights if the people were the state. But the people could only *be* the state, in literal terms, in the township. Protection of the rights of women and men could only be achieved practically in the township, the local republic, the authentic republic. Jefferson's ideal took for granted the principle discussed at length by Tocqueville, namely, that governmental structures condition political cultures. As one scholar has noted:

> If (as Tocqueville argued) administrative structures have implications beyond government alone—if they shape the political culture of a people—the undercutting of local power in the late nineteenth and early twentieth centuries perhaps caused or contributed to one of the most puzzling attributes of modern American politics. It might, in short, explain the persistent *civic malaise* of the late twentieth century, the widespread sense of individual detachment from government that contrasts so dramatically with the vibrant democracy Tocqueville observed— and that threatens to provoke yet another major restructuring of the American republic.[8]

The universal tone of this statement overlooks diversity among communities and the fact that some twenty-first-century American communities, especially those most prosperous and stable (one related to the other), do thrive. The existence of such communities does not, however, necessarily ensure that citizens participate to the degree envisioned by Jefferson in the public life of the community.

To render Jefferson's theory of the elementary republic plausible requires, first, that it be shown to be coherent, compatible with modern commercial life, and not antagonistic to the moral and political convictions of an advanced liberal democracy. Second, an account of the institutional arrangements that this theory implies must be drawn up and the resources of political science and sociology employed to rehearse the possible consequences of its institutionalization. This being a study in political theory, the concerns of political scientists and social analysts are employed to identify the problems of institutional arrangements, but the principal purpose remains to resurrect and render plausible a view of republican politics peculiar to Jefferson yet possibly more relevant to the current age than to his own.

The Republican *Polis* in Twenty-first-Century America

For anyone proposing to take Jefferson's republican ideal seriously in the current age, the temptation exists to attempt to construct the detailed Constitutional and institutional structures, both of the elementary republic and of its relationship to the national republic, required to bring it to life. But such an enterprise of translating Jefferson's ward republic ideal into detailed governmental structures would be, as stated above, an exercise in political science well beyond the scope of this work. Thought has been given, however, to the practical questions related to community scale by those who are concerned for the restoration of citizen participation and who share the conviction that participation builds community and community enables participation.[9]

Robert Dahl wrote *After the Revolution* (1970) during a period of social upheaval in the United States. Dahl struggles with two competing realities. First, "on the whole the ordinary man [and woman] is more competent than anyone else to decide when and how much he shall intervene on decisions he feels are important to him."[10] Second, "to insist on primary democracy as the exclusive form of democracy is to condemn 'the people' to impotence."[11] In short, in a democracy, people are the best judges of their own interests and how public policies affect them, but not everyone can participate in every decision. The solution is what he calls "the Criterion of Economy": "When in the course of the eighteenth century it came to be recognized that by means of elections you could join the aristocratic principle of representation to the democratic principle of political equality, democrats were exhilarated by the discovery that democracy need not after all be confined to the tiny city-state. In endorsing representative democracy, Jefferson accepted, as Rousseau did not, the Criterion of Economy."[12]

Dahl conceives of large-scale democracy in the image of a series of "Chinese boxes, the smaller nested in the larger." To increase opportunities for participation, he says, "We shall have to find ways by which citizens can participate more fully in smaller units, units smaller than nation-states or megalopolis[es]. These smaller units must be . . . neighborhoods and cities of human proportions."[13] Dahl concludes that the appropriate size for a city in which people can participate in matters important to them would be between fifty thousand and several hundred thousand. That city could be governed by an assembly composed of representatives of neighborhood units of approximately five hundred where immediate and direct citizen participation could take place. Even then, Dahl stresses, two reforms in city government are required: cities must have access to unencumbered and automatic equal shares of federal revenue, and citizens must take back crucial neighborhood decisions from professional managers.[14]

More recently, Richard Dagger has ventured a similar proposal designed to "convert the city from a prisoner's dilemma to an assurance game." He proposes that stable, well-defined, small cities—where they do not already exist in small-town America—can be created out of metropolises and their suburbs. He suggests, "in an unabashedly prescriptive manner, how this might be done. I hasten to note, however, that these prescriptions provide neither a utopian vision of a good city nor a detailed blueprint for 'practical' changes. They are instead a set of tentative, incomplete, and deliberately provocative suggestions that will serve . . . to focus and stimulate reflection on cities and citizenship."[15]

Dagger suggests that each metropolis be divided into districts of approximately fifty thousand population each and the districts subdivided into ten wards of five thousand people each. This scheme is neither unnatural nor arbitrary. Most American cities with council governments are already divided into council districts, constituencies from which council members are elected and to which they are accountable. Further, the oldest American metropolises—for example, New York, Boston, and Philadelphia—retain neighborhoods with identifiable names and fairly well-established boundaries, neighborhoods often of the approximate size of the prescribed wards. Consolidation of now widely dispersed "special service district" functions within the purview of the district and ward councils would overcome the growing problem of the fragmentation of government. And the wards and the districts within which they function can assume responsibility for, *inter alia*, local schools, health-care facilities, police and fire protection, and parks and recreational activities. Even within the context of the greater metropolis, district and ward governments would be readily available for citizen participation up to and including occupancy of elective office. A large number of representative positions from the wards to the districts would be made available, and monthly ward meetings would be open for direct citizen participation. Dagger suggests the additional possibility of coercive measures, such as compulsory local voting and mandatory community service for young people (to which the Jefferson of the *Bill of Rights* might object).

Dagger further suggests that national government measures, such as health and transportation grants, business tax subsidies, preferential mortgage programs, and so forth, can be used as incentives for the relocation of populations and for building up less desirable communities. He uses the illustration of Atlanta, Georgia, to emphasize the importance of urban and civic design. That city named its neighborhoods to give them pride of place and created distinct neighborhood boundaries. It created specific public meeting places, both formal and informal, in each neighborhood, and it attempted to identify and encourage neighborhood leaders and organizations as a means of providing stability, presumably in the spirit of Jefferson's natural aristocracy. This concept of civic design goes well beyond traditional urban planning, which is concerned with physical infrastructure, to encourage responsible citizenship, participation, civic virtue, and civic identity and memory.

Beneath the logistics and mechanics of the proposal, the political science of it, rests human desire: "Most Americans, like the citizens of other industrialized nations, would rather live in smaller settlements, something like an idealized Tocquevillian town," such a town being, of course, the New England township. National surveys over the last two decades of the twentieth century concluded that "if everyone were to live in the location that he or she preferred, the distribution of population would be different than current residence. In particular there would be considerably fewer people in large cities [i.e., with more than fifty thousand residents] and more people near large cities [i.e., within thirty miles]."[16]

The Jefferson ward republic is not examined here as the possible solution to a large nation's demographic ills, as a remedy for mass longing for a more ideal existence, nor as a utopian political scheme. Descriptions of possible formulas for achieving the Jeffersonian proposition are not put forward as definitive solutions. They are merely meant to show that the idea of authentic republicanism in a mass urban society is not impractical. For those concerned with political and social science, with urban government and political processes, a great deal of work on the practical questions should take place.

To extrapolate further on three specific governmental functions—public education, social welfare, and local security—there follows more detailed consideration of the challenges these social issues currently face and the way these problems might be managed in the *polis* of the ward.

Public Education in the Authentic Republic

Republican Education for Citizenship

Tocqueville was one of the earliest observers to appreciate the distinctive role that public education played in the new American republic: "It is the provisions for public education which, from the very first, throw into clear relief the originality of American civilization."[17] He noted both its elevating and leveling effects. "I think there is no other country in the world where, proportionately to population, there are so few ignorant and so few learned individuals as in America."[18] He later observes the same curiosity from a different perspective: "Anyone trying to find out how enlightened the Anglo-Americans are is liable to see the same phenomenon from two different angles. If his attention is concentrated on the learned, he will be astonished how few they are; but if he counts the uneducated, he will think the Americans the most enlightened people in the world."[19] However, Tocqueville also understood the close links between the federal republic and community republics and between local institutions, including those for public education, and the empowerment of people to preserve freedom. He discussed the factors that "seem to contribute more than all others to the maintenance of a democratic republic in the New World. The first is the federal form adopted by the Americans, which allows the Union to enjoy the power of a great republic and the security of a small one. The second are communal institutions which moderate the despotism of the majority and give the people both a taste for freedom and the skill to be free."[20] "The strength of a free people resides in the local community," he observed. And local institutions "are to liberty what primary schools are to science; they put it within the people's reach; they teach people to appreciate its peaceful enjoyment and accustom them to make use of it. Without local institutions a nation may give itself a free government, but it has not got the spirit of liberty."[21] The local communities most typifying Tocqueville's qualities were New England townships, among whose primary institutions were the public schools. These schools educated Americans to govern themselves at the community level and by so doing equipped women and men to protect their own liberty within the greater federal system. Education, for Tocqueville as well as for Jefferson, provided the equipment for participation, and participation was the guarantor of rights, not an encroachment upon them.

Where Hamilton carried over an Old World fear of democracy as simply another name for passionate, unruly mobs, Jefferson believed that enlightenment through education turned every person from simply a democrat into a democratic republican. Where Madison sought to shield government from the people by representation and by separation of powers, Jefferson sought to introduce people to wise government through education. Where others saw the solution to the problem of republican scale to be representation, Jefferson "preferred education to representation as democracy's guarantor."[22] Three principal pillars of Jefferson's political philosophy were participation, generational renewal and responsibility, and maintenance of the spirit of revolution. Participation could only occur directly in the ward republics. Each generation was responsible for reenacting the revolutionary process of adopting its own laws and constitution. The spirit of revolution and innovation was the best means for each generation to adapt to changing circumstances. This radically different outlook on democratic republicanism could only succeed in practice if citizens were uniformly and universally informed, enlightened, and educated. Both the foundation and the future of the American republic rested upon civic virtue, and civic virtue had to be learned through education in the community. Jefferson's object was to

> make revolution commonplace, to make it a permanent feature
> of the political landscape rather than just leaving it as a found-
> ing mechanism for a new, more legitimate politics of stasis.
> Democracy's chief guarantor was not accountability but partici-
> pation, not representation but local government. The cry "divide
> the country into wards" with which Jefferson liked to conclude
> letters and speeches during one phase of his career was a re-
> minder to the young republic that devolving power into the
> hands of citizens was a surer way to protect against the abuse
> of power than to insulate the power holders from popular prej-
> udice via representative institutions.[23]

The issue is whether the founding of a republic is an event or series of events anchoring the republic to a point in time and whose meaning must be preserved through constant conservation or whether the revolutionary founding is a perpetual process requiring innovation and renewal. The question, in a word, is whether the preservation of democracy is a static or a dynamic process.[24] If the former, then remote, representative government will suffice to protect interests and provide a static safeguard against a nation straying too far from its founding experience and the oligarchy of wealth that forms its base. If the latter, however, then the vitality of citizen participation in widespread self-government and the creation of active civic virtue are required to adapt a polity established for one original purpose to the new purposes demanded by changing times and events. Unlike Renaissance republicanism, Jefferson's American republicanism saw the founding as a revolutionary moment to be replicated through innovation and experimentation. This was the meaning of his insistence on each generation being required to revisit its laws and constitution. The exercise was both revolutionary and therapeutic, and it demanded civic virtue. "Jefferson saw democracy itself, more particularly ward government and active participation by citizens in self-governance, as the remedy to the inevitable ossification of a democratic constitution founded on an original compact that successor generations could only approach as an ancient artifact in a spirit of abstract loyalty."[25] But the dynamic, revolutionary spirit to emerge from the ward republics and percolate up through the pyramid of State and federal republics could evolve only from an educated citizenry. Simple participation, absent informed judgment, avails little.

In his age, Jefferson sought to eradicate the two remaining feudal barriers to the recreation of the authentic republic: dependence and ignorance. His solution to the problem of dependence was to make every man a landowner, in effect as independent as the yeoman who had been the backbone of English republicanism. His solution to the problem of ignorance was to educate all citizens, to educate them not only for the emerging commercial world but also for the role of citizen. Here his understanding anticipated Madison and the Federalists' anxiety that democracy would amount to mobocracy. The masses of people were a danger only when ignorant and particularly when ignorant of their responsibilities as citizens. Citizens educated *qua* citizens by definition could not form a mob nor be ruled by every passing passion. Those schooled in their responsibilities to the community, the common good, and the common interest would stand as a bulwark against self-interested or destructive movements. "Above all things," he wrote, "I hope the education of the common people will be attended to; convinced that on their good sense we may rely with the most security for the preservation of a due degree of liberty."[26] Popular enlightenment goes hand in hand with majority rule. As Jefferson insisted in his first inaugural address, all "should bear in mind this sacred principle, that though the will of the majority is in all cases to prevail, that will to be rightful must be reasonable."[27]

By linking rights to duties, duties to participation, participation to education, and education to the ward republic, Jefferson forged a logic chain relevant to a debate over the shape and future of democracy in the twenty-first century. According to Barber:

> Jefferson grounded liberty's claims in education, thereby giving
> to rights a living meaning and a defensible reality. Education
> makes citizens; citizens make a bill of rights; rights make de-
> mocracy. There is no democracy without citizens, no citizens
> without public education. The questions raised by this logic
> confront crucial democratic controversies of our own time no
> less than Jefferson's: how much democracy, and for whom?
> What kind of democracy—egalitarian or liberal?—and at what

price to reason? Who should be educated and how, and to what end?[28]

However, today, Jefferson's vision of independent property-owning citizens and citizens educated for self-governance has been largely overtaken by an alternative vision of citizens dependent on corporate employment and educated principally for commercial participation in the market economy. Though, in material terms, the alternative vision has proved relatively satisfying for a large majority, nevertheless it fails to equip citizens for active participation in self-governance. One scholar contrasts the two visions—representing the triumph of Hamilton over Jefferson—in this manner:

> The virtuous republic modeled on antiquity relied above all on the cultivation of citizenship and positive liberty and demanded civic education, civic participation, and sufficient civic activism to guarantee a responsible electorate. The new commercial republic, on the other hand, called for a limited state whose primary function was to protect the market and personal and private liberty, and for individuals whose primary motives were economic—the good citizen as the productive capitalist or the efficient worker—and who held the state and the democratic majority in suspicion.[29]

The commercial republic can sustain popular support so long as it provides the majority the opportunity for at least middle-class material status and the ever-distant possibility for great wealth. But its minimization of the potential for social progress, its relegation of government to the role of underwriter of commerce, its discouragement of active citizenship, and its elevation of individualism over the common good—all exact their price over time.

> The hostility to citizenship and the contempt for *res publica* has by now taken a toll even on the constrained notion of citizenship permitted by limited government and by the dominion of market over public sector forces. We have noticed that only half of the eligible electorate participates in presidential elections, and the numbers fall off quickly in lesser elections, plummeting to 10 or 15 percent in local primaries—where, however,

millions are spent by eager candidates trying to buy television time to win office.[30]

Nationalization of Education and the Rights Revolution

In the United States, as in other advanced democracies, citizens are compelled by the state (or the States) to submit their children to a system of education operated by local school districts.[31] In the context of this study, the long history of localism in the administration of public education in the United States is put forward as a prototype of and argument for the restoration of republican governance in other areas of community concern. However, this history of community control of public education has been systematically eroded by the demands of expanding rights and by centralized administration: "In the twentieth century, the universalist claims of national citizenship have preoccupied policy makers. The result may be that the community no longer recognizes the public schools as its own."[32]

Since the local public school has been a traditional venue for the dissemination of civic values, the weakening of community administration of public education also weakens the intergenerational link by which community civic values are conveyed. For Jefferson, schools were centers for training citizens, and participation in political life was itself an education: "In the political theories of Thomas Jefferson, John Stuart Mill, Jean Jacques Rousseau, Alexis de Tocqueville, and John Dewey, local self-government is the school in which citizens learn democratic virtues. When prescribing rules to themselves, citizens are at once free and governed by their noblest impulses. Practicing democracy makes the practitioners better democrats by forcing them to reckon with the aspirations of their fellow citizens. The result is a moral community of free, dignified, enlightened members."[33] According to John Stuart Mill, without mutual and collective experience in public life, a citizen "never thinks of any collective interest, of any objects to be pursued jointly with others but only in competition with them, and in some measure at their expense. ... A neighbor, not being an ally or an associate, since he is never engaged in any common undertaking for joint benefit, is therefore only a rival." That citizen participating in public affairs, however, "is called upon ... to weigh interests not his own; to be guided, in case of conflicting claims, by another rule than his private partialities. . . . He is made to feel himself one of the public, and whatever is for their benefit to be for his benefit."[34] John Dewey believed much the same: "Fraternity, liberty and equality isolated from communal life are hopeless abstractions. . . . Democracy must begin at home, and its home is the neighborly community."[35] Very much like Jefferson, Mill saw the profound importance that political participation held for education in citizenship: even though they might be less competent at a civic task than a government official, citizen action in public service was "a mode of strengthening their active faculties, exercising their judgment, and giving them a familiar knowledge of the subjects with which they are thus left to deal." Though, unlike Jefferson, Mill did not see civic participation as an issue of liberty, he did see it as

> part of national education; as being, in truth, the peculiar training of a citizen, the practical part of the political education of a free people, taking them out of the narrow circle of personal and family selfishness, and accustoming them to the comprehension of joint interests, the management of joint concerns—habituating them to act from public or semi-public motives, and guid[ing] their conduct by aims which unite instead of isolating them from one another. Without these habits and powers, a free constitution can neither be worked nor preserved.[36]

From the public school as a transmitter of civic values, the modern public school has become the locus for a more profound and far-reaching contradiction which forms the basis for this argument. The efforts to purge American politics and governance of bias and discrimination based upon race, gender, religion, and mental and physical capacity have unquestionably expanded the core of rights and liberties of the citizens of the nation, but to some extent they have done so at the expense of the authority and cohesion of the local community. As national mandates over local public schools have waxed, local responsibility has waned. As responsibility wanes, so does participation. Michael Sandel makes the point in this fashion:

Unlike the liberty of the early republic, the modern version permits—in fact even requires—concentrated power. This has to do with the universalizing logic of rights. In so far as I have a right, whether to free speech or a minimum income, its provision cannot be left to the vagaries of local preference but must be assured at the most comprehensive level of political association. It cannot be one thing in New York and another in Alabama. As rights and entitlements expand, politics is therefore displaced from smaller forms of association and relocated at the most universal form—in our case, the nation.[37]

Once rights are established, however, the question recurs as to whether they must be administered and protected by centralized governmental authority or whether they can be guaranteed with equal vigor by township and community governments and institutions, including schools, which also are the forums for and bearers of community values, civic virtues, and citizen duties in ways that centralized national governments cannot be. If the centralized national government, which has heretofore been the promoter and protector of universalist rights, has itself fallen prey to the dangers of corruptibility and interest, has contributed to the erosion of popular sovereignty, and has reduced the importance of civic virtue to the republic, then is it not necessary to recreate the township and its public institutions, including its schools, as the locus of citizen participation in guaranteeing rights as well as in perpetuating civic virtues and community values?

Though this struggle has been played out, perhaps beginning with Montesquieu, on the platform of the scale of the republic, more profound issues than the mechanics of democracy are at stake. In *On Democracy*, Robert Dahl discusses the dilemma of representative-versus-assembly democracies in terms of "the law of time and numbers," that is, the greater the number of citizens, the less they can participate in decisions and the more they must delegate (including in large-scale assemblies, where all cannot feasibly be heard): "The more citizens a democratic unit contains, the less that citizens can participate directly in government decisions and the more they must delegate authority to others." Yet, Dahl admits, in representative democracies, authority is delegated not only to elected representatives but also to "administrators, bureaucrats, civil servants, judges, and at a still further remove to international organizations." This extensive and nonrepresentative delegation of authority leads inevitably to a nondemocratic process—"bargaining among political and bureaucratic elites."[38] Confronted with this dilemma, Dahl heightens its extremes and finds no resolution. The "limited capacity of self-governing units small enough for assembly democracies have shown up time and time again," he says, in every kind of public matter from military defense to economic policy to human rights to education. He further finds it "impossible to foresee a world in which all large political units will have vanished, to be replaced *entirely* by completely independent political units with populations so small . . . that its citizens could govern themselves, and would choose to govern themselves, exclusively by a system of assembly democracies."[39] Modern democracy is thus left with Dahl's dilemma: representative democracy governed by "bargaining among [unelected and often unrepresentative] political and bureaucratic elites."

Curiously, in constructing this dilemma between large-scale representative democracies and small-scale assembly democracies, Dahl overlooks the resolution that he developed almost three decades earlier in *After the Revolution*, namely, "In a world with so many interdependencies, the hope for democracy cannot rest on total autonomy but . . . on democratic systems constructed like Chinese boxes, the smaller nested in the larger." This is the solution that was advocated by Thomas Jefferson and is explored here.

Jefferson did not argue for the outcome Dahl refutes—restoration of some form of autonomous city-states. Rather, Jefferson's pyramid of republics, transposed to the current age, offers a way out of Dahl's dilemma, and operation of the local public school system is representative of the kind of public enterprise best entrusted to the community republic under the rights—and resources—framework established by the national republic. By lumping national defense with economic policy, with human rights, and with transportation and communication networks and by lumping all of these with health, education, family planning, and criminal justice, Dahl misstates the problem and compounds the confusion. No one seriously argues for community control over foreign policy, monetary policy, rapidly internationalizing communication networks, or national security (except in the new threat to homeland security discussed later in this chapter). Such matters that are clearly for national cognizance should not be intermingled and confused with matters of more immediate community concern, such as schools, hospitals, local transport, environment, and social welfare. Contrary to Dahl's assumption that all public matters have necessarily become national (or even international), there are, as Jefferson recognized, matters requiring federal and therefore representative attention, and there are matters for the local community's oversight and concern. By expanding the jurisdiction of the township republic over these civil matters, one horn of Dahl's dilemma is diminished if not eliminated. Bargaining among [unelected] political and bureaucratic elites—the process that now dominates political life in mass democracies—is considerably reduced and exposed to community scrutiny, where all may participate. Community republics would still rely on representative centralized government to establish national baseline standards and to distribute resources. And the issue of the motivation of citizens to participate in community self-government will still be present.

The issue in question, public education, is instructive regarding a twentieth-century pattern of elevating national standardization and the universalization of rights at the price of republican values. With the exponential expansion of public school enrollment in the nineteenth century, bureaucratic educational hierarchies emerged to impose standards, professionalism, routines, pedagogical orthodoxies, uniformity, and "efficiency." The twentieth century brought laudable and necessary federally instituted and administered programs of racial integration, education methodologies, school financing equalization, gender neutralization, and access for handicapped children. In these and other instances federal standards were imposed upon State education departments and local school districts by statutory or judicial fiat. Few would quarrel with the intent or necessity of these actions, actions required to make democracy morally consistent. The question is whether the price of republican values is still required to be paid to maintain higher social objectives. Here it is argued that civic virtue and citizen participation are not incompatible with social justice and civil rights.

The price should be fully understood. "Polling data about schools, private-school enrollments, results of bond elections, and a growing home-school movement indicate that these developments may have provoked an adverse public response."[40] On average about 12 percent of all children of public school age in the United States are being educated in private, including parochial, schools and close to one million are now engaged in home schooling. Approximately one-fourth of all public school district bond elections were defeated during the five years at the close of the twentieth century, reflecting an ominous public resistance to, if not rejection of, public education. In recent years there has been a substantial growth in movements demanding parental choice of schools, educational vouchers, and charter schools. By 1996, twenty-five States had enacted authorization for charter schools, an approach that substitutes market mechanisms for national regulation and innovative methodologies for standardization of instruction. The price of choice is the replacement of democratic homogeneity with balkanization.[41] "In national U.S. polls conducted on education questions in 1995 . . . 64 percent of respondents favored more influence for local government in determining educational programs in schools. Seventy percent of respondents would favor a change to increase local school authorities' say over how federal funds are spent; 86 percent favor recent changes that increase local input into the way federal aid-to-education funds are spent."[42]

Every quantitative indication is to the effect that growing majorities of Americans are demanding greater community determination of the kind and quality of education their children receive. "Such patterns [as these data demonstrate] are inextricably bound up with the question of community conceived as an affective, moral social order based upon organic bonds and shared symbols. Parents seek such an order in private sectarian schools when they cannot find it in the public schools."[43] Thus, a public that applauds the goals of equality of opportunity and access, equal rights for all people, equalization of education financing, and similar social goals might also be a public concerned for the loss of community standards and values, local control, and educational quality. If a growing segment of the public opts out of the public school system, then social fragmentation, representing a fissure between township and nation, community and citizenship, takes place, and two vital forums for the cultivation of citizenship—public schools and communities—are weakened. The condition is summarized by one scholar in these words: "The quality of American education has been of growing concern in recent decades; in fact, many knowledgeable observers believe that public schooling has reached a crisis."[44] As several scholars concur, the current chasm between nation and place must not be permitted to widen. The net result is the destruction of both:

> In recent years both formal studies of collective action, such as [Michael] Taylor's and Mancur Olson's, and the experiments of social psychologists have born out the observation that size inhibits cooperation. The larger the group, the less likely are its members to cooperate for the good of the group. Small groups encourage solidarity and reciprocity because the individual's contribution is more visible and more meaningful—not the mere "drop in the bucket" that it is in a large group. For anyone who wishes to see the body politic resemble an assurance game rather than a prisoners' dilemma, the overwhelming size of the modern state, and even of many of its subordinate units, is a tremendous obstacle. That is why a number of analysts, wittingly or not, have followed the lead of Montesquieu or Tocqueville and suggested a greater and *more creative use of federalism* or local government, or both, to overcome the size problem.[45]

A "more creative use of federalism" is precisely the point. Underscoring the tension between civic duties and citizens' rights, the same point is made by those who view this tension within the arena of education:

> Local communities—affective, moral social orders identified with determinate small places—are highly desirable components of any political system; they are even more desirable in a democracy for their ability to raise and nurture citizens, to encourage the development of healthy civic and personal identities, and to serve as intermediary objects of attachment that provide individuals with concrete ways of belonging in the more abstract national political order. To perform these functions, however, they rely on affective bonds, many of which are organic. The tendency of such bases of membership is to create outgroups as well as ingroups. They invite the violation of widely-recognized citizen rights. Citizenship is another irreducible value in a federal, liberal, democratic political system. Hence any-

lessening of these tensions must take the form of an accommodation rather than a solution.[46]

The accommodation between citizenship and the organic bonds of specific groups, for example, ethnic or racial groups in a community, represents one of the principal challenges of the community-based republic. Republican government in its most immediate form of a modern city-state based on assembly negotiation and resolution of political issues will ultimately rely on the ability of individuals and groups to expand existing bonds and at least to deal respectfully, as required by law and social intercourse, with those not members of the ingroup(s). For this, no magic solution exists. But in the substantial number of instances where accommodation has been achieved, it resulted from a combination of public laws against discrimination, political leadership and will, and social goodwill. The national government, including both the Supreme Court and the Congress, has established the rules by which political and social life are to be lived. It is now for the people in their community republics to put those rules into concrete action. In the final analysis, where the practical aspects of social and political accommodation are concerned, "all politics is local."

Restoration of Republican Education within the Rights Framework

The proposed accommodation and the more creative use of federalism must be explored. If means can be found to restore to the township sufficient direction of public education matters to enable traditional civic virtues to be incorporated into an educational structure framed within established civil rights, using Jefferson's principle of the ward republic as the foundation for the federal republic, then hope exists for the resolution of the same tensions in other fields of democratic endeavor.

The argument here is not for a specific curriculum, style of education, or pedagogical method. It is rather an argument for a restoration of community responsibility for local schools so that they will once again become, at least in part, the locus of civic education and training in the duties and responsibilities toward the *res publica*. The centrality of the school to the community, after family and religious institutions, the centrality of community life to self-government, and the centrality of self-government to the restoration of democratic republican values in an age of global economics, ideological vacuum, and the declining authority of nation-states is very much what this argument is about. Putnam also links public schools with community solidarity: "School reform initiatives that encourage kids to attend smaller, more communal schools may have the unintended result of increasing both student and parental involvement in clubs, classroom activities, governing bodies, and education lobbying groups. In this way, such education reform could be an engine of civic reengagement."[47]

In the current age, the choice has wrongly been stated as between rights and duties, liberty and obligation, with duty and obligation somehow representing the commands of an authoritarian state. By so posing the choice, the individual must constantly guard against the state, be wary of government, protect his own autonomy, and seek security in individualism and material success. The role of the citizen is thus marginalized. Education, in this political economy, is principally the means toward individual achievement, material success, and isolation from public affairs.

In the contrary interpretation proposed here, however, duties are the guarantors of rights. Civic virtue, especially in the form of the citizen active in community self-governance, is the principal means to prevent the state from conditioning liberties. The republic is the political foundation for rights and the arena in which citizens actively protect their rights and perpetuate them for future generations. The only authentic republic, that is to say, the only republic in which there can be genuine citizen participation, is local. But the modern local republic must also be inclusive. It must, in other words, be democratic. To protect the modern local republic from factionalism, passing passion, and mobocracy, people must be educated as citizens. They must be instilled with the civic values required for intelligent self-governance. Education, particularly in its classic form of civic education, enables the republic to be democratic. In mass society, education enables people to participate in government as a means of protecting their own freedoms or, in Jefferson's admonition to Madison, to "educate and inform the whole mass of people" is to make them, as educated citizens, the "guarantor of liberty."

This linking of rights to duties, of duties to participation, of participation to the local republic, of education to participation, causes one to "ponder anew Aristotle's claim that nothing other than the provision of a common education (*paideia*) can turn a multitude (*plethos*) into a unit and constitute it as a polis."[48] The linking of freedom to education, once begun, becomes perpetual. "Liberty is the guarantor of education; . . . we not only have to educate every person to make him free, but we have to free every person to make him educable. Educated women and men make good citizens of free communities, but without a free learning community you cannot educate women and men."[49] The social and political objective is to bring the school into the community and, by so doing, bring the community into the school.[50]

From a Jeffersonian point of view, education has a broader function than the simple but still important goal of preparing students for the commercial world. With reference to its classic roots, education is at the same time the system for perpetuation of civic virtue. Its goals must be to produce not only the now-standard "productive member of society," in the capitalist sense, but also a participant in society, in the republican sense. If modern mass education in America has failed, it is in this latter duty.[51]

To reiterate, what is at issue is not education *per se* but education *for* citizenship as reflected by participation in the activities and affairs of the local community, if not also in the state and nation. It concerns the role of the local and therefore authentic republic in structuring the public school as a principal conveyor of civic virtue. In this regard it is instructive to note the evolution of the words *civic* and *civil*. The Latin *civilus* concerned that which had to do with being a citizen. By the eighteenth century, it had also come to mean educated or refined. It is now formally defined as "of or pertaining to citizens as a community; relating to the internal organization of a society." But the coin of citizenship has been devalued and has also been disassociated from civility. In the current age, it requires little more than birth in the nation-state or the simple process of naturalization. Locke, to the contrary, thought it not sufficient for citizenship to merely find it "convenient to abide for some time" in a place: "Submitting to the laws of any country, living quietly and enjoying privileges and protection under them, makes not a man a member of that society"[52]

While the rights revolution has placed greater emphasis on the role of public schools as social equalizing institutions, those schools have been increasingly losing their local identities. Instead of, as Jefferson would have it, building the local community, the ward, around the immediately available ward school freely available to all in the township or community, the second half of the twentieth century has seen regionalization, enlargement, and consolidation of school districts. "The number of general-purpose local governments . . . has been roughly constant since 1940, but the number of local school districts has contracted by 87 percent. Though the remaining local school districts are still the frontline vehicles of educational service delivery, they have been subjected to increasingly pervasive state and federal policy guidance."[53]

The challenge to neo-Jeffersonian republicanism (or "neoromanism," as Skinner would have it) is to discover whether the centralization and consolidation of national power during the rights revolution of the second half of the twentieth century, in this case in public education, can be reversed sufficiently to restore strong community control over public education without, at the same time, abandoning the aims, purposes, and achievements of that national revolution. In other words, can the centralizing tendencies of that revolution be reversed without sacrificing its standards? The goal is twofold: to reengage citizens in self-government and in the conduct of local public affairs and to restore civic education to the curriculum of the local public school.

Presuming democratic consensus on the need for the restoration of public education both as preparation for participation in the twenty-first-century commercial world *and* as civic education in preparation for participation in the life of the community (*paideia*) and presuming consensus that greater community supervision of local public education is desirable and necessary, how might such a system be structured so that national mandates for equal civil and educational rights are not sacrificed? Through the various statutory programs and judicial mandates already in existence, the national government can continue to establish standards for equal access to public education, for elimination of race and gender barriers, for financing educational activities and, where necessary, equalizing per pupil revenue bases, for improvement of teacher salaries and reduction of class sizes, for improvement of pupil performance and maintenance of standards for graduation, and for all those activities that guarantee equal access and opportunity to all students regardless of where they reside in the nation and that are deemed in the national interest.

Many of these initiatives are the product of federal judicial decisions and congressional actions in the second half of the twentieth century, some under the political guise of "national security." In more recent years, the trend has been for federal programs to establish general standards and goals and to provide revenues to the various States for their implementation. Predictably, these initiatives have greatly expanded both federal and state education bureaucracies and have, consequently, greatly increased the burden on local educators to comply with reporting requirements mandated by those bureaucracies. Thus, local public schools have been confronted with a classic Faustian bargain: they can receive the largesse of the national government but only in exchange for assuming a heavy burden of centralized control by both State and federal bureaucracies. Detailed, documented compliance with national mandates has been the price for federal largesse, and the guarantee of compliance has been the lever for federal and State hegemony over local public education.

However, compliance with national standards can be guaranteed in a variety of ways, not least through the federal and State judicial systems. Elaborate reporting requirements for local educators and school boards can be sharply reduced. The burden of proof can be shifted away from a standard of proving (by the grantee) that compliance has been achieved to one of proving (by the grantor, with the initiative of aggrieved parties) that compliance has not been achieved. In any case, problems of noncompliance with established national rights and norms would initially arise within the local community in the form of the local school board, and most could be resolved through the public airing of grievances in the local forum. Indeed, that is a central purpose of republican government: to empower the citizen to participate in the affairs of the local *polis* both as a forum for constructive service and as a forum for conflict resolution. The more successful the local community is at resolving grievances caused by purported violations of rights or standards, the stronger the ward republic would become in governing local affairs.

Public education must move a major step beyond the dominant influence of the national government as the implementor of individual rights and administrator of national programs. Reverting to a standard embodying republican qualities, this should be especially desirable when popular sovereignty has been steadily waning, when the national political system has succumbed to a sophisticated form of legalized corruption by interests operating through political party finance mechanisms, when civic virtue has been all but overwhelmed by the individual pursuit of material success, and when subtle forms of marketplace domination condition individual liberties, especially the republican liberty of self-governance.

The case of public education is important not only for the role it plays in the minds of thinkers from Aristotle to Jefferson in creating citizens, but also because it is an important link in a chain that leads from individual citizen at one end to township republic on the other. The half-century experiment in greater national control of education methodology, teacher training, and school curricula is increasingly seen by parents as having produced no greater excellence in the quality of public school instruction than the more locally governed schools that preceded the experiment. This has led to increased pressure, especially from middle- and upper-middle-class families, for privatization of education in the form of charter schools, private schools, and home schooling. The more this trend continues, the lower the quality of the remaining public schools, and thus the more the cycle continues downward.[54] "In the twentieth century, the universalist claims of national citizenship have preoccupied policymakers. The result may be that the community no longer recognizes the public schools as its own."[55]

An Operational Proposal

Were restoration (it cannot properly be called devolution since the township was the original locus) of local authority over public education to occur, local communities, local school boards, and teacher, parent, and administrator organizations, operating under the umbrella of national rights and opportunities mandates, would regain greater authority over and responsibility for establishing teacher qualification and compensation schemes, curriculums, student performance standards, and plans for civic education. The local community would thus be empowered to assume more responsibility for the public school as central to community life. Disgruntled parents could no longer blame "the federal government" or "Washington bureaucrats" for most problems occurring in the local school. The failure of students to meet national performance standards would be much more a matter for local correction. Teacher performance would be more immediately judged and rewarded or corrected. The role of national education organizations and national bureaucrats in the life of the local school would be diminished and put in proper perspective.

Disparities in resources remain a serious social and political concern. Not all communities enjoy the same income levels and standards of living. There are unquestioned correlations between community income levels and the quality of public educational institutions. Therefore, equity and justice require that the national government bring lagging community schools up to acceptable performance standards by the allocation of federal resources. Sufficient revenues must be allocated to every school district to ensure that the demands of a reasonably high-quality education can be met. With those resources must go administrative oversight to ensure wise allocations and investments in such areas as teacher salaries, quality of the school plant, up-to-date pedagogical equipment (including, especially, computers and computer learning), libraries, and at least basic athletic equipment. Revenue allocation should not be solely on a per-pupil formula basis, but should also take into account particular community needs and shortfalls. One district might need money for teacher salaries, one for a new school facility, and another for both. Expert technical advice should be available to all school districts from federal and State administrators.

The restoration of republican government to local communities, particularly in matters so crucial to community life as public schools, will do much to awaken citizen involvement and citizen responsibility. This may especially be true in poorer communities where substandard education is often taken for granted. If in poorer communities resources adequate to meet reasonable national standards are provided, and they are provided under conditions that require local citizen involvement and responsibility, there is every reason to believe that the outcome will be an awakening of community pride, participation, and empowerment, outcomes that can only benefit the greater national community.

There are, of course, no guarantees of this benign outcome. Indeed, there is ample evidence that impoverished and dependent communities have great difficulty in creating community spirit, in attracting capable managers, and in establishing confidence for self-government. However, the only remaining choice is not to relegate them to perpetual dependence on federal largesse and bureaucratic administration. The resources to be distributed by federal and state governments under the proposal here put forward include not only cash grants but also incentives for the relocation of industry, job-training centers, targeted development programs, programs for teaching entrepreneurship, bonuses for the relocation of teachers and managers, tax abatements, housing grants, and a wide variety of community improvement initiatives. Though there can never be guarantees of positive human response in every case, the Jeffersonian view is heavily based on an optimistic appreciation for the common sense and good judgment of ordinary people.

Social Welfare and Economic Justice in the Authentic Republic

Unequal Division of Property

The corruption and attendant poverty that Jefferson noted during his travels through Europe as U.S. ambassador to France were the products of the "unequal division of property" among the people, the dependency this created for laborers upon the landed few, and the consequent impoverishment created by an excess labor force and an inability of workers to bargain for fair incomes.[56] Almost thirty years later he proudly (and unrealistically) noted that "we [in the United States] have no paupers" and that "the old and crippled among us, who possess nothing and have not families to take care of them" are too few to constitute a separate portion of society or to constitute "a separate estimate."[57]

The issue of poverty arose most revealingly in one of the rare instances in which Jefferson acted as psychologist both for himself and humanity in general: the well-known "Head and Heart" dialogue drafted in the form of an extended letter to Maria Cosway. The Heart side of his nature recalls two, presumably real-life, incidents—one involving his failure to give a poor, weary soldier a ride in his carriage and the other involving his failure to give a poor woman money for her child—in which the Head argued successfully against these charitable gestures as useless. The Heart reflects, "Though we cannot relieve all the distressed, we should relieve as many as we can." It further concludes, using the experience of the American Revolution itself, that reason alone cannot be the basis for human action: "If our country, when pressed with wrongs at the point of the bayonet, had been governed by its heads instead of its hearts, where should we have been now? Hanging on a gallows as high as Haman's. You [the Head] began to calculate, and to compare wealth and numbers: we [the Hearts] supplied enthusiasm against wealth and numbers; we put our existence to the hazard, when the hazard seemed against us, and we saved our country."[58] The conclusion thus is to do what is right, including to the needy, and leave the result to Providence.

In the two instances where Jefferson outlined the duties of ward republics, he gave "the care of their poor" a prominent place.[59] Jefferson believed about great economic disparity as he did about slavery, that it corrupts both wealthy/master and poor/slave. Here he is in tune with traditional republican thought. For Aristotle, those who are "exceedingly poor or weak or of very mean station" turn often to "malice and petty wickedness" and, lacking a share of "fortune's goods," "those who are excessively in need" are "too humble to govern." "A state consisting of slaves and masters, not of free men, and of one class envious and another contemptuous . . . is very far removed from friendliness, and from political partnership—for friendliness is an element of partnership, since men are not willing to be partners with their enemies even on a journey."[60] Rousseau concurred, arguing that "no citizen should be so rich as to be capable of buying another citizen, and none so poor that he is forced to sell himself." Like Aristotle, he understood absolute equality to be unrealistic but abhorred the extremes. The community or state should "tolerate neither rich men nor beggars," for either condition is "equally fatal to the common good."[61] Extremes of wealth and poverty were destabilizing to Aristotle's *res publica*, to Rousseau's contractual society, and to the pure republic of Jefferson.

The Right to Labor the Earth

Europe, for Jefferson, demonstrated the outcome of the concentration of land ownership: a permanent, landless, impoverished class with no chance of rescue by themselves or others. Though not familiar with the neorepublican language of freedom-as-nondomination, Jefferson saw late feudalistic Europe as reducing men to the status of "bees," who labored for the profit of others. For him, concern for the needy in the neighborhood was both a legitimate and necessary function of the local republic.

Civic virtue, the exercise of citizen duties and responsibilities, also included moral virtue, the care for those in our midst who are in need. We have previously seen that Jefferson distinguished between the able-bodied poor and those poor by virtue of illness or age. For the former, his solution was radical. Give them land, of which there was plenty both in undeveloped regions of the new States and on the western frontier. Men had, he believed, a fundamental right to labor the earth and, given a surplus of that resource, the creation of a dependent class of the poor as in Europe could be avoided by division and subdivision of land ownership. That there might be those unwilling to work was not comprehensible within Jefferson's view of human nature. As for the rest—the ill, the old, or children without family support—they were, without question, the responsibility of the community, including the church, local families, neighbors, and local government.

Poverty as Domination

The foundational argument for an activist policy of social welfare, administered at the level of the local republic, is taken from Philip Pettit, who argues from the republican principle of freedom as nondomination as much as from the more traditional social-liberal, moral standpoint. Put simply, for Pettit, to be needy is to be vulnerable to domination either by the state or by those with wealth and the protection of the state. It is in the interest of the republic to foster individual socioeconomic independence because it will protect the citizen against the inevitable domination that would otherwise occur, and it will encourage undominated decisions and choice on the citizen's part. This same principle is central to Jefferson's insistence on a more equitable distribution of land. According to Pettit, "Republicans will require the state to provide more or less assistance for those in need; to provide it entirely in cash or at least partly in kind; to provide it directly or by means of independent civil agencies; to provide it subject to means-testing or as part of a universal form of provision; and so on. There is no direct argument from the republican ideal to decisions on such specific matters of policy; the policy decisions will be determined by empirical considerations as well as by philosophical."[62] Pettit argues that nondomination does not necessitate strict material equality but rather "the basic capabilities for functioning in society" and thus a "substantial reduction in material inequalities." For Pettit, republicanism is not merely form and process but also policy broadly defined and policy based upon the principle of the common good:

> Not only should the republic seek to remove domination from people's lives—not only should it try to reduce such compromises of people's freedom—it should also seek to increase the range and ease with which people enjoy undominated choice. It should seek to reduce the influence of factors like handicap and poverty and ignorance that condition people's freedom as non-domination, even if they don't actually compromise it. Otherwise put, it should promote people's *effective* freedom as non-domination, not just their *formal* freedom as non-domination.[63]

Even though laws may seek to protect all citizens, including the poor, against domination by the state, freedom is compromised if a citizen is so subject to domination by socioeconomic circumstances as to be *effectively* denied the rights of citizenship.

Economic Justice in the Twenty-first-Century Republic

Repeating his correlation of the early twentieth century with the early twenty-first century in America, Putnam asserts, "Some unexpectedly relevant—and in many respects optimistic—lessons can be found in a period uncannily like our own—the decades at the end of the nineteenth century and beginning of the twentieth century that American historians have dubbed the Gilded Age and the Progressive Era. In a number of deep respects the challenges facing American society at the end of the nineteenth century foreshadowed those that we face in our own time."[64] The great social programs of twentieth-century America largely grew out of the economic depression of the 1930s, which stretched across class boundaries. The New Deal was less about the distribution of income from the rich to the poor than it was about the distribution of income generally to all to stimulate economic activity along lines suggested by John Maynard Keynes. Jefferson, on the other hand, assumed the existence of the dependent in most communities and included their welfare among the duties of the ward government.

The historic antecedent of the New Deal was the Progressive movement of the early twentieth century which in turn drew its original energy from the populist causes of farmers and workers of the last quarter of the nineteenth century.[65] The Progressive movement was concerned with expanding the national government's role in guaranteeing the economic well-being of the nation's citizens. But its organizers and members demanded that any system of social insurance or welfare be the product of popular design and not a scheme devised in the remote national capital. In a speech to an annual dinner of the Progressive party in 1914, the social reformer Jane Addams demanded, as a fundamental tenet of progressivism, that no welfare state be created "unless the power of direct legislation is placed in the hands of the people, in order that these changes may come, not as the centralized government [gives] them, from above down, but may come from the people up; that the people shall be the directing and controlling factors in this legislation."[66] Two decades later, John Dewey echoed this theme in *Liberalism and Social Action*, a book he dedicated to Jane Addams: "These new liberals [Progressives] fostered the idea that the state has the responsibility for creating institutions under which individuals can effectively realize the potentialities that are theirs."[67] Despite the Progressive movement and the New Deal and Great Society programs that it eventually fostered, "The United States lagged behind other advanced democracies in adopting most elements of the welfare state." However, "it led the world in developing universal public education. And though the nation's income distribution is the most unequal in the developed world, the most conspicuous feature of its public education system is its leveling orientation—in the sense of emphasizing the needs of average and below-average students far more than those of gifted students."[68]

The most notable and lingering achievements of the New Deal and Great Society periods are the so-called middle-class entitlements, such as Social Security and Medicare. Efforts to expand government social policy to the bottom of the income ladder in the Great Society era of the 1960s proved less enduring, as the recent welfare "reform" initiatives of President Clinton have proved. It is those middle-class entitlement programs that have led some to abandon any hope for the renewal of local government: "The public's persistent commitment to middle-class entitlements . . . and its strong support for regulatory initiatives dedicated to environmental and consumer protection make the revival of local government unlikely."[69] But such conclusions overlook two crucial distinctions: that between enactment and administration and that between middle-class entitlements and aid to the dependent poor. In education, social welfare, consumer protection, environmental issues, and other public policy areas, uniformity requires national statutory and regulatory action and, often, appropriation of the financial resources necessary to achieve the mandated result. But the achievement of desired ends does not necessarily dictate a single set of means. In the interest of the revival of republican civic virtue, citizen participation, and township vitality, federal programs, including social welfare programs, can be locally administered within the context of particular local circumstances.

Before proceeding to examine the role of the local republic in achieving social justice, some quantification of present-day economic reality is required, especially in an age seemingly characterized by great wealth and prosperity. In the United States, fifteen million households headed by at least one full-time worker have annual incomes below the poverty line of $13,000 for a family of four. A total of thirty-five million Americans are living in poverty, including the largest number of children since the Great Depression. The number of children in families of the working poor has increased by 5.6 million. Twenty-one percent of all children under eighteen years of age live in families with incomes below the poverty line. The U.S. child poverty rate is the highest in the developed world, 50 percent higher than the next country. One out of every four American children under the age of three is growing up in poverty. Homicide is the largest single cause of death for children under eighteen. Twenty-six million people visit a relief center, food bank, or soup kitchen every day. More than five million working-poor families require housing assistance. Finally, there are direct correlations between poverty and illiteracy and between child abuse and crime. The number of abused children placed in foster homes increased by 86 percent in the 1990s, and 70 percent of the 1.8 million people in prison are illiterate.[70] Thus, it cannot be argued that economic prosperity has eliminated the need for concern about social misery.

These data are not presented for the purpose of opening an argument about the success or failure of capitalism but to establish the point that prosperous early twenty-first-century America is not prosperous for all. For a variety of reasons, poverty in measurable quantities, especially among dependent children and the elderly, exists as a social reality. This study does not undertake to determine why people are poor but rather to examine whether there might be some alternative way, founded in the community and consistent with republican values, for alleviating their condition in keeping with a fundamental commitment undertaken by the national government over the latter two-thirds of the twentieth century.

An Operational Proposal

Community republics, under guidelines provided by national and State governments and with the financial resources provided by both, can administer many aspects of poverty relief programs at least as well as, and in some cases better than, massive and therefore cumbersome federal bureaucracies. Local responsibility for local poverty will make local citizens much more familiar with the extent, nature, and causes of poverty in their midst.

From its founding, America incorporated the responsibilities for the establishment and maintenance of local public schools into its local communities. The same was not done on any systematic level with regard to social welfare. Depending in large part on local political belief systems and traditions, problems of poverty and dependence were dealt with on a varying scale ranging from total reliance on private charitable and religious institutions to publicly established and maintained relief agencies (including "poor houses," shelters, and soup kitchens). Local practices varied widely until the enactment of national welfare programs introduced more uniform measures, administered by federal authorities, across the country. As with public education, there seems little reason that the responsibility for administration of federally mandated social welfare programs cannot be restored to local republics.

Under a system of ward or community republics, local government might be given great flexibility in the methods for achieving federal goals. *Administration,* in the context used here, implies something more than mere bureaucratic distribution schemes. It is meant broadly to include innovative methods for identifying the particular needs of those receiving social assistance. Not all dependent children are in the same plight. Some are members of working-poor families, some are dependents of single, unemployed parents, and others are the product of generations of poverty.

The community republic should have the authority to deploy federal and local resources in creative new ways that acknowledge the uniqueness of virtually every case rather than simply following strict federal guidelines. The same can be said for assistance to the elderly, the other large population sector living in poverty. Some require food assistance, some medical assistance, and others simply basic human attention and concern. For the able-bodied of working age, community public works programs can supplement the private sector job market. Job-training centers can be established to create skills in particular demand in the region. New employers can be attracted to the area through a variety of incentive programs. Local republics administering federally mandated social relief programs should be more than mere pass-through agencies. They should be encouraged to tailor the national programs to local realities, and they should be rewarded for doing so.

Local responsibility would have the therapeutic effect of awakening local citizens to the dimensions and causes of social need in their communities in an immediate way. Given the responsibility for the administration of federal and State relief programs, local republican officials and citizens would confront the realities of unemployment, homelessness, child and spousal abuse, illiteracy, physical and mental illness, and hunger in more dramatically immediate ways than when, as now, these matters are left to remote authorities and regional bureaucracies. Indeed, by the enactment of national relief programs, which make use of federal resources and management, local citizens have managed to escape both attention and responsibility.

Today, many national assistance programs are administered in local regions, but the administrators are federal employees accountable through district managers to program administrators in the national capital. They may live locally, or at least regionally, but they are accountable nationally and not to the community. Under the proposal offered here, the managers of programs funded by federal authority would be employed by and accountable to the local republic, which itself would be responsible for satisfying the federal authorities as to the quality their stewardship.

In the last quarter of the twentieth century, poverty and welfare became an abstraction and a federal undertaking subject to political condemnation for waste, fraud, and abuse. It thus became too easy for local citizens to believe political nostrums that "a rising tide lifts all boats," that market capitalism, left to its own devices, would alleviate want, and that "trickle-down economics" had some resonance in reality. By restoring administrative responsibility—and, where successful communities are concerned, increased fiscal responsibility—to ward republics, citizens would once again be required to confront the immediate realities of want in their communities and thus be challenged to respond humanely, morally, and creatively, in short, to respond as citizens.

Disparities in community revenues and resources, as with education and other social undertakings, would have to be substantially reduced by federal authority. Where local communities lack the revenue base required to address local welfare needs, national and State governments must supply financial and technical assistance. Standards for sheltering, feeding, training, educating, and caring for the poor and needy would be established nationally. Financial resources required to meet these standards would be distributed by the national and State governments. Oversight by both levels of government would be required to guarantee that resources are properly administered to meet those standards. But with local responsibility would also go a substantial degree of local discretion in resource allocation, prioritization, and methodology. Incentives would be provided for constructive experimentation in new social welfare approaches. Local ingenuity and initiative, rather than the mechanical application of established administrative practices, would be strongly encouraged. Given wide discretion in method and application, local citizens would not only acquire responsibility, they would also be empowered to act creatively and imaginatively.

The political impact of republican responsibility for community social needs could be extensive. The reality and root causes of want would be revealed and would require realistic confrontation. Simple denial would not suffice. Community peer pressure would be brought to bear on those who advocated passivity or denied the existence of need. The breadth and depth of hunger, homelessness, the health needs of the elderly, and poverty among the young would be more starkly revealed, more demanding of response, and therefore less deniable.

For some, there would be a desire to avoid both reality and responsibility by escape to middle-class suburbs, upper-middle-class enclaves, or upper-class gated communities. To an unhealthy degree, this has already come to pass in America. Through their federal and State tax systems, however, those engaged in such flight would still be required to provide a reasonable share of their income to alleviate the misery that they have chosen to escape by abandoning their neighborhoods. *Over time*, however, through civic education, the elevation of civic virtue, more responsible political leadership at all levels, private sector leadership, community appeals to duty and responsibility, and concentration on the social dimensions and political implications of a society deeply divided between haves and have-nots, social, political, and even economic values can be transformed. If local political systems produce better results and more congenial community conditions, there will be less incentive for citizens to try to escape them.

To an even greater degree than the proposal for the restoration of genuine community-based education outlined above, shifting responsibility for the administration of social welfare back to ward republics would be a fundamental test of political values. If, as Jefferson believed and as republican theory supposes, the price of freedom is responsibility and the price of rights is duty, then the price should be paid. The twentieth century era of centralized responsibility for and therefore authority over a widening scope of social endeavors has unquestionably elevated the level of national economic and social progress. No effort is being made here to advocate a retreat from existing federally mandated rights or to call their wisdom or merit into question. Indeed, the question raised here is whether those commitments might be better met, under federal mandate, in the local community. Nor should any conclusion be drawn from the republican arguments contained herein that the government of the United States has exceeded its Constitutional authority in order to achieve much higher degrees of equality and social justice. There is neither explicit nor implicit suggestion in any argument herein for the restoration of any republican values that might require retreat by the national government from a commitment to full equality and justice for all. The argument here is quite the opposite.

However, in these two areas, public education and social welfare, centralized authority has not resulted in satisfactory education achievement or in substantial progress in combating systemic poverty. And the successes that have been realized have been achieved at the cost of increased corruption, diminished civic virtue and popular sovereignty, and the erosion of freedom as nondomination. They have been gained at the price of citizen participation, responsibility, and accountability.

There is no absolute guarantee that greater civic virtue would necessarily ensure reduced poverty or higher educational performance. But the restoration of civic virtue through citizen participation in the ward republic would counter apathy, irresponsibility, and social atomization. Theories of rights, justice, and equality generally insist on the uniform distribution of such goods. Few, if any, instances are available where such theories also seek to specify the nature or structure of the government, especially in a complex federal system, that must deliver them. Where the quality of the rights, the liberties, or the justice is secure, the structure of the government securing them becomes of only collateral consequence. Presuming that government to be itself right and just, its scale is irrelevant to the goods it secures for its citizens or that it empowers its citizens to secure for themselves. Scale is important to republican government because it directly affects the republican values of virtue, duty, responsibility, and participation. But there is no proof that a correlation exists between the scale of the government and the quality of the rights and liberties it guarantees. In other words, scale is central to republican values, such as duty, but not to democratic values, such as justice and equality of rights.

In commenting on civic virtue and the scale of government, one scholar reaches this conclusion: "Examining the rise and decline of local self-government in the United States demands that we come to terms with a legacy that yields a more active and better-equipped national state—the national resolve to tackle problems such as forced segregation at home and communism abroad—but one without adequate means of common deliberation and public judgment—the very practices that nurture a civic culture."[71]

Homeland Security and the Militia in the Authentic Republic

The Militia, Citizen-Soldiers, and the Republic

Following classic republican belief, Jefferson considered the first line of national defense to be the local militia. In his first annual address to Congress and the American people as president, he diminished the importance of a standing army, saying, "Nor is it conceived needful or safe that a standing army should be kept up in time of peace for that purpose.

Uncertain as we must ever be of the particular point in our circumference where an enemy may choose to invade us, the only force which can be ready at every point and competent to oppose them, is the body of neighboring citizens as formed into a militia."[72] Significant for republican thought is the phrase "needful and safe." If citizen-soldiers are properly trained and equipped, they will be as effectively motivated as a standing army to defend their homes and nation, while maintenance of a large standing army in a peacetime republic has consistently been considered a danger to republican liberties. Jefferson bracketed his presidential terms with the same thought in his eighth annual message to Congress and the country: "For a people who are free, and who mean to remain so, a well-organized and armed militia is their best security."[73] Freedom in the republican context is here meant to include freedom from the political influence to which a professional standing army might be put as well as freedom from foreign invaders.

A Permanent Standing Army within the Republic

What is to be done in a much more complex present age when war becomes domestic, when there is no longer the traditional and historic distinction between war, which involves states, and crime, which involves individuals? Where domestic terrorism is concerned, the role of the soldier and the role of the police officer begin to merge. The classic republican doctrine that holds that a standing army in a peacetime republic is a danger to republican liberty has been noted. Following this long tradition, U.S. statutory law restricts the deployment of national defense forces, short of an all-out attack by a hostile power, in the homeland. In post–Civil War America, the so-called Posse Comitatus Act (1878) forbade regular military forces from occupying or conducting operations on American soil: "From and after the passage of this act it shall not be lawful to employ any part of the Army of the United States, as a posse comitatus, or otherwise, for the purpose of executing the laws, except in such cases and under such circumstances as such employment of said force may be expressly authorized by the Constitution or by act of Congress."[74]

The Posse Comitatus Act resulted from the threatened use of military forces during and after the intense presidential contest of 1876: "But the principle behind the Act—excluding the military from the civilian

sphere—is as old as the United States."[75] Black's law dictionary defines
posse comitatus as "the power or force of the county. The entire population
of a county above the age of fifteen, which a sheriff may summon to his
assistance in certain cases, as to aid him in keeping the peace, in pursuing
and arresting felons, etc."[76] This concept was practiced in nineteenth-
century frontier America and has been enshrined in countless western
movies. Jefferson's own *Declaration of Independence* indicted George III
for using his armies "to compleat works of death, desolation and tyranny
... totally unworthy ... of a civilized nation," for keeping "among us, in
times of peace, Standing Armies without the Consent of our Legislature,"
for affecting "to render the Military independent of and superior to the
Civil Power," and for "quartering large bodies of armed troops among us:
For protecting them, by mock Trial, from Punishment for any Murders
which they should commit."[77] The Articles of Confederation, the Constitution, and the Bill of Rights all went to explicit lengths to restrict the
raising of armies, appointment of officers, appropriation of funds, and
quartering of soldiers. The principles underscoring the act were recon-
firmed as recently as 1994, when criminal penalties for its violation were
enacted: "Whoever, except in cases and under circumstances expressly
authorized by the Constitution or Act of Congress, willfully uses any part
of the Army or the Air Force as a posse comitatus or otherwise to execute
the laws shall be fined under this title or imprisoned not more than two
years."[78] Efforts were made as recently as 1995 to enact exceptions to the
Posse Comitatus Act when the Clinton administration, responding to the
bombing of the federal office building in Oklahoma City, proposed to use
federal military forces to investigate the use of weapons of mass destruction as part of the Counterterrorism Act of 1995. This proposal was with-
drawn in response to congressional resistance.[79]

Homeland Defense

But what of this new threat, the threat of nonstate actors, of terrorists,
using weapons of mass destruction against the homeland? What republican measures are at hand, short of martial law, to defend against this
threat? Here, the Jeffersonian republican insistence on citizen-soldiers,
the homeland militia, might prove its worth both in theory and in practice
more than two centuries later. In a curious twist of history, defense of

the U.S. homeland in the early twenty-first century may depend more on the National Guard, the Constitutionally recognized militia, than on the armed might of the superpower's permanent standing military forces. The threat to U.S. national security is increasingly emanating from terrorists with the potential to use weapons of mass destruction against domestic U.S. targets and the demonstrated willingness to do so. This threat has been documented by official U.S. sources and studies and was vividly demonstrated as a reality on September 11, 2001.[80] Those same sources have recommended that the first line of defense against such threats, the "first responders," be National Guard units specially trained and equipped to identify and isolate the threat, confine its affects, apprehend the perpetrators, maintain order, and respond to the needs of victims.

The current National Guard of the fifty States owes its existence to the Constitutional compromise among the founders over the nature of military forces in a republic. It was widely held that classic republican theory resisted a standing army in peacetime as a threat to republican government. Yet the Federalists, led by Alexander Hamilton, insisted on the need for a standing army and navy to protect U.S. international interests, largely commercial, and to defend against attacks on the homeland by aggressive foreign powers that maintained designs on the American continent. The Antifederalists, citing classic republican theory and following the English Country party's belief of a century earlier, saw the standing professional military as a tool for foreign adventure and for the suppression of political opposition at home.[81]

Thomas Jefferson stood firmly on the side of the classic republicans. His *Draft Constitution for Virginia*, dated June 1776, stated: "There shall be no standing army but in time of actual war." His consistent reliance on the homeland guard, the militia composed of citizen-soldiers, has been noted in his first and last annual presidential messages to Congress. As with those who saw standing armies in republics to be a danger, he had previously noted, in connection with the maintenance of order among Native Americans, the connection between a professional army and a national debt: "The least rag of Indian depredation will be an excuse to raise troops for those who love to have troops, and for those who think that a public debt is a good thing."[82]

That was then, and this is now. The United States of the twenty-first century is a world power with a plethora of international security agreements and commitments, such as the North Atlantic Treaty Organization, largely left over from the cold war. The United States is expected by most of its allies and most of its citizens to guarantee—with allies if possible, alone where necessary—the free flow of maritime commerce, the worldwide distribution of oil, the prevention of treachery and regional ambition, the suppression of terrorism, the protection of its diplomatic presence and of its citizens abroad, and a host of other tasks requiring considerable professional military capabilities. It is beyond the scope of this study to argue whether these are or are not necessary roles and missions for a modern superpower. Certainly nothing contained herein should be construed to suggest that the United States has entered an era without external threats or the potential for domestic economic or social unrest. No inevitable contradiction exists between a revival of democratic republicanism and America's role as the early twenty-first century's superpower. Consolidated authority in the national government is required for America to play its current stabilizing role in the world, as well as to ensure uniformity of the rights and opportunities of its citizens. But that consolidated power need not frustrate the republican values of civic virtue, duty, and citizen participation. The issue at hand, rather, is the most effective and Constitutionally sound method of defending the homeland against the new and real threat of terrorist attacks. Significantly, the new issue of homeland security underscores the opportunity for a restoration of the authentic republican ideal.

The homeland threat is both new and real. According to the National Intelligence Council report issued in late 2000 by the Central Intelligence Agency, "The risk will increase that organized criminal groups will traffic in nuclear, biological, and chemical weapons. The degree of risk depends on whether governments with WMD [weapons of mass destruction] can or will control such weapons and materials." Further:

> Chemical and biological threats to the United States will become more widespread; such capabilities are easier to develop, hide, and deploy than nuclear weapons. Some terrorists or insurgents will attempt to use such weapons against U.S. interests—against the United States itself, its forces or facilities overseas, or its allies. Moreover, the United States would be

affected by the use of such weapons anywhere in the world because Washington would be called upon to help contain the damage and to provide scientific expertise and economic assistance to deal with the effects. Such weapons could be delivered through a variety of means, including missiles, unmanned aerial vehicles, or covertly via land, air, and sea.[83]

The local militias under the control of the various States are the most constitutionally acceptable, the most compatible with the restoration of civic virtue in the township republic, and the most effective force to be used.

THE CONSTITUTIONAL AND LEGAL FRAMEWORK Conditions on the use of regular forces in domestic conflict are contained in the *Posse Comitatus* Act. Meanwhile, the Constitution clearly envisions the militias (hereafter called the "reserves" to include both the State militias, the modern National Guard, and, only under particular circumstances, the reserves of the standing forces) as the primary responders in domestic crisis. Congress is empowered "To provide [laws] for calling forth the Militia to execute the Laws of the Union, suppress Insurrections and repel Invasions" (Article I, sec. 8). The president is made commander in chief "of the Militia of the several States, when called into the actual Service of the United States . . ." (Article II, sec. 2). As creatures of the States, officers of the militia are appointed by the States, and the States are responsible for training the militia "according to the discipline prescribed by Congress." The Congress, however, is responsible for organizing, arming, disciplining, and governing such part of the militia "as may be employed in the Service of the United States" (Article I, sec. 8).

These provisions of the Constitution and a body of statutory law and judicial decisions make it clear that the reserve forces are to be the frontline response to domestic unrest or internal attack.

CIVIC DUTY AND THE MILITIA This being a discussion neither of military capabilities nor of Constitutional law, rather more attention must be given to the central argument that changing circumstances in the early twenty-first century may now make restoration of the authentic, local republic worthy of consideration. No public service more immediately and vividly demonstrates civic virtue than the citizen's defense of the homeland, both in prevention of treachery and in remediation of its consequences. The life of the defender is literally on the line and the lives of his family and neighbors equally so, as the Swiss, for example, have believed for centuries. Nothing more immediately engages the citizen's attention and energies than a threat to the well-being of family, community, and nation. This being so, it is reasonable to assume that a man or woman entrusted with the defense of the homeland—and more immediately of the local community—would also be more immediately interested in the total well-being of that community. If the responsibility for repelling or responding to attacks on the community sharpens the citizen's focus on community life, it is logical to assume that the citizen will be more attendant to the overall health of that community. Few activities bond citizens into communities more than participation in the common defense. Robert Putnam finds the same correlation between social cohesion and military cohesion: "Research has found that military units are more effective when bonds of solidarity and trust are high, and that communities with strong social networks and grassroots associations are better at confronting unexpected crises than communities that lack such civic resources. In all these instances our collective interest requires actions that violate our immediate self-interest and that assume our neighbors will act collectively, too."[84]

The distinction between republics and despotic regimes, according to Charles Taylor, rests in citizens in the former providing for themselves what are provided for them in the latter:

> A free, that is, participatory, regime calls on citizens to provide
> for themselves things that a despotism may provide for them.
> The foremost example of this is national defense. A despotic
> regime may raise money and hire mercenaries to fight for it; a
> republican regime will generally call on its citizens to fight for
> their own freedom. The causal links run in both directions. Citizen armies guarantee freedom because they are an obstacle to
> despotic takeover, just as large armies at the disposal of powerful generals invite a coup, as the agony of the Roman republic

illustrates. But at the same time, only people who live in and cherish a free regime will be motivated to fight for themselves. This relation between citizen armies and freedom was one of the main themes of Machiavelli's work.[85]

Searching for the common theme in writers from Machiavelli to Harrington to Milton, who espoused the self-governing republic as the best means of achieving both community fulfillment and individual liberty, Quentin Skinner finds it in Cicero's concept of *virtus*, the Italian *virtù*, or the English republican concept of civic virtue or public-spiritedness. The first specific capacity that civic virtue requires, according to Skinner, is "the need to defend our community against the threat of conquest and enslavement by external enemies. . . . no one else can be expected to care as much for our own life and liberty as we care ourselves. . . . It follows that a willingness to cultivate the martial virtues, and to place them at the service of our community, must be indispensable to the preservation of our own individual liberty as well as [to] the independence of our native land."[86] From the Renaissance republican tradition forward, indeed from the early Greek republics, an inseparable connection has existed between citizenship and homeland defense and, even more important, between the citizen-soldier and liberty itself.

EFFECTIVENESS The U.S. regular armed forces (hereafter referred to as the "regulars") maintain bases and training centers throughout the United States, although the number of such facilities has contracted since the end of the cold war. Both in theory and in practice, regular forces are available to the commander in chief (the president) for the security of the nation.

Given the legal restrictions on the deployment of regular forces domestically, however, the question foremost is a practical one. Can reserve forces respond effectively? Presuming attacks on one or more civilian targets—population centers, communications, transportation, or power systems, government facilities, and so forth—those most capable of responding quickly, in addition to local police forces, are the local reserve forces. The National Guard is made up of volunteers, often former members of the regular forces, who have normal civilian jobs, live in the community, and carry out training exercises throughout the year. As community citizens, they are available in unit sizes up to company strength or greater within a reasonable distance from any likely target. Properly trained and equipped for counterterrorist activities—isolation and apprehension of perpetrators, evacuation, damage limitation, triage, emergency medical treatment for victims, establishment of emergency communications systems, crowd and traffic control, and similar activities—these local reserve forces can be mustered and on the scene much more quickly, efficiently, and effectively than regular military units from distant bases.

To a substantial degree, National Guard units are already configured into the types of units most required to respond to a homeland attack and have at least some of the equipment necessary to do so. There are approximately twenty-seven hundred National Guard units spread (forward deployed) throughout every State of the United States. These units are capable of quick response in virtually every community of size in the country. If one or more targets are attacked with weapons of mass destruction, most immediately needed will be emergency medical systems, emergency communications systems, police and crowd management, transportation control systems, engineers, specialized capabilities for dealing with radiation, chemicals, or biological agents, and logistics. Among the fifty State National Guard components, there are currently fourteen medical companies, twenty-three signals and communications companies, twenty-six military police companies, twenty-eight transportation companies, seventy-one engineering companies, four supply companies, and thirty-two logistics support companies. Significantly, there are only three companies trained in chemical warfare. (Here, three companies equal a battalion.) There are, additionally, significant numbers of companies dedicated to infantry, mechanized infantry, armor/cavalry, and more conventional military missions.[87]

Critics argue that the National Guard is inadequate to undertake primary responsibility for homeland security. Throughout much of the twentieth century, when America was in conflict with both fascism and communism, the reserve forces, including the National Guard, were trained and equipped (not often well) as follow-up support for the regular military services in conventional warfighting roles and missions. In

NG also very often used like regular military for foreign purposes & not available to States.

NG are permanently under regular military. Command structure at the President's command. They are a select professional reserve - not a State militia. State Defense forces are permanently under Governor's authority.

World War II, Korea, and to some degree Vietnam, Guard units were mobilized wholesale. But the twenty-first century will look much different from the twentieth. There will be less necessity to prepare for major theater wars involving massive numbers of infantry and heavy mechanized divisions. Expeditionary forces will become much lighter, more agile, more quickly deployable, and less able to rely on the long time delays necessary to mobilize, train, lift, and deploy reserve forces (as occurred in the Persian Gulf war). Instead, reserve forces must assume the new primary responsibility for homeland defense. Given this mandate, and the resources and training it requires, the collective National Guard can reorganize itself into homeland defense units much more immediately dedicated to the missions required. Restoration of the National Guard, the Constitutional militia, to the mission for which it was originally intended—homeland security—will require the concurrence of the president as commander in chief and the Congress, the commitment of the Defense Department, and the dedication of the Guard itself to this mission.

Within thirty days of taking office, President George W. Bush made this statement in the context of a speech to the National Guard: "As threats to America change, your role will continue to change. The National Guard and Reservists will be more involved in homeland security, confronting acts of terror and the disorder our enemies may try to create. I welcome the important part you will play in protecting our nation and its people."[88] There seems little doubt that the current commander in chief is strongly inclined to make homeland security a primary duty of the National Guard.

Depending on the breadth, scope, and duration of an attack on the homeland, the reserves, the National Guard, can quickly be augmented, if necessary, by regular military units lifted in from other parts of the country. This may especially be the case where a catastrophic attack, such as the use of a nuclear device or persistent chemical or biological agents, is involved, where large-scale forces are required over time, or where widespread devastation or heavy civilian casualties require substantial, extended medical care. Any attack involving massive damage, multiple targets, or continuing devastation would necessarily engage virtually all of the resources of the nation. But the immediate and practical issue is the designation of the first responders. Logic, history, and practice argue for reserve forces locally deployed in the form of the National Guard and the reserve units of the regular forces.

AN OPERATIONAL PROPOSAL The militias were given privileged status under the Constitution for the principal purpose of defending the homeland. There was widespread acceptance among the founders, with the exception of Hamilton and a few others, of the republican belief that standing armies are a danger to republics in peacetime. The new century presents a clear and present threat to homeland security. The National Guard could be given the mission of preparing to respond to that threat, and by giving the citizen-soldier the mission of leading the homeland defense, a 2,500-year tradition of belief would be restored.

According to the recent recommendations of the U.S. Commission on National Security/Twenty-first Century:

> New actors, with deadly means both new and old, pose stark dangers to the security of our citizenry. The proliferation of missiles capable of reaching the United States is increasing, and the number of states and nonstate actors seeking capabilities proscribed by most conventions of warfare and the international community seem[s] to be accelerating. Almost all of the proliferants have interests inimical to those of the United States. The development of advanced weaponry is not limited to established states. Small groups are seeking lethal means that vary from chemical to nuclear devices to conventional explosives. Their goal is invariably mass casualties, mass effects and mass disruption. The relative low cost and greater availability of such disruptive technologies make them attractive tools for terrorists, fanatics and extremists. They can be easily produced and anonymously transported, and today's global economy makes even more people facile with the relevant technologies involved.[89]

To respond to this new security threat, the commission recommended the creation of a new homeland security agency, and after the September

2001 attacks, a Homeland Security Council was created.[90] Existing public safety, border security, and emergency preparedness organizations should be realigned into this single institutional entity, which has been given the authority, responsibility, and accountability for securing the homeland. However, all of these measures have to be carried out within a Constitutional and statutory framework that protects civil liberties, Constitutional government, and the privacy of individual citizens. The commission also recommended that the Department of Defense strengthen the existing Joint Forces Command/Joint Task Force–Civil Support and place it under the command of a senior National Guard general.

With specific reference to the lead role of the National Guard in twenty-first-century homeland security, the commission recommended:

> The National Guard, whose origins can be found in the states'
> militias authorized by the Constitution, should play a central
> role in the response component of a layered preventive defense
> strategy. It should designate homeland security as a primary
> mission and reorganize so that it is trained and equipped to
> undertake that mission. The National Guard should redistribute
> resources currently allocated to preparing for conventional wars
> overseas to provide greater support to civil authorities in pre-
> paring for and responding to disasters, especially weapons of
> mass destruction incidents within the United States.[91]

The commission's recommendations for carrying out this proposal include reequipping and retraining National Guard units for the homeland defense mission in contrast with conventional expeditionary war fighting. In practical terms, this means fewer infantry and mechanized units and more units prepared to prevent, respond to, and recover from a domestic attack. "Reorganized to recognize its historic and Constitutional mission of homeland security," the commission concluded, "the National Guard could provide an effective mobilization base with strong local ties and support." It is already forward deployed to achieve this mission and could

> participate in and initiate where necessary state, local, and regional
> planning for responding to a weapons of mass destruction incident;

train and help organize local first responders;

maintain an up-to-date inventory of military resources and equipment available in the area on short notice;

obtain emergency protective gear from the National Homeland Security Agency and maintain it in functioning condition; and

plan for rapid interstate support and reinforcement and develop an out-of-CONUS [continental United States] capability for international humanitarian assistance and disaster relief.[92]

Viewing the resumption of nonstate, almost tribal, warfare in the form of terrorism against civilian populations, current expert opinion in the United States concludes that citizen-soldiers in the form of the fifty state National Guards, billeted in their home communities (indeed, under most circumstances, billeted in their own homes), are the most immediately available first responders to an attack on the American homeland. After a century of conventional and potentially strategic warfare employing massive numbers of troops in nation-state conflicts, history has now taken a distinctly republican turn and made important once again the Jeffersonian militia, the citizen-soldier.

The Militia and the Future Ward Republic

On the relationship of the military to democracy, Tocqueville's perceptiveness is acute. In aristocratic armies, he wrote, the officer corps is the most conservative force in that officers retain a strict connection with civil society with the intent eventually to reenter it. By contrast, in democratic armies, "the private soldiers stand in this position, and from the same cause." Additionally, in democratic armies, private soldiers, in contrast to noncommissioned officers, "will carry with them into military life the strength or weakness of the manners of the nation; they will display a faithful reflection of the community." If the community is ignorant and weak, the private soldiers will permit themselves to be drawn into conflicts unnecessarily. But if the community from which these soldiers come is enlightened, "the community will itself keep them within the bounds of order."[93] Still cogent in the American democracy, these observations argue in favor of reliance on the citizen-soldiers of the National Guard as the first responders when the mission is defense of the homeland.

J. G. A. Pocock restates the classic republican argument reflected in both Tocqueville and the Posse Comitatus Act restricting the deployment of regular military forces within the homeland without specific congressional authorization:

> The Second Amendment of the Constitution, apparently drafted to reassure men's minds against the fact that the federal government would maintain something in the nature of a professional army, affirms the relation between a popular militia and popular freedom in language directly descended from that of Machiavelli, which remains a potent ritual utterance in the United States to this day. The new republic feared corruption by a professional army, even while—like England a century before—it saw no alternative to establishing one; and the implications of the rhetoric employed in this context were to be fully worked out in the debates and journalism of the first great conflict between American parties.[94]

The duties of citizenship and the arena in which to exercise civic virtue may vary due to circumstance. But in most democracies there are some constants, including the duty to pay taxes and the duty to defend the homeland. Some democracies add the duty to vote. In the democratic republic envisioned by Jefferson, to these would be added the duty to attend to the public affairs of the republic of the ward. Though he did not suggest coercive measures to guarantee performance of this duty, he suggests that, given the opportunity, most citizens would willingly choose to participate. To the followers of Jefferson, the Hamiltonian insistence on a permanent standing army was not only proof of Hamilton's ambition for an empire of commerce but also a signal that he believed the defense of the nation to be too important to be left to the citizen-soldier. By relieving the citizen of this crucial duty, Hamilton thereby diminished civic virtue and undermined the foundation of the republic. If the people at large could not be trusted to defend their families, their property, their community, and their nation, they could not be trusted with anything, including self-government. Indeed, believing as he did that "the advantage of character belongs to the wealthy" and that "the rich and well-born" should be given a "distinct, permanent share in the government," he could not but believe the country to be safer in the hands of a professional army procured by the powerful interests than in the hands of a militia of citizen-soldiers.

Such has it been in modern times—but at the cost of duty, responsibility, and civic virtue. The class divisions brought on by the selection of those who fought in the Vietnam War resonate in America even today. *Amen!* And, given the reliance on a large standing professional army, when the ranks of those willing to volunteer for service grow thin, as they are currently, the defensive capabilities of the nation suffer. A renewed republican spirit, inspired by a call for citizens to train and equip themselves for the defense of their communities, however, might both release the standing regular forces for legitimate expeditionary duties and reawaken a civic vitality among citizens at large.

Education, Welfare, Homeland Defense,
and the Republican Spirit

Within the context of the American federal system, the local republic is incapable of performing many functions of the nation-state. It cannot conduct relations with foreign nations, participate in global wars, negotiate treaties, or defend the homeland's borders. It cannot devise national economic policies, stabilize currencies, negotiate trade agreements, regulate interstate commerce, lower unemployment rates, regulate monetary policy, or stimulate an economy in recession. It cannot establish uniform national standards for the environment, health and safety, civil rights and workers' rights, education, or any of a plethora of national undertakings. Nor can it establish or maintain a federal judicial system. National governments, especially in the last century, have increasingly created uniform national mechanisms and standards for dealing with national issues.

However, within this national context, there is much for which the local republic can assume greater responsibility in the interest of reawakening the republican values of civic virtue and citizen participation. As argued here by way of illustration, those responsibilities may include greater community responsibility for public educational institutions, greater participation in the remediation of poverty, and greater citizen participation in defense of the community. Similar arguments could be raised for greater responsibility by the local republic for community health-care facilities, local transportation systems, local environmental protection and the protection of immediate natural resources, and a wide variety of other governmental activities increasingly assumed by the federal government during the twentieth century. The results, in Jefferson's terms, would be to relieve higher levels of government of administrative responsibilities. It would also enable a plethora of local service districts to be consolidated into a single, local governmental unit, thus increasing accountability and locating responsibility. More important, it would make "every citizen an acting member of the government, and in the offices nearest and most important to him, will attach him by his strongest feelings to the independence of his country, and its republican constitution." Thus, the whole pyramid of republics—federal, State, county, and ward—is cemented by this measure, "by giving every citizen, personally, a part in the administration of the public affairs."[95]

Why, it will be asked, would citizens unwilling even to vote in national elections be willing to invest the time required to participate in local self-governance? Robert Dahl makes this argument:

> It would be wrong . . . to deprecate the importance of developing governments more accessible and responsive to the politically weak simply because their initial participation would, foreseeably, be low. . . . if we were to abolish democracy wherever substantial segments of the population failed to use their opportunities to participate, there might not be much in the way of rule by the people left standing anywhere in the world. Neighborhoods help to civilize [the] megalopolis, and neighborhood governments will help to restore citizenship to the noncitizens of [the] megalopolis.[96]

There are many reasons, including a sense of empowerment, ready access to the levers of authority, and the simple sense of responsibility, why a citizen might wish to participate. Perhaps most important, however, is the desire for self-esteem and the esteem of others, the more positive side of the peer pressure coin. Tocqueville recognized this readily in the New England townships: "It is in the township, the center of the ordinary business of life, that the desire for esteem, the pursuit of substantial interests, and the taste of power and self-advertisement are concentrated; these passions, so often troublesome elements in society, take on a different character when exercised so close to home and, in a sense, within the family circle."[97] Natural ambition for power and position is tempered by the immediate opinion of neighbors. An ego can more easily become grander than it deserves at a distance from home.

The ward republic operates not only as the base for the federal republic but also as a therapeutic corrective to unwise or unjust national policies. The local republic, politically referred to as the *grassroots*, is the best forum for organizing citizen protest against unjust national policies, including, in more recent times, those regarding the civil rights of minorities, women's rights, the Vietnam War, environmental abuse, and the movement for minimum wages for workers. Citizens express opposition and can best organize themselves on a local not a national basis. The power of locally organized citizen opposition is ultimately felt when like-minded citizens across the nation join in protest and demonstrate their opposition to a government policy on a national basis. But in virtually every case, citizen opposition and protest begin at home and find their roots and strength in the local community. The most effective political movements in the past half century have grown from the bottom up and have not been imposed from the top down. The role of the local republic can be a positive one as well. Citizens currently isolated from the levers of power can, as active participants in their local governments, be fountains of new ideas, policies, and initiatives. At their best, local republics can become fountains of political energy and creative experimentation in ways that the cumbersome national bureaucracy never can. As James Q. Wilson writes: "People with a shared sense of community will be more likely, I conjecture, to have a shared sense of efficacy. People who feel they can influence their neighbors will be more likely to feel they can influence distant officials, if for no other reason than their ability to mobilize neighbors to act upon officials." He continues: "Small-scale politics teaches something else—the importance of direct knowledge, firsthand experience, long-term commitments, and communal preservation. Localistic politics is rarely about abstractions, the knowledge that informs it is not controlled by the media, and the participants must live with the consequences. It is about the quality of local schools, the use of local land, and the protection of familial interests."[98]

As he interpreted it, republicanism came to underlie Thomas Jefferson's own liberalism: "All men are created equal, . . . they are endowed by their Creator with certain inalienable rights, . . . among these are Life, Liberty, and the Pursuit of Happiness" and "To secure these Rights, Governments are instituted among Men, deriving their just Powers from the Consent of the Governed."[99] The government best suited to secure these rights is republican government, for it is dependent upon those citizens whose rights are at stake to participate in that government as immediately and directly as possible. And the most direct participation possible is in the elementary republic, the republic of the ward. Unlike comprehensive theories of liberalism, Jefferson's republican ideal presupposed no comprehensive scheme of political morality beyond the values assumed in civic virtue, citizen duty, and citizen participation. His theory of government placed ultimate trust in the common sense and good judgment of a democratic people. Were the people themselves to betray that trust, it would be at the sacrifice of their own rights and liberties.

The Jeffersonian democratic republic is an ideal, but that may or may not mean it is also utopian. Quentin Skinner has rightly responded to the following argument: "That an equal right to participate in government is indispensable to the maintenance of civil liberty is so utopian as to make it irrelevant to the political world in which we live." He does so by observing:

> I have never understood why the charge of utopianism is necessarily thought to be an objection to a theory of politics. One legitimate aspiration of moral and political theory is surely to show us what lines of action we are committed to undertaking by the values we profess to accept. It may well be massively inconvenient to suggest that, if we truly value individual freedom, this commits us to establishing political equality as a substantive ideal. If this is true, however, what this insight offers us is not a critique of our principles as unduly demanding in practice; rather it offers us a critique of our practice as insufficiently attentive to our principles.[100]

Utopia is defined as "an imaginary or hypothetical place or state of things considered to be perfect; a condition of ideal (esp. social) perfection," and *utopianism* is defined as "advocating or constituting an ideally perfect state; impossibly ideal, visionary, idealistic."[101] This chapter has shown how the Jeffersonian notion of the ward republic might function in the modern, complex, federal nation-state. It is nowhere suggested that this ideal is either perfectionist or beyond reach in practice.[102] On the contrary, it is discussed here because it may be a practical, even if also idealistic, response to a new set of economic, social, and political realities, among which are the globalization of capital and markets, the information-driven economic revolution, fragmentation of the political authority of the nation-state, and the rise of terrorism as a new, though primitive, kind of warfare. Two sets of arguments have been put forward. First, the restoration of the republican values of citizen responsibility, duty, and participation is required to offset the corruption of democratic political systems, the erosion of popular sovereignty, the loss of civic virtue, and the subtle domination of liberty by special interests. Second, revitalization of authentic republicanism is a possible means of governing in a new world, which is characterized by the erosion of national authority and the weakening of national sovereignty.

The age of Enlightenment enshrined the analytic method, scientific thought, and human reason over medieval superstition and prejudice. Reason in turn elevated the rights of individuals by relieving humanity, in the minds of some, of the baggage of theological and metaphysical systems of belief. As a result, however, "In a liberal and pluralistic culture which is devoid of either a theological or metaphysical view about the definitive nature and work of human beings the attempt to ground political theory in a doctrine about human nature is bound to fail and the common good relating to this definitive work of man to be secured by the state is an illusion."[103]

There are further consequences for the effort to devise a political theory in an age characterized by individual autonomy, an autonomy only a short step away from alienation:

> Modernity has undermined both the practical moral agreements about the purposes of individuals which may have characterized some earlier societies and made the claim for a shared human essence appear plausible, and equally philosophical speculation and the growth of scientific secularism have undermined the intellectual assumptions on which such theories of the human

essence are based. . . . With the collapse of religious or even mythological bases of political legitimacy, it has been part of the quest of political philosophy to provide universal reasons for political legitimacy and this perhaps comes out most clearly in doctrines about human rights which are thought to apply to all persons everywhere.[104]

This search for political legitimacy through a liberal theory premised on rights, both universal and individual, has, however, been based upon "a principled but very insubstantial theory of the self."[105]

As pointed out by Raymond Plant, a culminating trend in the late Enlightenment era was the introduction of psychoanalytic theory to social thought. "This link between political theory and a psychoanalytic theory of human nature has led to a change in the language of political theory away from talk of good, bad, right, wrong, that is to say moral categories, towards a set of quasi-medical categories such as drives, impulses, sanity, neurosis and the pathologies of political life."[106] Plant notes Erich Fromm's view that liberal capitalist societies especially deny the individual a community in which basic desires and instincts can be rooted: "Sanity and mental health depend upon the satisfaction of those needs and passions which are specifically human and which stem from the conditions of the human situation: the need for a framework of transcendence, rootedness, the need for a sense of identity, and the need for a frame of orientation and devotion." A sane society, argues Fromm, is "one which puts a man to operate within manageable and observable dimensions and to be an active participant in the life of society as well as in his own life."[107] This language of modern psychology, especially its latter phrase, might have come directly from Jefferson.

In this, as in many other ways, the language of Jefferson's republican theories has modern currency. For example, his views on generational accountability are existential in the sense that they require that each generation cope with the particular realities of its own age through new laws and constitutions. The previous generation's laws and constitution are to be called into question and examined for their applicability to the inevitability of changing conditions and circumstances. Jefferson's radical notion presupposes no superior *a priori* human laws and structures. Instead, change is seen as an eternal truth and premise. Yet, each generation is morally bound to obey nature's laws and to operate within the rule of reason. The guiding political frame of reference and foundation of legitimacy is to be found in the community republic governed by free and virtuous citizens.

Jefferson's political philosophy, though rooted in classical, especially Aristotelian and Roman, language and values, foresaw an age in which the boundary between human individualism and alienation and isolation might become thin. He balanced human reason with human virtue and individual rights with individual responsibilities and duties. Here, he follows the Aristotelian mean that incorporates both reason and virtue. "The function of man," said Aristotle, "is a certain form of life, namely an activity of the soul exercised in combination with a rational principle or reasonable ground of action. The function of a good man is to exert such activity well. . . . If these assumptions are granted, we conclude that the good for man is an activity of soul in accordance with goodness."[108] As political animals, humans cannot exercise their virtue, their goodness, in isolation or as autonomous beings. The *polis*, or state, has a greater purpose than merely as the guarantor of each individual's rights against all others. The *polis* is not merely "an association for residence on a common site, or for the sake of preventing mutual injustice and easing exchange." Instead, "a *polis* is an association of households and clans in a good life, for the sake of attaining a perfect and self-sufficing existence."[109]

Thus, Jeffersonian republicanism represents more than utopian perfectionism or a revisiting of a political road not taken at America's founding. It is put forward as a response to two realities: the separation of reason from virtue and rights from duties, which have resulted in the alienated citizen, and the emergence of an era in which governance is beginning to escape even national boundaries and thus the grasp of national citizens. Jefferson favored the *res publica* because he suspected the state. Its moral fiber was highly dependent on the quality of the representatives elected by the people to manage it. If those representatives themselves lacked virtue, then the state would as well. Indeed, virtue could survive intact only in the authentic republic of the wards. Madison's system of checks and balances, designed to create an equilibrium of power and to prevent any branch from falling sway to unruly democracy, has not prevented the modern state from concentrating economic, political, and military power within itself.

Modern republican theorists accept Jefferson's reasoning in altered forms. Traditional republicans, claims Philip Pettit, argue that

> a state would not itself dominate its citizens—and could provide a unique protection against domination based on the private power of internal or external enemies—provided that it was able to seek only ends, and employ only means, that derived from the public good, the common weal, the *res publica*. In effect their view was that in order to satisfy the requirements of freedom as non-domination the state had to be constrained so far as possible to track the common interests—the common, recognizable interests, as they were assumed to be— of its citizens.[110]

Pettit defines common interests, in contrast with special interests, as those goods—such as domestic peace and external defense—that are best provided for everyone collectively in their pursuit of their cooperative enterprise.

For Pettit, freedom as nondomination is a positive not a negative value. It is preferable over a conservative theory of freedom as noninterference in that the former requires a polity actively engaging the lives of its citizens, whereas the latter restricts the lawmaking activity of the polity as a coercive venture. The former view enables republicanism, that is, a vital state; the latter reduces the state to the role of night watchman. But this view requires the polity to promote effective, not just formal, freedom, that is, it should seek to remove factors that condition freedom: "Not only should the republic seek to remove domination from people's lives—not only should it try to reduce such compromises of people's freedom—it should also seek to increase the range and ease with which people enjoy undominated choice. It should seek to reduce the influence of factors like handicap and poverty and ignorance that condition people's freedom as non-domination, even if they don't actually compromise it. Otherwise put, it should promote people's *effective* freedom as non-domination, not just their *formal* freedom as non-domination."[111]

It has been argued here that in some areas of social and political endeavor, such as public education and the remediation of poverty, the local republic of dedicated citizens may, under national guidelines and with national resources, better reduce the factors of domination, including handicap, poverty, and ignorance, than the cumbersome and remote nation-state. And it may do so with the added gain of restored civic virtue and citizen participation. With citizen responsibility comes citizen accountability. In a complex system of government, such as today's federal system in America, no one person or no single interest bears responsibility for the function of the whole. Thus, each participant in public policy, whether the president, members of Congress, members of the cabinet, civil servants, or an interest group from the private sector, can say, "I only did what the system required me to do to protect my interest." If the net result of this atomization of responsibility is corruption, or a system that does not protect the common good, no one is then responsible. There is no accountability.

In the authentic republic, however, the citizens assume responsibility for the common good, including the quality of local public education, the care of the dependent poor and the employment of the able poor, and the defense of their own communities against attack. The proper functioning of the local republics does not require or produce a weakening of the national republic; indeed, it strengthens it. The greater republic is strengthened by substantially increased citizen participation in and responsibility for public life in the local community.

Robert Dahl understands the principal beneficiary of the republic of the neighborhood: "To the middle-class resident of a suburb or a smaller city, neighborhood government might seem to offer little beyond what he already has. But among those who now have little influence, it could dramatically increase opportunities to participate in decisions."[112] Those today who have little influence have the most at stake in the restoration of the true republic.

THOMAS JEFFERSON proposed an Aristotelian theory of the republic based upon civic virtue exercised in the ward or local community. He believed that men, "endowed by their Creator with certain unalienable Rights," could best protect those rights "by making every citizen an acting member of the government" in a "pure republic, . . . a state of society in which every member . . . has an equal right of participation, personally in the direction of the affairs of society." Rights were inextricably linked with—and were best protected by—duties. Liberty could not be separated from responsibility, nor freedom from obligation.

Conclusion

Jefferson reconciled Aristotle to Locke with little conscious effort. Humans were political animals living in a civil society with duties and responsibilities to participate in the public life of that society but also possessing individual rights endowed by the Creator. Those rights were best protected by republican democracy or democratic republicanism, that is, in a forum providing the opportunity to be a participant in government and that most effectively at the local level. Not all decisions affecting the commonwealth could be made locally. For those matters affecting a wider scale than the local republic, representative government within a federative framework was available. But representative government became less republican the further from direct citizen control it became.

Can there be a system of government, Jefferson asked, that combines representative democracy with assembly democracy? He found the answer in the ward or authentic republic, which exchanged duty for empowerment. The novel eighteenth-century principle of representation permitted democracy on a large scale, but at the cost of republican values. The concept of the local republic was meant to restore the balance between the political economy of representation and delegation, which involves selecting a representative to deliberate on national issues, and the duty of the individual citizen to participate in the public life of the society on the issues of immediate local importance.

On the issue of scale, Jefferson found support from a variety of thinkers who spanned the ages. Aristotle distinguished between the best regimes—those of tiny size and limited franchise, "established according to our prayers" for good fortune—and otherwise acceptable political communities that do not meet this ideal:

> Aristotle does not deny that larger poleis such as Athens are political communities, nor does he say that it is impossible for a very large city, one more the size of the nations of Asia and Northern Europe, to form a political community. He merely says that "it is not easy" for so large a group "to be ruled in a political way." . . . Modern political communities cannot, given their size, meet the requirements of Aristotle's conception of either the best regime or extreme democracy. But they can develop within them the distinctive sense of political justice that Aristotle associates with political community.[1]

Jefferson drew further from Montesquieu: "It is in the nature of a republic to have only a small territory; otherwise, it can scarcely continue to exist,"[2] and from Rousseau:

> If I had to choose my place of birth, I should have chosen a society of a size confined to the range of human faculties, that is to say to the possibilities of being well governed, and where, everyone being equal to his task, no one would have been com-

pelled to commit to others the functions with which he was himself entrusted: a State where, since all individuals know one another, neither the shady strategems of vice nor the modesty of virtue could have escaped the Public's gaze and judgment, and where this gentle habit of seeing and knowing one another would have made the love of one's Fatherland a love of the Citizens rather than of the soil.[3]

And, to a lesser degree, from Locke:

Men united into Societies, that they may have the united strength of the whole Society to secure and defend their Properties, and may have *standing Rules* to bound it, by which every one may know what is his. To this end it is that Men give up all their Natural Power to the Society which they enter into, and the Community puts the Legislative Power into such hands as they think fit, with this trust, that they shall be govern'd by *declared Laws*, or else their Peace, Quiet, and Property will still be at the same uncertainty, as it was in the state of Nature.[4]

Yet, Jefferson departed from Locke and, to a lesser degree, from Rousseau on the role of the state. For Locke, the citizen is dependent on his trust relationship with the state. For Rousseau, citizens contract with each other to establish governments to promote and protect their common interests. Neither a trust nor a contractual relationship was, for Jefferson, sufficient to replace the immediate participation of the individual citizen in the active life of the local republic. Rights and liberties required protection from a government in which the citizen does not or cannot participate. But the republican form of government with its emphasis on citizen virtue, exercised through participation, duty, and obligation to the society, offered the best—perhaps the only—hope of securing those unalienable rights with which individuals are endowed by their Creator.

Jefferson's construct of the virtuous republic was opposed to and supplanted by the Hamiltonian commercial republic: "The virtuous republic modeled on antiquity relied above all on the cultivation of citizenship and positive liberty and demanded civic education, civic participation, and sufficient civic activism to guarantee a responsible electorate. The new commercial republic, on the other hand, called for a limited state whose primary function was to protect the market and personal and private liberty, and for individuals whose primary motives were economic—the good citizen as the productive capitalist or the efficient worker—and who held the state and the democratic majority in suspicion."[5] Two centuries of American history—spanning continental expansion, civil war, economic turmoil, and eventual world leadership—have confirmed the commercial republican model, underwritten by a liberal political philosophy of individual rights, though at the expense of the Aristotelian mean established on virtue: "Since this liberalism asserts the priority of fair procedures over particular ends, the public life it informs might be called the procedural republic."[6] The rights-based public philosophy of the procedural republic provided a framework for economic expansion and eventual global democratic championship. Moreover, in the second half of the twentieth century, it provided the basis for the expansion of civil and economic rights across racial and gender lines, and on that plane it has achieved great success. But the procedural republic spread its rights-based net largely absent an emphasis on the substantive republican values of duty and participation.

Now, however, economic, social, and political revolutions threaten to expose the procedural republic as hollow, fragile, and possibly incapable of sustaining the rights it espouses: "The procedural republic cannot secure the liberty it promises, because it cannot sustain the kind of political community and civic engagement that liberty requires."[7] But what if liberty does not require engagement? What if individual autonomy, for those who have it, and the promise of individual autonomy, for those who do not, are of greater value than engagement? Mediocre public schools can be replaced by higher-performance private schools. Endemic social misery can be abandoned in the inner city as we move to suburban precincts. Chronic crime can be escaped by seeking sanctuary in the gated community. These and other social ills all lend themselves to the same solution for the atomized rights-valuing citizen. That solution is social, political, and economic insularity acquired through wealth. Sufficient wealth can guarantee a republic featuring superior education, the elimination of poverty, and guaranteed personal security. Such republics are, in fact, being created in suburban and semirural areas near America's great cities. Consideration might be given as to whether they are also democratic republics. In any case, inhabitants of the insular republics increasingly seek relief from the burdens of financing public schools other than their own private or semipublic ones. They strongly support measures to reduce social relief programs.[8] And they maintain their own private police forces. Contrary to Jefferson, who saw the ward republics as the foundation of the national republic, the inhabitants of the insular republics see themselves as distinct and apart from the national republic and its duties and burdens. The national republic is primarily meant to protect their right to create and inhabit secure republics separate from the greater society.[9]

The national republic, the Hamiltonian federal or commercial republic, has sustained its claim on citizen loyalty through two centuries of collective endeavor, through westward expansion and national destiny, through civil war and assertion of the union, through social and economic stabilization, and through global combat against fascism and communism. It has done so primarily by offering individual economic opportunity and the personal freedom to pursue it. New realities, however, are challenging this claim:

> National sovereignty is eroded from above by the mobility of capital, goods, and information across national boundaries, the integration of world financial markets, the transnational character of industrial production. At the same time, national sovereignty is challenged from below by the resurgent aspirations of subnational groups for autonomy and self-rule. As their effective sovereignty fades, nations gradually lose their hold on the allegiance of their citizens. Beset by the integrating tendencies of the global economy and the fragmenting tendencies of group identities, nation-states are increasingly unable to link identity and self-rule. Even the most powerful states cannot escape the imperative of the global economy.[10]

If this view proves correct, as I argue here, the insular republics of wealth and class will become even further isolated from the national community. This result then takes the political form of a new kind of feudalism rather than that of traditional republicanism. This neofeudalism features isolated walled cities, which draw from the urban areas (rather than from the neighboring peasant farms) the work force required to serve its needs and maintain its lifestyle. But for its fragmented political purposes, the neofeudal enclave relies upon itself for governance and the maintenance of its autonomy and increasingly does not concern itself with the cares of the greater community or nation.

The most ardent republican founders of the new nation feared the classic threats to republican government: corruption, interest, the loss of popular sovereignty, and the sacrifice of the rights of self-government. These led, inevitably they believed, to the restoration of autocratic government and the sacrifice of freedom. Early twenty-first-century Americans cannot be said to be less free as individuals, but they do not necessarily identify their individual interests with those of the national state. Through the extravagant costs of political campaigns, candidates and parties have dramatically increased their reliance on special interests for financial support. Successful candidates and parties assume the responsibilities of public office already beholden to those who have provided that financial largesse. Citizens know that a direct correlation exists between specific industries and interest groups and the amount of money contributed to members of specific congressional committees which have jurisdiction over matters of importance to those interests and industries. Successful presidential candidates reward their most important contributors with privileged access to the corridors of power.

This sophisticated form of corruption has been sanctioned by campaign contribution laws and is therefore not illegal. But it is massively corrosive to public trust. It is virtually impossible to prove that specific contributions lead to specific favorable decisions, but it can be established beyond question that political contributions buy access. Those who contribute to campaigns, parties, presidential libraries, and a wide variety of political causes are those who gain access to the executive and legislative branches of government at all levels. This access is not available to ordinary citizens and thus inevitably disadvantages them in the contest for influence on public policy decisionmaking. From the perspective of the ancient republicans, corruption need not sink to the level of outright bribery. Corruption consists in placing narrow or special interests above the common good and the commonweal. Quentin Skinner provided a definition of *corruption*, a term habitually used by republican theorists, as "our natural tendency to ignore the claims of our community as soon as they seem to conflict with the pursuit of our own immediate advantage."[11] Only the most cynical or the most foolish would argue today that this form of corruption has not permeated national and state governments in America. And only the most cynical and foolish argue that this process, acknowledged at the founding by the Hamiltonian faction as the inevitable outcome of governance in the commercial republic, produces out of the clash of interest against interest decisions for the national good. "Nowhere is the need to restore connectedness, trust, and civic engagement clearer than in the now often empty public forums of our democracy," Robert Putnam writes.[12]

Charles Taylor arrives at the same conclusion concerning the hollowing out of the American republic:

> America has moved in the last century more and more toward a definition of its public life based on Model A [focused on individual rights and equal treatment]. It has become a less participatory and more procedural republic. Judicial retrieval has become more important; at the same time, participation in elections seems to be declining. Meanwhile, political-action committees and lobbyists threaten to increase the leverage of single-issue politics. These are exactly the developments that republicans deplore, seeing in them a decline in civic spirit and ultimately a danger for a free society.[13]

There is, however, a different ideal and a different model never seriously considered during the founding era, one that does not require any fundamental Constitutional rearrangement. Even assuming a revival of democratic republicanism, the national government remains the powerful, unifying national force. This different model, however, opens up the base of the republican pyramid to local citizen involvement in the creative and innovative administration of national undertakings best carried out by those actively concerned with the local common good. Thereby, the national community is strengthened rather than weakened, and neorepublicanism becomes a means of enhancing citizenship and national unity.

This alternative vision is based upon the Jefferson ideal. Isolated, neofeudal communities of affluence might be increasingly augmented and surrounded by authentic republics of the ward, which seek, by their exercise of civic engagement (in contrast with individualism), both to secure rights and liberties and to weave together a national community increasingly under pressures of fragmentation and challenges to its legitimacy and sovereignty. The revival of the radical republican ideal in the form of the authentic republic of the ward would, at the very least, leaven the influence of interests in national politics. The more dispersed government is, the more it becomes self-government, the more difficult it is for powerful, concentrated private interests to permeate the council halls of a multitude of dispersed communities. Jefferson's radical republicanism, linking people's unalienable rights to their exercise of civic virtue, suggests a path circumventing and surmounting the procedural and commercial republic. Restoration of citizen duty and engagement and participation in the authentic republic of the community are the means of strengthening the weave of a national fabric under stress from new global and old local forces. This same vision, Robert Dahl believes, can and must be carried over even to modern, urbanized America:

> I do not see how we can do what needs to be done until an integral part of our culture and habits of thought is a vision of the potentiality of the city as a major civilizing force; a unit of human proportions in a world grown giant, demonic, incomprehensible; an optimal site for democratic life; an association in which citizens can learn that collective benefits from cooperation and peaceful conflict are so great that rational self-interest must act as a restraint on self-destructive egoism; an opportunity to engage in creating a new kind of community the shape of which no expert can foresee and to which every citizen can contribute.[14]

According to Putnam: "Government authority should be decentralized as far as possible to bring decisions to smaller, local jurisdictions, while recognizing and offsetting the potential negative effect of that decentralization on equality and redistribution. Indeed, liberals alert to the benefits of social capital should be readier to transfer governmental authority downward in exactly the same measure that compassionate conservatives should be readier to transfer resources from have to have-not communities."[15]

There is a logic and a strategy to the Jefferson republican ideal. Republican government is dependent upon civic virtue. Civic virtue is best exercised through citizen participation in the functions of government.

As a practical matter, citizens cannot participate directly in the workings of the remote State government or the even more remote national government. There they must rely on elected representatives, but at the cost of diminishing the purity of the republican ideal. Since individual rights are best protected by individual participation in the affairs of government, the responsibility of the ward republic and citizen participation in it grows even greater. Thus, for the preservation of a republic of citizens and a democracy of rights, the venue for direct citizen involvement must be the community republic. Upon it, all else is based. In the straightforward formulation of Skinner, "Performance of our public duties is indispensable to the maintenance of our own liberty."[16]

Hannah Arendt uniquely notes the failure of the Constitution to create a "public space" for the local republic and citizen participation. It is interesting, but futile, to speculate on whether Jefferson, had he been present for the Constitutional debates, might have pressed for formal Constitutional recognition of the ward republics as a separate and distinct unit of government. It is far from clear that he would have succeeded had he tried. However, she notes with approval Jefferson's fear of "an elective despotism" and his instinctive reliance on the people. From Paris, prior to the Constitutional debates, he reflected on the corruption of European governments and the division of their nations between "wolves and sheep." "Cherish therefore the spirit of the people," he wrote to Edward Carrington, "and keep alive their attention. . . . If once they become inattentive to the public affairs, you & I, the Congress & Assemblies, judges & governors shall all become wolves."[17] The spirit of the people, as measured by their attention to and participation in public affairs has declined measurably in the era of individualism, obsession with rights (especially at the expense of or without acknowledgment of duties), atomization, loss of national purpose, and government by interests. It is not too great a reach to conclude, therefore, that Jefferson's feared characterization of "Congress & Assemblies, judges & governors" has also come true.

Republican theory, particularly as interpreted by Jefferson for the evolving federal construct, offers an alternative vision of the polis, indeed, offers restoration of the very nature and meaning of the polis. According to this alternative, in Skinner's words, it is "open to us to meditate on the potential relevance of a theory which tells us that, if we wish to maximize our own individual liberty, we must cease to put our trust in princes, and instead take charge of the public arena ourselves."[18] Modern political thought will object to the restoration of republicanism in the Jeffersonian form as idealistic in the extreme, utopian, and nostalgic. Clearly, governance in a complex, increasingly international, and technological age will require large, powerful, and sophisticated national and international public agencies. However, the republican ideal proposed here is avowedly not utopian, unrealistic, or nostalgic. In many ways, it fits the current age even better than it fit the age of national founding and national unification. It is a response to the capture of the national interest by special interests. It is a means of encouraging greater accountability by elected representatives. It is a political framework in which citizens can achieve common objectives and goals by means tailored to the particular needs and natures of their local communities. And it is a structure in which the linkage between rights and duties, liberties and responsibilities, is restored: "The reason for wishing to bring the republican vision of politics back into view is not that it tells us how to construct a genuine democracy, one in which government is for the people as a result of being by the people. That is for us to work out. It is simply because it conveys a warning which, while it may be unduly pessimistic, we can hardly afford to ignore: that unless we place our duties before our rights, we must expect to find our rights themselves undermined."[19]

The vision of the American ward republic, a republican "city on a hill," was not realized in the Constitution. Its author was not present to press for an acknowledged public space for the pure republic, the democratic self-governing community uniquely combining the individual liberty only achieved through the power of self-government with the civic duty known from antiquity as the guarantor of the republican commonwealth. The grand commercial republic as the guarantor of procedural rights has largely succeeded in its mission and its promise but at the cost of the substitution of the autonomy of the individual for the common good and at the price of the virtue of participation. Whether, in a revolutionary age, that cost and price still represent a political bargain—particularly given the available alternative—remains to be seen.

Jeffersonian republicanism is not a threat to rights, does not erode the authority of the national republic, is not a formula for chaos, is compatible with justice, and does not threaten national purpose. Instead, restoration of this ideal is a means for securing individual rights, is potentially a way to reawaken a sense of economic justice at the community level, and is a forum for strengthening national purpose.

The author of the *Declaration of Independence*, who recognized at the outset the unalienable rights of individuals, believed the best, perhaps the only, way of securing those rights was through the exercise of responsibility for self-governance in the authentic republic of the ward: "Divide the counties into wards of such size as that every citizen can attend, when called on, and act in person. Ascribe to them the government of their wards in all things relating to themselves exclusively . . . and by making every citizen an acting member of the government, and in the offices nearest and most interesting to him, [it] will attach him by his strongest feelings to the independence of his country, and its republican constitution."[20]

1. Quentin Skinner, "The Republican Ideal of Political Liberty," in *Machiavelli and Republicanism*, ed. Gisela Bock, Quentin Skinner, and Maurizio Viroli (Cambridge, 1990), 309.

2. Michael Kammen, *People of Paradox: An Inquiry Concerning the Origins of American Civilization* (New York, 1972), 215–16.

3. "New World Coming," first report of the U.S. Commission on National Security/ Twenty-first Century, September 15, 1999, Washington, D.C.

4. Posse Comitatus Act, 20 Stat. L., 145, June 18, 1878.

5. Skinner, "The Republican Ideal of Political Liberty," 303.

6. In his writings on the subject, Jefferson referred to the local republic as the "ward republic," the "pure republic," or occasionally the "elementary republic." All meant the community republic in which all voting citizens could participate. He used the phrase *ward republic* most frequently. In early twentieth-century America, ward politics got a bad name. In many big cities, corruption at the ward level was endemic, especially among new immigrants and the poor, who could be manipulated by ward bosses to trade their votes for coal in winter, ice in summer, shelter, help with the police, jobs, and any of a number of services. Because many students of American politics are familiar with this history, I have often chosen to use phrases such as the *authentic republic* or the *true republic* to denote Jefferson's ideal of the local republic.

7. Garrett Ward Sheldon, *The Political Philosophy of Thomas Jefferson* (Baltimore, Md., 1991), 146–47.

8. Herbert Croly, *The Promise of American Life* (Indianapolis, Ind., 1909), 272–75.

9. Letter to James Madison, December 20, 1787, in Merrill D. Peterson, ed., *Thomas Jefferson: Writings* (New York, 1984), 914–18.

10. Though not central to this study, it might further be pointed out that the States' rights argument against federal domination was, throughout the second half of the nineteenth and the first half of the twentieth centuries, so identified with the cause of racial segregation that it rendered any republican argument for local empowerment suspect. Additionally, the New Deal era sealed the role of the national government as the provider of both a ladder up for and a safety net under the middle classes and as a regulator of capitalism's excesses. Even the most ardent of the twentieth-century Antifederalists came to embrace Social Security and all that it symbolized. Nothing in this study is meant to support a reversal of the progressive achievements of the federal government during the twentieth century.

11. These scholars include, for example, Garrett Ward Sheldon and Richard K. Matthews.

12. Here, I am referring to Locke's sense of "the People are at Liberty to provide for themselves by erecting a new Legislative."

Chapter 1

1. Ian Clark, *Globalization and Fragmentation: International Relations in the Twentieth Century* (Oxford, 1997), 11.

2. Ibid., 21.

3. Ibid., 202.

4. Jeffrey Garten (dean of the Yale School of Management), "Mega-Mergers, Mega-Influence," *New York Times*, October 26, 1999.

5. Robert A. Dahl, *On Democracy* (New Haven, Conn., 1998), 115.

6. "Global Trends 2015: A Dialogue about the Future with Nongovernment Experts," prepared under the direction of the National In-

telligence Council and approved for publication by the National Foreign Intelligence Board under the authority of the director of Central Intelligence, December 2000, Washington, D.C., 24.

7. Martin van Creveld, *The Rise and Decline of the State* (Cambridge, 1999), 389, citing "Change and Development in the International Economy," C. Mulhearn, *Global Politics*, 160–65.

8. "Global Trends 2015," 24.

9. Garten, "Mega-Mergers, Mega-Influence." Neither the ancient Greeks nor the Romans knew of the "nation-state." States—or the permanent bureaucracies by which peoples are governed—were cities in early Greece and republican Rome. Beyond that, the world knew empires, principalities, feudal states, kingdoms, theocracies, and a panoply of political constructs usually organized around a single powerful figure. Then, sometime between that brilliant Florentine father of modern political thought, Niccolo Machiavelli, and the dour English determinist Thomas Hobbes, the idea of a nation-state was born, and it has been the principal political building block of the modern world since the Peace of Westphalia in 1648. So accustomed are policymakers to thinking of the world as a collection of nation-states—many as artificial as Yugoslavia and as arbitrary as colonial powers could make them—that they cannot envision a world organized around any other political construct.

10. "Global Trends 2015," 12. The report further concludes: "States with competent governance, including the United States, will adapt government structures to a dramatically changed global environment—making them better able to engage with a more interconnected world. . . . Shaping the complex, fast-moving world of 2015 will require reshaping traditional government structures."

11. Garten, "Mega-Mergers, Mega-Influence."

12. "Global Trends 2015," 7.

13. Clark, *Globalization and Fragmentation*, 194.

14. "A Single Market in Crime," *The Economist*, October 16, 1999, 23–28.

15. van Creveld, *Rise and Decline*, 396.

16. "Global Trends 2015," 25.

17. van Creveld, *Rise and Decline*, 395.

18. Jean-Marie Guehenno, *The End of the Nation-State* (Minnesota, 1995), x. The author is the former French ambassador to the European Union.

19. Ibid., 56.

20. Ibid., 16

21. Ibid.

22. Bill Bruger, *Republican Theory in Political Thought: Virtuous or Virtual?* (London, 1999), 123.

23. Philip Selznick, "Afterword," in *Dilemmas of Scale in America's Federal Democracy*, ed. Martha Derthick (Washington, D.C., 1999), 360–61.

24. Ibid.

25. Daniel Bell, *The End of Ideology* (Cambridge, Mass., 1988), 400.

26. Ibid., 404.

27. Francis Fukuyama, *The End of History and the Last Man* (New York, 1992).

28. Samuel P. Huntington, *The Clash of Civilizations and the New World Order* (New York, 1997).

29. Bob Herbert, "A Nation Loosening Its Bonds," *New York Times*, August 26, 1999.

30. Marlise Simons, "In New Europe, a Lingual Hodgepodge," *New York Times*, October 17, 1999.

31. Ibid.

32. Yet, recently, the U.S. Congress was debating how many more billions to spend on cold war–era weapons, none of which will counter this threat.

33. Robert Kaplan, "Could This Be the New World?" *New York Times*, December 27, 1999.

34. Peter F. Drucker, "The Rise, Fall and Return of Pluralism," *Wall Street Journal*, June 1, 1999.

35. Robert D. Putnam, *Bowling Alone: The Collapse and Revival of American Community* (New York, 2000), 382.

36. *The Federalist Papers*, ed. Clinton Rossiter (New York, 1961), no. 49 (Madison), 285.

37. Eric Foner, *The Story of American Freedom* (New York, 1998), 22–23.

38. Rossiter, *The Federalist Papers*, no. 10 (Madison), 45.

39. "By a faction I understand a number of citizens, whether amount-ing to a majority or minority of the whole, who are united and ac-tuated by some common impulse of passion, or of interest, adverse to the rights of other citizens, or to the permanent and aggregate interests of the community" (Ibid., 46).

40. Ibid., no. 6 (Hamilton), 24.

41. Ibid., no. 11 (Hamilton), 58–59.

42. Ibid.

43. Ralph Ketcham, ed., *The Anti-Federalist Papers and the Constitutional Convention Debates* (New York, 1987), 287–88.

44. "The powers not delegated to the United States by the Constitu-tion, nor prohibited by it to the States, are reserved to the States respectively, or to the people" (Tenth Amendment, often called the "reserved powers" amendment, Constitution of the United States of America).

45. Herbert Croly, *The Promise of American Life* (Cambridge, Mass., 1965), xv.

46. Ibid., 29.

47. Ibid., 45.

48. Ibid., 152.

49. Ibid., 214. Given all that, one is prompted to wonder how Croly could identify anything in Jefferson worthy of synthesis.

50. See, for example, correspondence from Jefferson to Madison in this book's introduction regarding Jefferson's fundamental approval of basic elements of the proposed constitution.

51. This is an allegation whose echoes were employed against anyone questioning weapons systems or advocating arms control in cold-war America.

52. This is the modern day equivalent of saying that Ronald Reagan's political philosophy was clearer than Franklin Roosevelt's. It is pos-sibly true, but it is also irrelevant.

53. To assert, as Croly does, that radical American democrats, presum-ably led by Jefferson, the arch "democrat," were "opposed to the es-sential political need of the time—viz. the constitution of an effi-cient Federal government" is not only wrong but wrongheaded. Though it is difficult to take seriously, Croly claims to believe that national purpose must emanate from a formidable central govern-

ment, or not at all, and that Jeffersonian democracy was inimical to this goal.

54. Joseph J. Ellis, *American Sphinx: The Character of Thomas Jefferson* (New York, 1997), 182.

55. Since there is little evidence that Croly majored in the perverse, bias conditioned by lack of thorough scholarship must account for this unacceptable lapse.

56. Croly, *Promise of American Life*, 419.

57. Ibid.

58. Ibid., 23.

59. Ibid., 25. This is language that only someone like William Randolph Hearst might fully appreciate.

60. "A World without Virtue: Mandeville's Social and Political Thought," in Shelley Burtt, *Virtue Transformed: Political Argument in England, 1688–1740* (Cambridge, University Press, 1992), 128–49.

61. "Virtue Transformed," in Burtt, *Virtue Transformed*, 150–64.

62. Ibid.

63. Putman, *Bowling Alone*, 337.

64. Theda Skocpol, "Advocates without Members: The Recent Transformation of American Civic Life," quoted in Putnam, *Bowling Alone*, 344.

65. Article I, sec. 8, Constitution of the United States of America.

Chapter 2

1. Joyce Appleby, *Liberalism and Republicanism in the Historical Imagination* (Cambridge, Mass., 1992), 321.

2. Quoted in Hannah Arendt, *On Revolution* (New York, 1963), 169.

3. Richard K. Matthews, *The Radical Politics of Thomas Jefferson* (Lawrence, Kans., 1984), 121. Such rhetoric is alive and well in post–cold war America.

4. Max Farrand, ed., *The Records of the Federal Convention of 1787* (New Haven, Conn., rev. ed. 1966), 1:381.

5. Ibid., 1:436.

6. Ibid., 1:299.

7. Letter to Samuel Kercheval, September 5, 1816, in *Jefferson: Political Writings*, ed. Joyce Appleby and Terence Ball (Cambridge, 1999), 219.

8. Lance Banning, *The Jeffersonian Persuasion: Evolution of a Party Ideology* (Ithaca, N.Y., 1978), 205.

9. Letter to John Taylor, May 28, 1816, in Appleby and Ball, *Jefferson*, 206–8.

10. Bill Bruger, *Republican Theory in Political Thought: Virtuous or Virtual?* (London, 1999), 181.

11. Ibid., 20.

12. Ibid., 20–21.

13. The U.S. system, it must be said, still permits a degree of public participation in candidate selection not experienced in parliamentary systems such as the French republic or the Constitutional monarchy of the United Kingdom. Yet, a large majority of voters chooses to focus on available candidates only after those candidates have been produced by intricate party nomination processes.

14. Federal Election Commission statistics for 2000, www.fec.gov.

15. Robert D. Putnam, *Bowling Alone: The Collapse and Revival of American Community* (New York, 2000), 287. The earliest definition of social capital cited by Putnam occurred in the writings of a Progressive Era reformer, L. J. Hanifan, who used it to mean, "those intangible substances [that] count for most in the daily lives of people: namely good will, fellowship, sympathy, and social intercourse among the individuals and families who make up a social unit. . . . The individual is helpless socially, if left to himself. . . . If he comes into contact with his neighbor, and they with other neighbors, there will be an accumulation of social capital, which may immediately satisfy his social needs and which may bear a social potentiality sufficient to the substantial improvement of living conditions in the whole community. The community as a whole will benefit by the cooperation of all its parts, while the individual will find in his associations the advantages of the help, the sympathy, and fellowship of his neighbors" (quoted in Putnam, 19).

16. Richard Dagger, *Civic Virtues: Rights, Citizenship, and Republican*

Liberalism (Oxford, 1997), 14–15. Authentic republicanism suffers when a narrow preoccupation with sin replaces a concern for genuine public morality.

17. The net political effect of this primitive form of libertarianism is, to strengthen a certain kind of government, a government of, for, and by powerful private interests and special pleaders, who see citizen alienation as an opportunity, to plunder the common wealth for private gain. Those who preach the government-as-enemy seldom do so to congregations of military contractors, mining and timber companies, or licensors of pharmaceuticals.

18. The Reform party, protests against the World Trade Organization, citizen uprisings on controversial local issues, and growing disgust at uncontrolled campaign finance abuse—all provide evidence of a latent populism abroad in the United States. This populism has yet to reach movement status because it lacks several key ingredients: a manifesto, a catalytic event, and a leader. Late nineteenth-century agrarian, labor, and other movements had issues, such as the silver standard, monopoly corporate power, and financial market manipulation, to unite them. Depression in the 1880s and 1890s provided the catalyst, and leaders such as William Jennings Bryan provided the voice. In twenty-first-century America those ingredients are missing, but globalization, the outmigration of capital, and massive job terminations a could prove to be unifying forces. Certainly a substantial national or international recession or a major political scandal involving a serious and wholesale breach of trust could supply the catalyst. A variety of these forces together might also raise up a charismatic leader.

19. Though conservative America deplores "liberalism," read to mean government activism in market regulation, consumer and environmental protection, and social justice for the poor, it very much favors classic liberalism. The late twentieth-century conservative ascendancy restored the liberal priority of noninterference over civic virtue and citizen participation.

20. Putnam, *Bowling Alone*, 398.

21. Ibid. Putnam concludes his comparison of the Progressive Era to current America with this exhortation: "Just as did our predeces-

sors in the Progressive Era, we need to create new structures and policies (public and private) to facilitate renewed civic engagement" (403).

22. Martin van Creveld, *The Rise and Decline of the State* (Cambridge, 1999), 408.

23. Arendt, *On Revolution*, 218 n. 2.

24. John Rawls, *Political Liberalism* (New York, 1993), 206, quoted in Dagger, *Civic Virtues*, 186 n. 11.

25. William Galston, *Liberal Purposes: Goods, Virtues, and Diversity in the Liberal State* (Cambridge, 1991), 225, quoted in Dagger, *Civic Virtues*, 187 n. 11.

26. Quentin Skinner, "The Republican Ideal of Political Liberty," in *Machiavelli and Republicanism*, ed. Gisela Bock, Quentin Skinner, and Maurizio Viroli (Cambridge, 1990), 306. Some, however, might quarrel with Skinner's further conclusion that republican theory contemplates that citizen duty can be imposed by coercion and constraint.

27. J. G. A. Pocock, *The Machiavellian Moment: Florentine Political Thought and the Atlantic Republican Tradition* (Princeton, N.J., 1975), 56.

28. Ibid., 212.

29. Appleby, *Liberalism and Republicanism*, 23 n. 1.

30. Charles de Secondat, baron de Montesquieu, *The Spirit of the Laws* (Cambridge, 1989), 124. Montesquieu continues: "In a large republic, there are large fortunes, and consequently little moderation in spirits; the depositories are too large to put in the hands of a citizen; interests become particularized; at first a man feels he can be happy, great, and glorious without his homeland; and soon, that he can be great only on the ruins of his homeland."

31. Ibid., 131. Joyce Appleby offers this interpretation: "Republics . . . by their very nature had no such tripartite division [the Constitutional balance of the one, the few, and the many recommended by Aristotle and Polybius], and the moderating influence had to come from another source. A virtuous citizenry could sustain a republic through the disorders endemic in human society, but this essential civic virtue could survive only among a people of frugal habits who

lived in a limited area where a rough equality of property prevailed. From this chain of reasoning came Montesquieu's celebrated small-republic theory" (Appleby, *Liberalism and Republicanism*, 293 n. 1).

32. Montesquieu, *Spirit of the Laws*, 143.
33. Pocock, *Machiavellian Moment*, 546, 541 n. 17.
34. Letter to Samuel Kercheval, July 12, 1816, in *The Works of Thomas Jefferson*, ed. Paul L. Ford (New York, 1904), 12:12.
35. Ibid., 12:8–9.
36. Joseph J. Ellis, *American Sphinx: The Character of Thomas Jefferson* (New York, 1997), 261.

Chapter 3

Portions of the section "The Mature Jefferson and the Radical Republic" are the product of research carried out in residence at Pembroke College, Oxford, during Michaelmas term 1996. Some of this material appears, in somewhat altered form, in Gary Hart, *The Minuteman* (New York, 1998).

1. Letter to John Taylor, May 18, 1816, in *Jefferson: Political Writings*, ed. Joyce Appleby and Terrence Ball (Cambridge, 1999), 206–8.
2. Letter to James Madison, September 6, 1789, in *The Life and Selected Writings of Thomas Jefferson*, ed. Adrienne Koch and William Peden (New York, 1993), 448–53. This letter contains perhaps the most succinct statement of Jefferson's radical notion that each generation inherits the earth and is accountable and responsible for it. The full implications of this idea transcend the bounds of most Western political ideologies and deserve comprehensive elucidation separately.
3. Ibid.
4. Letter to Isaac H. Tiffany, April 4, 1819, in Appleby and Ball, *Jefferson*, 224–25.
5. Letter to Joseph C. Cabell, February 2, 1816, ibid., 202–6.
6. Letter to Isaac H. Tiffany, ibid., 217–18.
7. Letter to Joseph C. Cabell, ibid., 202–6.
8. Letter to John Taylor, ibid., n. 1.

9. Letter to Samuel Kercheval, September 5, 1816, ibid., 219.

10. Ibid.

11. Max Beloff, *Thomas Jefferson and American Democracy* (New York, 1949), 251.

12. Joyce Appleby, *Liberalism and Republicanism in the Historical Imagination* (Cambridge, Mass., 1992).

13. Garrett Ward Sheldon, *The Political Philosophy of Thomas Jefferson* (Baltimore, Md., 1991).

14. Merrill D. Peterson, *Thomas Jefferson and the New Nation* (New York, 1970), 94–95.

15. "The Americans had come to believe that the Revolution would mean nothing less than a reordering of eighteenth century society and politics as they had known and despised them—a reordering that was summed up by the conception of republicanism" (Gordon Wood, *The Creation of the American Republic: 1776–1787* [New York, 1969], 48). See also Wood's chapter 15, "The American Science of Politics," for the notion that Americans of the revolutionary era envisioned a social as well as a political revolution.

16. Letter to Benjamin Franklin, August 3, 1777, *The Papers of Thomas Jefferson*, ed. Julian P. Boyd (Princeton, N.J., 1950).

17. Wood, *Creation of the American Republic*, 93.

18. Ibid. Wood's emphasis on the social revolution is not in contrast to the political but is connected with it. He does not seem to be saying that one was more remarkable than the other. Though Wood does not feature it at length, the social revolution certainly did not include the substantial loyalist community in America and the class structure it represented.

19. Gordon Wood, *The Radicalism of the American Revolution* (New York, 1992), 96–97.

20. Letter to Lafayette, November 4, 1823, in *The Writings of Thomas Jefferson*, ed. Paul L. Ford (New York, 1898), 10:281, quoted in Wood, *Radicalism*, 97.

21. Ford, *Writings*, 1:68–69.

22. Carl J. Richard, *The Founders and the Classics: Greece, Rome, and the American Enlightenment* (Cambridge, Mass., 1994), 53.

23. Ibid., 57.

24. Ibid., 7–8.
25. Bernard Bailyn, *The Ideological Origins of the American Revolution* (Cambridge, Mass., 1967), 22–24.
26. Ibid., 25.
27. Wood, *Radicalism*, 101.
28. J. G. A. Pocock, *The Machiavellian Moment: Florentine Political Thought and the Atlantic Republican Tradition* (Princeton, N.J., 1975), 506–7.
29. "Modern and effective government had transplanted to America the dread of modernity itself, of which the threat to virtue by corruption was the contemporary ideological expression" (ibid., 509).
30. Aristotle, *Politics* (Cambridge, Mass., 1923), 9. Jefferson's Aristotelianism is not cited here as a rigid, orthodox, or doctrinaire position in opposition to other forms of republicanism, especially the Roman. Indeed, Jefferson wrote, "So different was the style of society then [in Aristotle's time] . . . from what it is now and with us, that I think little edification can be obtained from their writings on the subject of government. They had just the idea of the value of personal liberty, but none at all of the structure of government best calculated to preserve it" (Sheldon, *Political Philosophy*, n. 13).
31. Aristotle, *Politics*, 69.
32. Ibid., 77.
33. Cicero, *De Re Publica* (Cambridge, Mass., 1928), 29.
34. Ibid., 77. Aristotle's version says, "The proper thing is for the state, while being a multitude, to be made a partnership" (*Politics*, 91).
35. Cicero, *De Re Publica*, 169.
36. Ibid., 79.
37. Ibid., 17.
38. Quoted in Quentin Skinner, *Liberty before Liberalism* (Cambridge, 1998), 31.
39. Niccolo Machiavelli, *Discourses on Livy*, 280; quoted in Skinner, *Liberty*, 62.
40. Algernon Sidney, *Court Maxims*, ed. Hans W. Blom, Eco Haitsma Mulier, and Ronald Janse (Cambridge, 1996), 65.
41. Ibid., 35.
42. Ibid., 16.
43. Ibid., 24. "It is not known beyond doubt whether Sidney actually

was involved in the Rye House Plot to kill Charles. But we are reasonably sure that he played a role in the attempts of the Whigs to stage a general uprising in England" (xvi).

44. *Thomas Jefferson: Writings*, ed. Merrill D. Peterson (New York, 1984), 479.

45. Quoted in Richard, *Founders and the Classics*, 175.

46. *The Federalist*, ed. Edward Meade Earle (New York, 1941), no. 71.

47. Wood, *Creation of the American Republic*, 508.

48. *The Works of John Adams*, ed. Charles Francis Adams (Boston, 1850–1856), 5:183.

49. Appleby, *Liberalism and Republicanism*, 200.

50. *The Adams-Jefferson Letters*, ed. Lester J. Cappon (Chapel Hill, N.C., 1959), 2:332.

51. Merrill D. Peterson, *The Jefferson Image in the American Mind* (Charlottesville, Va., 1998), 89.

52. Calvin Colton, quoted in ibid.

53. Bailyn, *Ideological Origins*, 282.

54. Michael Kammen, *People of Paradox* (New York, 1972), 215.

55. Sheldon, *Political Philosophy*, 143.

56. Earle, *The Federalist*, no. 39.

57. *The Writings of James Madison*, ed. Gaillard Hunt (New York, 1904), 5:376–77.

58. Wood, *Creation of the American Republic*, 605.

59. Kammen, *People of Paradox*, 89–90. For its powerful analysis of the social and political paradoxes and cultural contradictions that have characterized America throughout its history, this work won the Pulitzer Prize for history.

60. Pocock, *Machiavellian Moment*, chap. 15.

61. Ibid., 527.

62. John Locke, *Two Treatises of Government*, ed. Peter Laslett (Cambridge, 1988), 350.

63. Aristotle *Politics*, III. iv; Aristotle *Nicomachean Ethics* I.1099b.

64. Sheldon, *Political Philosophy*, 11.

65. Aristotle *Politics* VII. iv.

66. Appleby, *Liberalism and Republicanism*, 300.

67. Michael J. Sandel, *Democracy's Discontent* (Cambridge, Mass., 1996), 330.

68. Letter to James Madison, October 28, 1785, in Peterson, *Thomas Jefferson*, 840–43.

69. "More than any other figure in his generation Jefferson integrated a program of economic development and a policy for nation-building into a radical moral theory" and "a fairly coherent description of the kind of economic base that would support a democratic republic" (Appleby, *Liberalism and Republicanism*, 300–301).

70. Ibid., 304.

71. Sheldon, *Political Philosophy*, 42–48.

72. "The Autobiography," in Peterson, *Thomas Jefferson*, 38–44.

73. Richard K. Matthews, *The Radical Politics of Thomas Jefferson* (Lawrence, Kans., 1984) 35.

74. Letter to Francois de Marbois, in Peterson, *Thomas Jefferson*, 1409–10.

75. Matthews, *Radical Politics*, 18.

76. Letter to P. S. Dupont de Nemours, April 24, 1816, in Peterson, *Thomas Jefferson*, 1387.

77. Letter to Justice William Johnson, June 12, 1823, in Peterson, *Thomas Jefferson*, 1470.

78. Appleby, *Liberalism and Republicanism*, 301.

79. Drew R. McCoy, *The Elusive Republic: Political Economy in Jeffersonian America* (Chapel Hill, N.C., 1980), chaps. 1, 2.

80. Ibid., 134.

81. Charles de Secondat, Baron de Montesquieu, *The Spirit of the Laws*, ed. Anne M. Cohler, Basia Carolyn Miller, and Harold Samuel Stone (Cambridge, 1989), 124.

82. Ibid., 131. Montesquieu knew of Harrington's efforts, in *The Commonwealth of Oceana* (relying on Moses for the Israelites, Lycurgus for the Greeks, and Romulus for the Romans), to devise a mathematical formula for subdivisions of the republic using parishes, precincts (or "hundreds"), and tribes. In his "Idea of a Perfect Commonwealth," David Hume, in turn, followed Harrington by proposing a hundred counties each divided into a hundred parishes, "refuting the falsehood of the common opinion that only a city or small territory can be a commonwealth. . . . Though it is more difficult to form a republican government in an extensive country than in a city, there is more facility, once it is formed, of

preserving it steady and uniform, without tumult and faction" (David Hume, *Selected Essays* [Oxford, 1993]).

83. See Appleby, *Liberalism and Republicanism*, 294–96, for a concise but learned summary of the factors influencing Jefferson's altered views, especially his perception while in Paris of the elitism explicit in Montesquieu's civic humanism.

84. Letter to Francois D'Ivernois, February 6, 1785, in Peterson, *Thomas Jefferson*, 1024.

85. Letter to Joseph C. Cabell, February 2, 1816, in Appleby and Ball, *Jefferson*, 203.

86. Destutt de Tracy, *A Commentary and Review of Montesquieu's Spirit of the Laws* (Philadelphia, 1811), cited in Adrienne Koch, *The Philosophy of Thomas Jefferson* (Gloucester, Mass., 1957), 152.

87. Letter to Robert Williams, November 1, 1807, in *The Writings of Thomas Jefferson*, ed. Albert Ellery Bergh (Washington, D.C., 1903), 11:389.

88. Letter to Dupont de Nemours, April 24, 1816, in Appleby and Ball, *Jefferson*, 290–94.

89. John Stuart Mill, "Concerning Representative Government," in *On Liberty and Other Essays* (Oxford, 1991), 244.

90. Ibid., 254.

91. Ibid., 423–24.

92. Ibid., 240.

93. Appleby, *Liberalism and Republicanism*, 290.

94. *The Papers of James Madison*, ed. Robert A. Rutland et al. (Chicago, 1977), 10: 163–64, quoted in *The Federalist Papers*, ed. Charles R. Kesler and Clinton Rossiter (New York, 1999), vii.

95. Kesler and Rossiter *Federalist Papers*, no. 85.

96. Ibid., no. 10. Unless otherwise designated, the following Madison quotes are from this source.

97. Ibid., no. 9.

98. Hamilton quoted Montesquieu's statement from *The Spirit of the Laws*: "It is very probable that mankind would have been obliged at length to live constantly under the government of a Single Person, had they not contrived a kind of constitution that has all the internal advantages of a republican, together with the external force of a monarchical, government. I mean a Confederate Republic" (I.9.1).

Though Hamilton cited Montesquieu regarding *confederations*, he seemed to be implying that Montesquieu would have also endorsed federation to achieve the same purpose.

99. *The Anti-Federalist Papers and the Constitutional Convention Debates,* ed. Ralph Ketcham (New York, 1986), 199.

100. Ibid.

101. Ibid., 205.

102. Ibid., 208.

103. Thomas Jefferson, *Notes on the State of Virginia,* 8:404.

104. Sheldon, *Political Philosophy,* 121. "In colonial Virginia, bordering a vast virgin wilderness, the plantation leisure was necessarily purchased with slavery. When the reality of an open frontier allowed even indentured servants to escape to farmland of their own, an enslaved working class of identifiable color became the convenient means of replicating the English country life in the New World."

105. This circumstance did in fact occur some fifty years later on the eve of the Civil War when whole counties in slave states joined the Union cause against the very slave states in which they were located, and, in a few cases, communities in the North joined with southern secessionists.

106. Peterson, *Thomas Jefferson and the New Nation,* 44. For his trouble, Bland was condemned as "an enemy of his country."

107. Jefferson, *Notes on the State of Virginia,* 87, quoted in Alf J. Mapp, Jr., *Thomas Jefferson: A Strange Case of Mistaken Identity* (Lanham, Md., 1987), 168.

108. Peterson, *Thomas Jefferson and the New Nation,* 91.

109. Jefferson, *Notes on the State of Virginia,* where Jefferson restated his plan for gradual emancipation. But his notorious observations on the presumed natural inferiority of the African race, contained in this same work, were too much even for one of his most admiring biographers: "Honest, disinterested, and no doubt true to his personal observation and knowledge, Jefferson's opinion was also a product of frivolous and tortuous reasoning, of preconception, prejudice, ignorance, contradiction, and bewildering confusion of principles" (Peterson, *Thomas Jefferson and the New Nation,* 262).

110. Quoted in Sheldon, *Political Philosophy,* 133.

111. Ford, *Writings*, 9:477.

112. Peterson, *Thomas Jefferson*, 528.

113. Ibid., vol. v, p. 66.

114. Quoted in Peterson, 998.

115. "Answers to Demeunier's Queries," June 22, 1786, in Peterson, *Thomas Jefferson*, 592.

116. Eric Foner, *The Story of American Freedom* (New York, 1998), 40.

117. John Chester Miller, *The Wolf by the Ears: Thomas Jefferson and Slavery* (New York, 1977), frontispiece, taken from Jefferson, *Notes on the State of Virginia*. Though neither consolation to nor absolution of Jefferson, his views concerning emancipation and colonization were shared, into the first years of the Civil War, by Abraham Lincoln (Miller, *Wolf by the Ears*, 90–92).

118. Quoted in Peterson, *Jefferson and the New Nation*, 927. "His learned letters ranged over a wide, and generally familiar, terrain: the 'poison' of Hume and Blackstone, the moral sense, Epicurean philosophy, the history of the Greek ablative, Lord Napier's theorem for the solution of right-angled spherical triangles, the superiority of the American and Siberian mammoth, the new Spanish constitution, the history of hopperboys, weights and measures on a universal standard, and the value of neology in the enrichment and growth of language" (Ibid., 951–52).

119. Ibid., 961.

120. Peterson, *Thomas Jefferson*, 900. This precept is one of many found in Jefferson's writings that have direct roots in Locke.

121. Ibid.

122. Ibid., 961–62.

123. Wood, *Creation of the American Republic*, 192.

124. Quoted in *Dilemmas of Scale in America's Federal Democracy*, ed. Martha Derthick (Washington, D.C., 1999), 7.

125. Pauline Maier, "Early American Local Self-Government," in ibid., 72.

126. Letter to Samuel Kercheval, July 12, 1816, in Peterson, *Thomas Jefferson*, 1399.

127. Letter to John Tyler, May 26, 1810, in Peterson, *Thomas Jefferson*, 1226.

128. Letter to John Tyler, May 26, 1810, in Appleby and Ball, *Jefferson*,

183. Jefferson proceeded to say: "Could I once see this I should consider it as the dawn of the salvation of the republic, and say with old Simeon, 'nunc dimittas Domine.' "

129. Letter to John Adams, October 28, 1813, in Appleby and Ball, *Jefferson*, 189.

130. Ibid.

131. Letter to Charles Yancey, in Bergh, *Writings*, 6: 517.

132. Thomas Jefferson, "Notes on the State of Virginia," in *The Complete Jefferson*, ed. Saul K. Padover (New York, 1943), 668.

133. James Harrington, *The Commonwealth of Oceana and a System of Politics*, ed. J. G. A. Pocock (Cambridge, 1992), 197.

134. Montesquieu, *The Spirit of the Laws*, 35–36.

135. Letter to Wilson Nicholas, April 2, 1816, in Sheldon, *Political Philosophy*, 67. Sheldon's footnote misspells Nicholas's name as "Nicholes."

136. Wood, *Creation of the American Republic*, 72.

137. Letter to Peter Carr, September 7, 1814, in Peterson, *Thomas Jefferson*, 1346–52.

138. "Report of the Commissioners for the University of Virginia," in Peterson, *Thomas Jefferson*, 457–73.

139. Ibid., 461–62.

140. Letter to Richard Price, January 8, 1785, in Koch and Peden, *Life and Selected Writings*, 418.

141. Letter to William Jarvis, September 28, 1820, in *Works of Thomas Jefferson*, ed. Paul L. Ford (New York, 1904), 12:163.

142. Matthews, *Radical Politics*, 115.

143. Letter to Joseph Cabal, January 22, 1820, in Koch, *Philosophy*, 168.

144. Ibid., 162.

145. Sheldon, *Political Philosophy*, 146.

146. "First Inaugural Address," in Peterson, *Thomas Jefferson*, 492–96.

147. He would be amazed, but not amused, by a plan that featured the deployment of regulars abroad to be supported eventually by reservists—the precise opposite of his vision.

148. Russell F. Weigley, *History of the United States Army* (New York, 1967), 104.

149. Jerry Cooper, *The Militia and the National Guard in America since Colonial Times* (Greenwood, 1993), 16.

150. E. Wayne Carp, "Early American Military History: A Review of Recent Work," *Virginia Magazine of History and Biography* 94 (July 1986): 276.

151. Cooper, *The Militia*, 15.

152. Ibid., 44.

153. John Rich and Graham Shipley, *War and Society in the Roman World* (London, 1993), 95–96.

154. Ibid., 7.

155. Pocock, *Machiavellian Moment*, 202–3. The *virtù*-less mercenary, Machiavelli well knew, suffered also from inclinations toward cowardice, unreliability, and a tendency to abandon an employer for a more lucrative offer.

156. Ibid., 406, 412.

157. Ibid., 386.

158. "A Letter from a Parliament Man to His Friend," in ibid., 410.

159. Allen Millet and Peter Maslowski, *For the Common Defense: A Military History of the United States of America* (New York, 1984), 62. Despite Washington's ambiguities concerning the militia's effectiveness, militiamen early on penned Gage's forces inside Boston; later, under the leadership of Ethan Allen, they overwhelmed the British garrison at Ticonderoga, annihilated a Burgoyne detachment outside Bennington, Vermont, and fought splendidly under Greene in the Carolinas.

160. Pocock, *Machiavellian Moment*, 528.

161. William Blackstone, *Commentaries on the Laws of England* (1783). The echo of Machiavelli almost three centuries before—himself echoing Greek and Roman republicans—is remarkable.

162. Millet and Maslowski, *For the Common Defense*, 86.

163. Rossiter, *Federalist Papers*, no. 24.

164. John K. Mahon, *History of the Militia and the National Guard* (New York, 1983), 3.

165. Bailyn, *Ideological Origins*, 338.

166. *The Anti-Federalist Papers and the Constitutional Convention Debates*, ed. Ralph Ketcham (New York, 1986).

167. Ibid., "Brutus," no. 10, January 24, 1788.

168. Bailyn, *Ideological Origins*, 340.

169. Ketcham, *Anti-Federalist Papers*, introduction.

170. Weigley, *History of the United States Army*, 104. Although seemingly quaint to the modern age, Jefferson clearly saw defense as exactly that, a military capable of repelling attack but not of attacking anyone else. Thus, he stands modern defense on its head—the militia will hold off invaders until the regulars arrive.

171. Pocock, *Machiavellian Moment*, 528–29.

172. Ketchum, *Anti-Federalist Papers*, 221. The Second Amendment reads: "A well regulated Militia, being necessary to the security of a free State, the right of the people to keep and bear Arms, shall not be infringed."

173. Using the same calculation today, the United States would have citizen militia numbering more than 40 million.

174. Alexis de Tocqueville, *Democracy in America* (New York, 1985), no. 49.

175. Ibid., no. 23.

176. Ibid., no. 22.

177. Ibid., no. 49.

178. Peterson, *Thomas Jefferson*, 530–31.

179. Ibid., 547.

180. Appleby, *Liberalism and Republicanism*, 300–301.

181. McCoy, *Elusive Republic*, 127.

182. Thomas Jefferson, "Travel Journal," Champagne, March 3, 1787, in Koch and Peden, *Life and Selected Writings*, 127.

183. Letter to Reverend James Madison, ibid., 361–62.

184. Appleby and Ball, *Jefferson*, 450–51.

185. Appleby, *Liberalism and Republicanism*, 301.

186. See Koch, *Philosophy*, 21.

187. Koch and Peden, *Life and Selected Writings*, 375.

188. C. B. Macpherson, *Political Theory of Possessive Individualism: Hobbes to Locke* (Oxford, 1962), 135, quoted in Matthews, *Radical Politics*, 51.

189. Jefferson, "Notes on the State of Virginia," in Peterson, *Thomas Jefferson*, 258–60.

190. Sheldon, *Political Philosophy*, 68–69.

191. Aristotle *Politics* II. iv.9–11.

Chapter 4

1. Robert D. Putnam, *Bowling Alone: The Collapse and Revival of American Community* (New York, 2000), 411.

2. Richard Dagger, *Civic Virtues: Rights, Citizenship, and Republican Liberalism* (Oxford, 1997), 159.

3. *Thomas Jefferson: Writings*, ed. Merrill D. Peterson (New York, 1984), 1380.

4. Alexis de Tocqueville, *Democracy in America*, ed. Phillips Bradley (New York, 1985), 236.

5. Hannah Arendt, *On Revolution* (New York, 1963), 238–39.

6. Ibid., 255.

7. This synthesis anticipated by two centuries a similar one put forward in the form of "republican liberalism" by Dagger in *Civic Virtues*.

8. Pauline Maier, "The Origins and Influence of Early American Local Self-Government," in *Dilemmas of Scale in America's Federal Democracy*, ed. Martha Derthick (Washington, D.C., 1999), 88, emphasis added. The sweeping nature of this judgment neglects the reality that some modern-day communities do flourish. These are, by and large, prosperous, stable, and civically active polities of the sort that would be models for the rest of the nation under the proposal put forward by this work.

9. "Political participation is clearly one of the most effective ways of building community among neighbors. And involvement in neighborhood associations is a particularly effective way of building community among those who are willing to participate in the political process" (Jeffrey M. Berry, Kent E. Portnoy, and Ken Thompson, *The Rebirth of Urban Democracy* [Washington, D.C., 1993], 290), quoted in Dagger, *Civic Virtues*, 224 n. 34.

10. Robert A. Dahl, *After the Revolution* (New Haven, Conn., 1970), 35.

11. Ibid., 88.

12. Ibid., 41.

13. Ibid., 153.

14. Ibid., 164. "The city will never begin to meet its problems or attain a satisfactory level of self-government until it has a generous and

predictable flow of unencumbered funds—an automatic share of federal tax revenues."

15. Dagger, *Civic Virtues*, 166–71.

16. Quoted in ibid., 229 n. 32.

17. Tocqueville, *Democracy in America*, 45.

18. Ibid., 55.

19. Ibid., 302.

20. Ibid., 286–87.

21. Ibid., 63.

22. Benjamin R. Barber, *A Passion for Democracy* (Princeton, N.J., 1998), 163.

23. Ibid., 164.

24. Cf. Arendt, *On Revolution*, 248–55.

25. Barber, *Passion for Democracy*, 165.

26. Letter to James Madison, December 20, 1787, in Peterson, *Thomas Jefferson*, 918.

27. *The Life and Selected Writings of Thomas Jefferson*, ed. Adrienne Koch and William Peden (New York, 1993), 298.

28. Barber, *Passion for Democracy*, 170.

29. Benjamin R. Barber, *An Aristocracy of Everyone* (Oxford, 1992), 241.

30. Ibid., 244.

31. In recent years, this process has begun to be eroded by provisions in most states for "home schooling" approved and monitored by government education officials.

32. Gregory R. Weiher and Chris Cookson, "Local Self-Government in Education: Community, Citizenship, and Charter schools," in Derthick, *Dilemmas of Scale*, 268.

33. Ibid., 262–63.

34. John Stuart Mill, "Considerations on Representative Government," quoted in Putnam, *Bowling Alone*, 337.

35. John Dewey, "The Public and Its Problems," quoted in Putnam, *Bowling Alone*.

36. "On Liberty," in *Mill*, ed. Alan Ryan (New York, 1997), 127.

37. Michael Sandel, "The Procedural Republic and the Unencumbered Self," in *Communitarianism and Individualism*, ed. Shlomo Avineri and Avner de-Shalit (Oxford, 1992), 27. The sweeping conclusion of this quotation clearly overlooks the role of local politics in such

administrative functions as enforcement of criminal laws and such regulatory functions as zoning, as well as a large number of other public activities that are the responsibility of municipal and local governments. But those activities also support this argument: that the local republic can and should undertake greater administrative responsibilities.

38. Robert A. Dahl, *On Democracy* (New Haven, Conn., 1998), 101–18. It should be noted, though Dahl does not, that the assembly in ancient times did not necessarily guarantee universal participation in all debates but often relied on a selected few to frame issues and define questions while the entire assembly, as in Athens, voted the question up or down or functioned as jury.

39. Ibid., 112.

40. Weiher and Cookson, "Local Self-Government," 274.

41. Jeffrey R. Henig, *Rethinking School Choice: Limits of the Market Metaphor* (Princeton, N.J., 1994), 23, quoted in Derthick, *Dilemmas of Scale*. "Making government work is difficult. It especially is difficult to work through democratic procedures that invite and accept as legitimate views from disparate actors with conflicting agendas and incompatible styles. Calls for radical restructuring [of] education through market processes appeal in part because they promise to sidestep this process. In the grand bazaar of education, families would be free to negotiate their own bargains on their own terms, paying only so much attention as they wish to the hubbub around them" (289).

42. Weiher and Cookson, "Local Self-Government," 279.

43. Ibid., 277. There is also the phenomenon of parents supporting a variety of equal rights initiatives and sending their children to schools that resist them.

44. Putnam, *Bowling Alone*, 299.

45. Dagger, *Civic Virtues*, 113, emphasis added.

46. Weiher and Cookson, "Local Self-Government," 291–92.

47. Putnam, *Bowling Alone*, 305. Putnam, however, warns against the negative consequence of civically engaged parents removing their children into these kinds of schools. He further notes the striking correlation between States with high "social capital" indices and those where children flourish generally: "Statistically, the correla-

tion between high social capital and positive child development is as close to perfect as social scientists ever find in data analyses of this sort" (296–97).

48. Paul A. Rahe, *Republics Ancient and Modern* (Chapel Hill, N.C., 1994), 3:62.

49. Barber, *Passion for Democracy*, 224.

50. Ibid., 229.

51. Serious critics argue that it is not performing its utilitarian function nearly well enough either.

52. John Locke, *Two Treatises of Government*, ed. Peter Laslett (Cambridge, 1988), bk. II, par. 122.

53. Alan A. Altshuler, "The Ideo-Logics of Urban Land-Use Politics," in Derthick, *Dilemmas of Scale*. "The peak period of school consolidation was 1939–1940 to 1970–1971, when the number of districts contracted by 85 percent, from 117,108 to 17,995. As of 1992–3, the number stood at 15,205. *Digest of Educational Statistics*, U.S. Department of Education, National Center for Educational Statistics, 1994. Meanwhile, the number of incorporated municipalities rose from 16,220 in 1942 to 19,296 in 1992. *Statistical Abstract of the United States*, 1994" (201 n. 6).

54. Cf. Weiher and Cookson, "Local Self-Government," n. 22.

55. Ibid., 268.

56. Letter to Reverend James Madison, October 28, 1785, in Koch and Peden, *Life and Selected Writings*, 361.

57. Letter to Dr. Thomas Cooper, September 10, 1814, ibid., 594.

58. Letter to Maria Cosway, October 12, 1786, ibid., 375.

59. Letter to John Adams, October 28, 1813, and letter to Samuel Kercheval, July 12, 1816, in *Jefferson: Political Writings*, ed. Joyce Appleby and Terence Ball (Cambridge, 1999), 189, 213.

60. Aristotle, *Politics* IV. 11. 1295b, ed. Stephen Everson (Cambridge, 1996).

61. Jean Jacques Rousseau, "On the Social Contract," quoted in Michael Sandel, *Democracy's Discontent: America in Search of a Public Philosophy* (Cambridge, Mass., 1996), 330.

62. Philip Pettit, *Republicanism: A Theory of Freedom and Government* (Oxford, 1997), 160–61.

63. Ibid., 289, emphasis added.

64. Putnam, *Bowling Alone*, 367.

65. Richard Hofstadter, *The Age of Reform* (New York, 1955). Hofstadter documents the degree to which the populist movement, though it largely failed politically, laid the groundwork for the progressive movement that succeeded it. By and large the populists drew strength from distressed farmers and workers, while the progressives appealed to urban professionals and reformers.

66. Quoted in Sidney Milkis, "Localism, Political Parties, and Civic Virtue," in Derthick, *Dilemmas of Scale*, 114.

67. Ibid., 117; and John Dewey, *Liberalism and Social Action* (New York, 1935).

68. Altshuler, "Ideo-Logics," 201.

69. Milkis, "Localism," 119.

70. Cited in A. Huffington, *Los Angeles Times*, April 15, 2000.

71. Milkis, "Localism," 124.

72. "First Annual Message," December 8, 1801, in *Thomas Jefferson: Writings*, ed. Merrill D. Peterson (New York, 1984), 505.

73. "Eighth Annual Message," November 8, 1808, ibid., 547.

74. 20 Stat. L., 145, June 18, 1878.

75. Matthew Carlton Hammond, "The Posse Comitatus Act: A Principle in Need of Renewal," 75 *Washington University Law Quarterly* 953, no. 2 (1997).

76. 1162 (6th ed., 1990).

77. *Declaration of Independence*, pars. 12–19.

78. U.S. Code, sec. 1385 (1994). Regarding restrictions on standing armies and other prohibitions against a military establishment contained in the Constitution and Bill of Rights, it should be pointed out that similar restrictions were contained in the English Declaration of Right (1689).

79. S. 735, 104th Cong., 1st sess., sec. 908 (June 5, 1995).

80. U.S. Commission on National Security/Twenty-first Century, Washington, D.C., January 31, 2001, and statement by Secretary of Defense William S. Cohen, April 2000, Pentagon Press Release.

81. See chapter 1 and Bernard Bailyn, *The Ideological Origins of the American Revolution* (Cambridge, Mass., 1967), 338–39. "There is simply no way to measure the volume and fervor of the antifederalists' denunciation of this provision [Article I, sec. 8, of the Consti-

tution, which authorizes Congress "to raise and support armies"]
which revived for them not simply a general fear of military power
but the specific danger of 'standing armies,' a peculiar and distinctive threat to liberty that had been formulated for all time, they believed, in England in the 1690s, and had been carried forward intact to the colonies" (338–39).

82. See Chapter 2 of this book for a detailed discussion of the Constitutional debate and the two-army compromise and for the roots of
resistance to the combination of a standing army, national debt,
national bank, foreign adventure, and eventual domestic repression
found in early eighteenth-century English radical thinking.

83. "Global Trends 2015: A Dialogue about the Future with Nongovernment Experts," prepared under the direction of the National Intelligence Council and approved for publication by the National
Foreign Intelligence Board under the authority of the director of
Central Intelligence, December 2000, Washington, D.C., 25, 35.

84. Putnam, *Bowling Alone*, 349.

85. Charles Taylor, *Philosophical Arguments* (Cambridge, Mass., 1995),
193.

86. Quentin Skinner, "The Republican Ideal of Political Liberty," in
Machiavelli and Republicanism (Cambridge, 1993), 303.

87. Colonel James Barrineau, chief of Force Management Division
(NGB-ARF), Army National Guard Readiness Center, Washington,
D.C., October 20, 2000.

88. President George W. Bush, "Address to the National Guard,"
Yeager Field, Charleston, West Virginia, February 14, 2001.

89. Final report, USCNS/21C. Also see "Roadmap for National Security,"
Report of the National Defense Panel, Washington D.C., December
1997, 17: "These challenges are real. Terrorists, foreign and domestic,
state and nonstate, have already demonstrated the ability to strike
at us at home and abroad. Their sophistication, access to technologies that could include weapons of mass destruction and frequent
state sponsorship give them great potential to do us harm."

90. "Recommendation 2. A National Homeland Security Agency
(NHSA) should be established that appropriately realigns our out-
dated and fragmented domestic security and response mechanisms.
This realignment will build upon and strengthen existing public

safety, border security, and emergency preparedness capabilities. The mission of the NHSA will be to assist in the prevention of crises, and to ensure a more effective response and recovery from either an attack using weapons of mass destruction or disruption of the United States" ("Roadmap for National Security").

91. Ibid.

92. Ibid.

93. Tocqueville, *Democracy in America*, 2:272–74. Cf. also General (and then President) Dwight Eisenhower's famous admonition against the establishment of a "military-industrial complex." Regarding democratic armies, Tocqueville continued, "There are two things that a democratic people will always find difficult, to begin a war and to end it." War, he wrote, does not always lead democratic governments to militaristic qualities, but it almost surely increases and concentrates the powers of the civil government, and thus, "all those who seek to destroy the liberties of a democratic nation ought to know that war is the surest and the shortest means to accomplish it" (268).

94. J. G. A. Pocock, *The Machiavellian Moment: Florentine Political Thought and the Atlantic Republican Tradition* (Princeton, N.J., 1975), 528. Though resisted by the Anti-federalists, the standing army and navy established by the new nation were modest in size and more symbolic than real. The infant United States desired to participate in world commerce but to "avoid foreign entanglements" with European powers, some of which maintained territorial designs on its borders. The small initial forces were a hedge against this. Few, if any parallels can be drawn between America of the late eighteenth century and America of the twenty-first.

95. Letter to Samuel Kercheval, July 12, 1816, Appleby and Ball, *Jefferson*, 213–214.

96. Dahl, *After the Revolution*, 160.

97. Tocqueville, *Democracy in America*, 69 n. 70.

98. James Q. Wilson, "City Life and Citizenship," in Derthick, *Dilemmas of Scale*, 21–22.

99. *Declaration of Independence*.

100. Quentin Skinner, *Liberty before Liberalism* (Cambridge, 1998), 77–79.

101. *The New Shorter Oxford English Dictionary* (Oxford, 1993).

102. Raymond Plant, *Modern Political Thought* (Oxford, 1991), 74–75. "Plato, Aristotle, Marcuse, and Fromm accepted that values could be given a foundation and this led them to a communitarian conception of politics, that is to say that the basic political project should be the building of a political community within which these basic virtues, which constitute the common human good, could flourish." Plant then cites communism and Islamic fundamentalism in this same context and describes both as the "kind of political thought . . . sometimes known as perfectionism—concerned with the institutional structure necessary to fulfil [*sic*] or to perfect, in the sense of complete, human nature" (74–75).

103. Ibid., 34–35.

104. Ibid., 36.

105. Ibid., 54.

106. Erich Fromm, *The Sane Society* (London, 1963), 19, quoted in Plant, *Modern Political Thought*, 58–61.

107. Fromm, *Sane Society*, 276. Fromm, of course, is speaking psychoanalytically, not politically. Though he is making a point about human health, he also supports a political point of view expressed long before by Jefferson, among others.

108. Aristotle, *Nicomachean Ethics*, trans. J. A. K. Thomson (London, 1953), 38.

109. Aristotle, *The Politics*, trans. E. Barker (Oxford, 1946), 119.

110. Pettit, *Republicanism*, 287 n. 46.

111. Ibid., 289, emphasis added.

112. Dahl, *On Democracy*, 159.

Conclusion

1. Bernard Yack, *The Problems of a Political Animal* (Berkeley, Calif., 1993), 73.

2. Charles de Secondat, baron de Montesquieu, *The Spirit of the Laws*, ed. Anne M. Cohler, Basia Carolyn Miller, and Harold Samuel Stone (Cambridge, 1989), 124.

3. Jean Jacques Rousseau, "To the Republic of Geneva," in *The Dis-*

courses and Other Early Political Writings, ed. Victor Gourevitch (Cambridge, 1997), 114.

4. John Locke, *Two Treatises of Government*, ed. Peter Laslett (Cambridge, 1989), 359.

5. Benjamin R. Barber, *An Aristocracy of Everyone: The Politics of Education and the Future of America* (Oxford, 1992), 241.

6. Michael J. Sandel, *Democracy's Discontent: America in Search of a Public Philosophy* (Cambridge, Mass., 1996), 4.

7. Ibid., 24.

8. Social needs are to be addressed by the private charity implicit in "a thousand points of light" and "faith-based charities."

9. "More and more, the affluent evacuate public spaces, retreating to privatized communities defined largely by income level, or by the zip code direct-mail marketers use to target likely customers" (Sandel, *Democracy's Discontent*, 331 n. 5). Such enclaves of wealth and privilege are now even the basis for television programming, e.g., "Beverly Hills 90210."

10. Ibid., 344–45.

11. Quentin Skinner, "The Republican Ideal of Political Liberty," in *Machiavelli and Republicanism*, ed. Gisela Bock, Quentin Skinner, and Maurizio Viroli (Cambridge, 1990), 304.

12. Robert Putnam, *Bowling Alone: The Collapse and Revival of American Community* (New York, 2000), 412.

13. Charles Taylor, *Philosophical Arguments* (Cambridge, Mass., 1995), 201.

14. Robert A. Dahl, *After the Revolution? Authority in a Good Society* (New Haven, Conn., 1970), 165.

15. Putnam, *Bowling Alone*, 412–13.

16. Skinner, "Republican Ideal," 304.

17. Letter to Edward Carrington, January 16, 1787, in *Thomas Jefferson: Writings*, ed. Merrill D. Peterson (New York, 1984), 880–881; see also Hannah Arendt, *On Revolution* (New York, 1963), 232.

18. Skinner, "Republican Ideal," 308.

19. Ibid., 309.

20. Letter to Samuel Kercheval, July 12, 1816, in Peterson, *Thomas Jefferson*, 1399.

Adams, Henry. *History of the United States during the Administrations of Thomas Jefferson.* New York, 1986.

Appleby, Joyce. *Liberalism and Republicanism in the Historical Imagination.* Cambridge, Mass., 1992.

Appleby, Joyce, and Terence Ball, eds. *Jefferson: Political Writings.* Cambridge, 1999.

Arendt, Hannah. *On Revolution.* New York, 1963.

Aristotle. *The Politics and the Constitution of Athens,* ed. Stephen Everson. Cambridge, 1996.

Bailyn, Bernard. *The Ideological Origins of the American Revolution.* Cambridge, Mass., 1967.

Banning, Lance. *The Jeffersonian Persuasion: Evolution of a Party Ideology.* Ithaca, N.Y., 1978.

Barber, Benjamin R. *An Aristocracy of Everyone: The Politics of Education and the Future of America.* Oxford, 1992.

———. *A Passion for Democracy.* Princeton, N.J., 1998.

Beiner, Ronald, and William James Booth, eds. *Kant and Political Philosophy.* New Haven, Conn., 1993.

Bell, Daniel. *The Coming of Post-Industrial Society.* New York, 1999.

———. *The Cultural Contradictions of Capitalism.* New York, 1996.

———. *The End of Ideology.* Cambridge, Mass., 1988.

Beloff, Max. *Thomas Jefferson and American Democracy.* New York, 1949.

Bock, Gisela, Quentin Skinner, and Maurizio Viroli, eds. *Machiavelli and Republicanism.* Cambridge, 1990.

Bolingbroke, Viscount Henry St. John. *Political Writings*, ed. David Armitage. Cambridge, 1997.

Boorstin, Daniel J. *The Lost World of Thomas Jefferson*. Chicago, 1981.

Bruger, Bill. *Republican Theory in Political Thought: Virtuous or Virtual?* London, 1999.

Burtt, Shelley. *Virtue Transformed: Political Argument in England, 1688–1740*. Cambridge, 1992.

Cicero. *De Re Publica*, trans. C. W. Keyes. Cambridge, Mass., 1928.

Clark, Ian. *Globalization and Fragmentation: International Relations in the Twentieth Century*. Oxford, 1997.

Commager, Henry Steele. *Jefferson, Nationalism and Enlightenment*. New York, 1975.

Crawford, Michael. *The Roman Republic*. Cambridge, Mass., 1993.

Dagger, Richard. *Civic Virtues: Rights, Citizenship, and Republican Liberalism*. Oxford, 1997.

Dahl, Robert A. *After the Revolution? Authority in a Good Society*. New Haven, Conn., 1970.

———. *On Democracy*. New Haven, Conn., 1998.

de Grazia, Sebastian. *Machiavelli in Hell*. Princeton, N.J., 1989.

Derthick, Martha, ed. *Dilemmas of Scale in America's Federal Democracy*. Washington, D.C., 1999.

Diggins, John Patrick. *The Lost Soul of American Politics*. New York, 1984.

Ferguson, Adam. *An Essay on the History of Civil Society*, ed. Fania Oz-Salzberger. Cambridge, 1995.

Green, Thomas Hill. *Lectures on the Principles of Political Obligation*. London, 1931.

Hamilton, Alexander, James Madison, and John Jay. *The Federalist*. New York, 1971.

Harrington, James. *The Commonwealth of Oceana and a System of Politics*, ed. J. G. A. Pocock. Cambridge, 1992.

Hartz, Louis. *The Liberal Tradition in America*. New York, 1955.

Heffner, Richard D., ed. *A Documentary History of the United States*. New York, 1999.

Hofstadter, Richard. *The Age of Reform*. New York, 1955.

Hyneman, Charles S., and Donald S. Lutz, eds. *American Political*

Writing during the Founding Era: 1760–1805. Indianapolis, Ind., 1983.

Kammen, Michael. *A Machine That Would Go of Itself*. New York, 1986.

———. *The Origins of the American Constitution: A Documentary History*. New York, 1986.

———. *People of Paradox: An Inquiry concerning the Origins of American Civilization*. New York, 1972.

Koch, Adrienne. *The Philosophy of Thomas Jefferson*. Gloucester, Mass., 1957.

Koch, Adrienne, and William Peden, eds. *The Life and Selected Writings of Thomas Jefferson*. New York, 1993.

Lintott, Andrew. *The Constitution of the Roman Republic*. Oxford, 1999.

Locke, John. *Two Treatises of Government*, ed. Peter Laslett. Cambridge, 1988.

McDonald, Forrest. *Novus Ordo Seclorum: The Intellectual Origins of the Constitution*. Lawrence, Kans., 1985.

———. *The Presidency of Thomas Jefferson*. Lawrence, Kans., 1976.

Machiavelli, Niccolo. *The Discourses*, ed. Bernard Crick. New York, 1970.

———. *The Prince*, trans. W. K. Marriott. New York, 1992.

MacIntyre, Alasdair. *After Virtue*. Notre Dame, Ind., 1984.

Maier, Pauline. *American Scripture: How America Declared Its Independence from Britain*. New York, 1999.

Malone, Dumas. *Jefferson and His Times*. 5 vols. New York, 1951.

Mansfield, Harvey C. *Machiavelli's Virtue*. Chicago, 1996.

Mapp, Alf J., Jr. *Thomas Jefferson: A Strange Case of Mistaken Identity*. Lanham, Md., 1981.

Matthews, Richard K. *The Radical Politics of Thomas Jefferson*. Lawrence, Kans., 1984.

Mayo, Bernard, ed. *Jefferson Himself*. Charlottesville, Va., 1942.

Mill, John Stuart. *On Liberty and Other Essays*. Oxford, 1991.

Montesquieu, Baron Charles de Secondat. *The Spirit of the Laws*, ed. Anne M. Cohler, Basia Carolyn Miller, and Harold Samuel Stone. Cambridge, 1989.

Ohmae, Kenichi. *The End of the Nation-State*. New York, 1996.

Paine, Thomas. *Collected Writings*, ed. Eric Foner. New York, 1995.

Peterson, Merrill D. *The Jefferson Image in the American Mind.* Charlottesville, Va., 1998.

——, ed. *Thomas Jefferson: Writings.* New York, 1984.

Pettit, Philip. *Republicanism: A Theory of Freedom and Government.* Oxford, 1997.

Plant, Raymond. *Modern Political Thought.* Oxford, 1991.

Plato. *Statesman,* ed. Julia Annas and Robin Waterford. Cambridge, 1995.

Plutarch. *The Lives of the Noble Grecians and Romans.* 2 vols. New York, 1992.

Pocock, J. G. A. *The Machiavellian Moment: Florentine Political Thought and the Atlantic Republican Traditon.* Princeton, N.J., 1975.

Rahe, Paul A. *Republics Ancient and Modern.* 3 vols. Chapel Hill, N.C., 1994.

Rawls, John. *Lectures on the History of Moral Philosophy,* ed. Barbara Herman. Cambridge, Mass., 2000.

Rosenfeld, Richard. *American Aurora.* New York, 1997.

Rousseau, Jean Jacques. *The Discourses and Other Early Political Writings,* ed. Victor Gourevitch. Cambridge, 1997.

Ryan, Alan, ed. *Mill.* New York, 1997.

Sandel, Michael, J. *Democracy's Discontent. America in Search of a Public Philosophy.* Cambridge, Mass., 1996.

——. *Liberalism and the Limits of Justice.* Cambridge, 1982.

Sheldon, Garrett Ward. *The Political Philosophy of Thomas Jefferson.* Baltimore, Md., 1991.

Sidney, Algernon. *Court Maxims,* ed. Hans W. Blom, Eco Haitsma Mulier, and Ronald Janse. Cambridge, 1996.

Sisson, Donald. *The American Revolution of 1800.* New York, 1974.

Skinner, Quentin. *Liberty before Liberalism.* Cambridge, 1998.

Syme, Ronald. *The Roman Revolution.* Oxford, 1939.

Taylor, Charles. *Philosophical Arguments.* Cambridge, Mass., 1995.

Tocqueville, Alexis de. *Democracy in America.* 2 vols. New York, 1985.

Trenchard, John, and Thomas Gordon. *Cato's Letters.* ed. Ronald Hamowy. Indianapolis, Ind. 1995.

van Creveld, Martin. *The Rise and Decline of the State.* Cambridge, 1999.

Viroli, Maurizio. *For Love of Country: An Essay on Patriotism and Nation-alism.* Oxford, 1997.

Wood, Gordon S. *The Creation of the American Republic: 1776–1787.* New York, 1969.

———. *The Radicalism of the American Revolution.* New York, 1992.

Yack, Bernard. *The Problems of a Political Animal.* Berkeley, Calif., 1993.

Index

contemporary disinterest in, 16, 20

corruption as failure of, 66

Jeffersonian view of, 65, 103, 116, 171, 227, 229

military service and, 5, 6–7, 209–11

in republicanism, 7, 12, 61, 247n.26

restored republicanism and, 10, 11, 23, 222, 234, 236

as rights guarantor, 4, 12, 23, 171, 188, 236

civic education, 23, 187–90

civic humanism, 92, 105–11

civic virtue, 4, 51

Aristotelian theory on, 106–7

contemporary perspectives on, 20, 38, 71, 72, 75

as corruption, 94

dependence of republicanism on, 7, 12, 44, 61, 92, 97–98

education and, 177, 188, 189, 203–4

homeland defense as, 9, 210, 211, 217

Jeffersonian view of, 57–58, 65, 68, 84, 103, 104, 108, 116, 160, 224, 227, 229, 234

restored republicanism and, 10, 11, 23, 59, 61, 73–74, 77, 170, 222

rights and, 88, 188

civil rights, 5, 184, 187, 190, 230

Civil War, American, 20, 51, 52, 124, 254n.105, 255n.117

Civil War, English, 146

Clark, Ian, 26–27

classical texts. *See* Greece, ancient; Roman republic

Clausewitz, Carl von, 148

Clinton, Bill, 10, 198, 206

Coast Guard, U.S., 7

cold war, 20, 37–38, 52, 243n.51

Coles, Edward, 126

colonization of African slaves, 124, 255n.117

commerce. *See* trade and commerce

commercial republic, 47–48, 64–65, 78, 99–100, 116, 229–30

Commission on National Security/ Twenty-first Century, U.S., 7, 41–42, 214–16, 264–65n.90

common good, 61, 98

individual rights vs., 20

in Jeffersonian theory, 9, 57, 65, 84, 95, 97, 103

restored republicanism and, 23, 45, 73, 163–64, 226

common interests, 225, 229

Commonplace Book (Jefferson), 111, 136

commonwealth, 16, 61

formation reasons, 106, 108

in Jeffersonian theory, 58, 65, 84, 101, 103, 227–28

restored republicanism and, 10, 23, 73

communications technology, 33, 35, 76, 165–66

communism, 5, 6, 37, 52, 266n.102

communitarianism, 18–19, 266n.102

community building, 172, 190, 259n.9

community service, 10, 174

competence, in representative democracy, 114, 115

confederation, republics and, 117, 121–22, 253–54n.98

Congress, U.S., 150, 156, 187, 209, 213

Connecticut, 132
conservatism, 37, 246n.19
Constitution, U.S.
  armed forces and, 51, 150, 156,
    206, 209
  checks and balances in, 4, 12,
    104–5
  as compromise document, 65–
    66, 118, 120
  congressional powers and, 150
  equal protection and, 167
  federal powers and, 25, 61
  militia authority and oversight
    in, 51, 209, 214
  national unification and, 13
  participatory democracy and,
    169, 235, 236
  radical republican values and,
    22
  republican government
    guarantee, 4, 65–66, 75, 76,
    113
  restored republicanism and, 167–
    68
  rights of special communities
    and, 168
  state powers and, 51, 113,
    243n.44
  See also Bill of Rights; Second
    Amendment
Constitutional convention (1787),
    46, 50, 51, 66, 113
  Jefferson and, 12, 22, 54–55, 58,
    117–23, 243n.50
Constitution for the Commonwealth
    of Virginia (1776), 108–9
Continental army, 149
corporations, multinational, 27–30
corruption
  American Revolution as
    response to, 93–94
  campaign financing and, 9, 69–
    70, 192, 232–33

contemporary perspectives, 69–
    71, 72, 75
  economic disparity as cause of,
    195
  Jeffersonian view of, 13, 85–86
  in local government, 43
  as republican threat, 7, 12, 61,
    66–67, 68, 71, 92, 93–94,
    245–46n.16, 250n.29
  restored republicanism and, 10,
    77, 170, 222, 23
  special interests and, 9, 16, 20,
    38, 67, 191–92
  ward politics and, 239n.6
Cosway, Maria, 160, 194
Counterterrorism Act of 1995,
    206
counties, role of, 133–34
crime
  changing scope of, 32–33, 34
  poverty and, 199
"Criterion of Economy" (Dahl
    concept), 172–73
Croly, Herbert, 16–17, 53–57, 243–
    44n.53, 244n.55
Cromwell, Oliver, 50, 97, 146,
    152
currency, 29, 33, 41, 99
Customs Service, U.S., 7

Dagger, Richard, 166–67, 173–74,
    259n.7
Dahl, Robert, 172–73, 182–84, 219,
    226, 234
debt, national, 99, 141
Declaration of Independence
  Jeffersonian liberalism and, 21,
    86–87, 161
  Lockean influences on, 88, 107,
    108, 110, 86
  natural law theories and, 98
  rights espoused in, 15, 88, 107,
    110

isolationism, 20
Italian Renaissance, 92

James II, king of England, 151
Jay, John, 63, 118
Jefferson, Thomas
    Antifederalists and, 17–18, 54,
        58, 60, 94
    Constitutional debates and, 12,
        54–55, 58, 117–23, 243n.50
    Croly's critique of, 17, 53–57,
        243–44nn.44, 53, 55
    education's importance to, 21,
        131, 133–40, 155, 176–80, 189,
        192
    elements in political philosophy
        of, 116
    first inaugural address of, 53, 55–
        56
    "Head and Heart" dialogue of,
        160, 194–95
    individualism and, 53, 56, 88
    intellectual influences on, 83,
        86–87, 88, 92, 93, 94–98,
        106–8, 110, 112, 117–18, 128–
        29, 161, 224, 227, 250n.30,
        255nn.118, 120
    liberalism of, 21, 86–88, 221
    militias' role and, 6, 140–41,
        152, 155–56, 204–5, 207,
        258n.170
    popular sovereignty view of, 25,
        67–68, 86, 102–3
    property ownership beliefs of,
        15, 21–22, 88, 95, 107–11, 128,
        157–61, 194–96
    republic conception of, 11, 22,
        65, 67–68, 78, 94, 118–19,
        128–32, 221–25, 227–29
    rights philosophy of, 12, 14–15,
        86–88, 107, 108, 116, 140,
        171, 227, 229, 234
    scholarly literature on, 21

slavery views of, 21, 124–28,
    255n.117
    See also democratic
        republicanism; ward republic
Johnson, William, 159
Joint Forces Command/Joint Task
    Force–Civil Support, 215
judiciary, Jefferson's view of, 117
jury service, 7, 134
justice systems, international, 34
Justinian, emperor of Rome, 92

Kammen, Michael, 5, 103
Kercheval, Samuel, 132
Keynes, John Maynard, 197
Koch, Adrienne, 140
Korean War, 212–13
Kosovo, 42
Kurds, 39

labor movement, 20
land ownership. See property
language revival, 39–40
Latin American Free Trade
    Association (LAFTA), 30
legislatures
    standing army consent by, 150–
        51
    See also Congress, U.S.
Lewis and Clark expedition, 21, 55,
    109
liberalism, 230, 246n.19
    aristocratic, 5, 103
    Jefferson and, 21, 86–88, 161,
        221
    protection of autonomy in, 74
    republican, 7, 14, 259n.7
libertarianism, 246n.17
liberty, 61, 68, 71–75, 116, 227. See
    also freedom
Lincoln, Abraham, 255n.117
Livy, 63, 90, 91, 92
lobbyists, 7, 9, 59–60, 69

local government, 260–61n.37
  citizen participation in, 73
  contemporary political power
    and, 40, 60
  corruption of, 43
  government fragmentation and,
    18, 166–67
  in Mill's theory, 114–15
  restored republicanism and,
    164, 166, 168–69, 218–19
  social welfare and, 200–202
  ward republic practicality and, 18
  See also municipal government;
    township government
Locke, John, 15, 106, 189, 229,
    240n.12
  as Jefferson influence, 86–87,
    88, 98, 107, 108, 110, 227,
    255n.120
Louisiana Purchase, 21, 55, 109
Lucan, 91
Lucian, 91

Machiavelli, Niccolo, 99, 241n.9,
    257n.161
  American Revolution and, 93
  Aristotelian theory vs., 74
  common good and, 97
  militia's importance and, 144–
    46, 211, 217, 257n.155
  republican values and, 92, 93
Madison, James, 11, 46–47
  checks and balances conception
    of, 12, 78, 84, 94, 104–5,
    224
  elected representation and, 86,
    176
  factionalism fears of, 47, 59
  Federalist papers and, 63, 104,
    119, 153
  Jefferson's counseling of, 17, 54,
    117, 118

mobocracy fears and, 178
  republican government concept
    and, 64, 65–66, 78, 84–85,
    94, 117–21, 123
Mandeville, Bernard, 57
Marbois, Francois de, 109
Marcus Aurelius, 92
Marcuse, Herbert, 266n.102
Marx, Karl, 107
Marxism, 90
Maryland, 150
Massachusetts, 150
Matthews, Richard, 64
Medicare, 198
mercenaries, 143–46, 257n.155
MERCOSUR, 30
military, 5–7, 99
  citizen duty and, 5, 7
  Constitutional authority for, 51
  Federalist support for, 6, 48, 50,
    64, 65, 150, 152–53, 156, 207
  national defense and, 25
  Posse Comitatus Act and, 8,
    205–6, 209, 217
  recent foreign experiences of,
    35, 42
  reform recommendations, 42
  reserve forces, 209, 211–14,
    256n.147
  See also militias; National Guard;
    standing military; war
military-industrial complex, 6, 67,
    265n.93
militias
  American Revolution and, 142,
    149, 257n.159
  Antifederalist view of, 50, 51
  British, 142, 146–48
  civic duty and, 209–11
  constitutional authorization of,
    51, 142, 149, 153, 209, 214,
    217, 258nn.172, 173

popular sovereignty
  candidate selection process and,
    245n.13
  contemporary perspectives on,
    69, 70, 72, 75
  Jefferson and, 25, 67–68, 86,
    102–3
  Madison and, 104–5
  in Mill's theory, 114–15
  opinion polls and, 38
  in republicanism, 7, 12, 61, 101–
    2
  restored republicanism and, 10,
    23, 61, 73, 77, 163, 170, 222
  voter apathy and, 9, 38, 69, 70,
    179–80
populism, 72, 246n.18
populist movement, 263n.65
Posse Comitatus Act of 1878, 8,
  205–6, 209, 217
poverty
  as domination, 196–97
  land ownership as reduction of,
    159, 196
  restored republicanism and, 199–
    201, 203, 218, 225–26
  unequal property division and,
    157, 194–95
primogeniture, 109, 134, 137, 158,
  160
private security industry, 33–34
private virtue, 57–58
privatization, 31–32, 33, 71, 192
procedural republic, 3, 20, 230
Progressive Era, 52–53, 72–73, 197–
  98, 246–47n.21, 263n.65
progressivism, 37, 72, 198
property
  government and role of, 105–11
  importance in Jeffersonian
    philosophy, 15, 21, 88, 95,
    107–11, 157–61, 162, 178, 194–
    96

inheritance of, 109, 134, 137,
  158, 160
militia membership based on
  ownership of, 147
as participatory citizenship
  basis, 63, 109
unequal division of, 157, 194–
  95
Prussia, 148
psychoanalytic theory, 223
public debt, 99, 141
public education, 21, 198
  citizenship and, 175–81, 188
  community responsibility and
    restoration of, 187–92, 218,
    225–26
  greater civic virtue and, 203–4
  Jefferson's view of, 131, 133–40,
    155
  local control of, 170
  nationalization of, 180–87, 192–
    93
  national standards for, 164, 184,
    190–91, 192–93
  operational proposal for, 192–94
public service, 7, 181
  contemporary perspectives on,
    4, 10, 71
  expansion of, 44
  mandatory, 174
Putnam, Robert, 45–46, 59, 70,
  72–73, 165–66, 188, 197, 210,
  233, 234, 261–62n.47

racial segregation, 124, 125,
  240n.10
radicalism, 38
radical republicanism, 22
Rawls, John, 74
Reagan, Ronald, 243n.52
Reconstruction, 20, 52
regionalism, impact of, 32–33, 36
religious freedom, 160

206–9, 211–16, 242n.32,
264n.89
Posse Comitatus Act and,
206
Thebes, 92
Thucydides, 90, 91, 98
Tocqueville, Alexis de, 132, 153–55,
169, 171, 175–76, 180, 186,
216, 219–20, 265n.93
total ideology, 37
town meetings, 165
township government, 26
Jeffersonian theory of, 77, 81,
85, 123, 132, 169–70
in New England, 77, 81, 132,
176, 219–20
restored republicanism and, 61–
62
trade and commerce, 99–100
Antifederalist view of, 50, 51
expansion of, 20
Federalist view of, 48, 50, 150
free markets and, 32, 41
globalization and, 28–30
tribalism, 38
tyranny, resistance to, 169

Ulpian, 91
Union Douaniere et Economique
de l'Afrique Central
(UDEAC), 30
United Kingdom. *See* Great Britain
United Nations, 30
human rights initiatives, 34
international security forces
and, 42
United States government. *See*
federal government
universal military training, 141
University of Virginia, 131
urban conflict, 9, 32
urban design, 174

urban society, 18, 52
Utopia (More), 96
utopianism, 221–22

van Creveld, Martin, 73
Venice, Italy, 82
Vietnam War, 35, 212–13, 218
Virgil, 90, 91, 92
Virginia
Bill for More General Diffusion
of Knowledge, 135, 136
constitution, 108–9, 125–26
Jefferson's policies in, 117, 122,
125–26, 134, 160
virtue
moral, 196
private, 57–58
true republic of, 92
See also civic virtue
voting
apathy concerning, 9, 38, 69,
70, 179–80
as citizen participation, 7
compulsory, 174
land ownership and, 63, 109
See also elections
vouchers, educational, 185

Wales, 39
Walpole, Robert, 100
war
changing nature of, 9, 32, 33,
242n.32
as democractic government
threat, 265n.93
national governments and, 43
See also military; standing army;
specific wars
ward politics, 239n.6
ward republic
citizen protest organization and,
220